problems of the Reconstruction continuing, but new problems were confronting the Administration, such as the beginning of the Civil Service and monetary policy. The Hayes diary also reveals a somewhat lesser, but fascinating, part of the presidency—the social life of the White House, perhaps one of the fullest records of that side of the presidency ever put down. Hayes was a good writer, about men and events and about himself, and, as Mr. Williams comments, the diary is "an astonishingly frank and introspective portrait of Hayes himself."

T. Harry Williams, the editor, is Boyd Professor of History at Louisiana State University and author or editor of a number of well-known studies in American history, including *Lincoln and His Generals*.

HAYES

The Diary of a President

Books by T. Harry Williams

LINCOLN AND THE RADICALS, 1941

LINCOLN AND HIS GENERALS, 1952

P.G.T. BEAUREGARD, 1955

AMERICANS AT WAR, 1960

A HISTORY OF THE UNITED STATES WITH R. N. CURRENT
AND FRANK FREIDEL, 1959

AMERICAN HISTORY: A SURVEY WITH R. N. CURRENT
AND FRANK FREIDEL, 1961

ROMANCE AND REALISM IN SOUTHERN POLITICS, 1961

McCLELLAN, SHERMAN, AND GRANT, 1962

THE UNION SUNDERED, 1963

THE UNION RESTORED, 1963
(Vols. 5 and 6 of The Life History of the United States)

Books Edited by T. Harry Williams

SELECTED WRITINGS AND SPEECHES OF
ABRAHAM LINCOLN, 1943

WITH BEAUREGARD IN MEXICO, 1956

ABRAHAM LINCOLN: SELECTED SPEECHES, MESSAGES,
AND LETTERS, 1957

MILITARY MEMOIRS OF A CONFEDERATE
BY E. P. ALEXANDER, 1962

EVERY MAN A KING BY HUEY P. LONG, 1964

HAYES

The Diary of a President

1875-1881

COVERING THE DISPUTED ELECTION, THE END
OF RECONSTRUCTION, AND THE BEGINNING
OF CIVIL SERVICE

Edited by

T. HARRY WILLIAMS

DAVID McKAY COMPANY, INC.

New York

HAYES: THE DIARY OF A PRESIDENT

COPYRIGHT © 1964 BY T. HARRY WILLIAMS

LIBRARY OF CONGRESS CATALOG CARD NUMBER: 64-10784

MANUFACTURED IN THE UNITED STATES OF AMERICA

To

WATT P. MARCHMAN

PREFACE

This volume puts together as a continuous narrative the
diary of Rutherford B. Hayes from March, 1875, to March,
1881—covering his nomination as the Republican candidate,
the campaign of 1876, the disputed election and its compromise, and his Presidency. It is based on a typed copy of the
original manuscript supplied by The Rutherford B. Hayes
Library of Fremont, Ohio, and its director, Watt P. Marchman. Hayes was an inveterate diary keeper from his youth to
his old age. Large chunks of all the diaries have previously
appeared in print. The Ohio State Archaeological and Historical Society published in five volumes (1922–1926) the
Diary and Letters of Rutherford Birchard Hayes, edited by
Charles R. Williams. Although the collection has some merit,
it contains serious flaws and does not measure up to modern
scholarly standards. The diary entries are incomplete, practically no notes are supplied, and Mr. Williams chose to edit
freely the language of the diarist. From the viewpoint of
readability, much was lost by interspersing sections of the
diary with letters from Hayes's correspondence.

In this record of the presidential years the diary is reproduced virtually in facsimile form. All misspellings, errors in
punctuation, and other eccentricities have been retained, as
have the deletions and gaps in the original copy. The arrange-

ment of entry dates has been altered to achieve uniformity and ease in reading. Hayes, like some other diarists, had a habit of abbreviating proper names and even ordinary words. In many of these cases, explanatory or identifying material has been added in brackets. The use of notes has been held to a minimum. Hayes himself usually provided fairly full descriptions of major men and episodes in his story. The editor has supplied amplifying information in a *Dramatis Personae* and a *Chronology of Events*. He has also attempted in an introduction to trace Hayes's career and to evaluate the significance of this man for his own time and in the perspective of history.

Grateful acknowledgment is returned to the Hayes Library and to Mr. Marchman for aid in preparing the manuscript and for patient advice at all turns and on all points. Appreciation is due to the late Mr. John L. B. Williams of the David McKay Company for his sensitive understanding of the need to reproduce the diary as an exact historical source.

CONTENTS

INTRODUCTION

He became President in the strangest circumstances in American history, and he entered the office under a cloud that never entirely lifted. Some proposed that he should be addressed as "His Fraudulency," and others sneered that he might well change the spelling of his name to "Rutherfraud" B. Hayes. The irony of it all was that he was a singularly upright man, too much so, in fact, to be a competent or constant politician. His reputation had always been, as he intended it always should be, synonymous with reform. Rutherford B. Hayes attained the Presidency as a result of the only disputed American election, after a special process was devised to determine whether he or his Democratic opponent should receive the contested electoral votes, and after frenzied negotiations by both parties to gain those votes for their candidate. He took over the chief office at a critical moment in national history—at the end of reconstruction and in conditions of economic recession, when searching decisions on monetary policy had to be made, and at a time when the prestige of the Presidency was at one of its lowest levels. He met his problems not with brilliant daring, but squarely and as best he could, and when he retired he had the satisfaction of knowing that he was respected, if not admired, and that he was immeasurably more popular than he had been at the beginning of his administration. The verdict of his time has become the judgment of history: He was not a great President but he was a good one; solid and capable, he grew in his office and left that office stronger than he found it.

Hayes was born October 4, 1822, in Delaware, Ohio, into a family of Vermont extraction. He was born posthumously and was raised in a protectively feminine atmosphere. The only male influence was his uncle on the maternal side, Sardis Birchard. But Sardis' influence was strong, and Hayes would never forget it. Because of this uncle and because his family was above average in worldly means, young Hayes received a good education at private schools and at Kenyon College in Gambier. After graduating from Kenyon, he studied law in legal offices and put in a period at the Harvard Law School. He hung out his first shingle in the little town where Sardis lived, Lower Sandusky (later Fremont). Here for several years he practiced the small cases of a country lawyer, and then in 1850 he made what he obviously considered a decisive plunge. He moved his office and his ambitions to Cincinnati. In the state's metropolis he prospered almost from the first, and soon was regarded as one of the city's leading legal lights. With economic security came greater personal confidence, and in 1852 he married Lucy Webb, attractive and vivacious and a perfect complement to his sometimes studied seriousness. She had a seriousness of her own, perhaps stronger than his because it was more natural and often repressed, and they were as well suited as two people could be. It was a marriage whose attachments were never strained.

As Hayes rose in his profession, so also did his political stock, his availability rise. But for some reason he spurned office and the life of the officeholder, although he could have had his choice of several posts. He was first a Whig, then a Republican, and a firm but not an extreme antislavery advocate. He spoke and worked for his party in campaigns but always with a certain restraint. In fact, restraint is the word that most aptly characterizes everything about Hayes in this period. This impression of a man under discipline emerges from the diaries that he began to keep at an early age and that he continued to keep throughout his life. In these documents he sometimes revealed himself with a frank introspection that was perhaps unconscious. At the age of nineteen he wrote that he was determined to acquire a character distinguished by energy, firmness, and perseverance. He worked toward that goal methodically. He worked to acquire other ends in the same spirit, and always he seemed to be moving toward something, yet not giving himself completely to anything. He was, in 1860, successful and respected; a man of depth and power and even fire, who was under wraps of some kind.

The Civil War changed Hayes's life and personality, as it did the lives of countless others. In a mood of indignant determination after the firing on Sumter, he resolved to offer his services as a soldier. He would rather die, he wrote in his diary, than stay out of it. Though he meant every word, at the same time he had a good enough opinion of his abilities to think he should go in as an officer. He and his close friend Stanley Matthews talked the matter over with Governor William Dennison, and the upshot was that they were offered commissions in a three-year regiment, the Twenty-third Ohio, Matthews as lieutenant colonel and Hayes as major. Matthews soon decided he was not cut out to be a soldier and resigned. But Hayes loved military life from the start. He studied the art of war assiduously, became a good officer, and rose to be colonel and commander of his regiment. Before the war was over, he commanded a brigade and then a division, and he was mustered out as a brevet major general of volunteers. Unfortunately for Hayes's military fame, he spent most of his war years in the mountain fastness of West Virginia, a kind of pocket away from the main conflict, where reputations were hard to make. He entered the big picture only twice. In 1862 he participated in the Antietam campaign and was wounded at

South Mountain. Then, in 1864, he served under General Philip Sheridan in the Shenandoah Valley, playing a part in the battles that finally ended the Confederate threat in western Virginia. In many and vital ways the experience of the war changed Hayes. It made him more assured, more open and less restrained, more desirous of being with his fellow men and winning their favor. And it pushed forward his career as nothing else could have. As General Hayes and a legitimate military hero, he was now a prime political prospect. The people and politicians of his district had recognized his new status by electing him to the national House of Representatives in October, 1864, while he was still in uniform.

Hayes did not take his seat in Congress until December, 1865. There was principle in this—he did not want to leave his post in the field—and also clever politics. He could not be accused of putting office above duty. Hayes was, indeed, a curious mixture of idealism and practicality. At times he was too high-minded for his own advancement, and at others he was the most adept of politicians. This would not be the last time that he would demonstrate the more calculating side of his nature. He served two terms in the House, being re-elected in 1866. His tenure was respectable but not prominent. He faithfully supported all the Radical Republican measures for the reconstruction of the South, although he privately had some doubts about the extremism of some of them. He was most active personally in advocating bills for the betterment of the Library of Congress.

A call for larger service came in 1867. The Republicans of Ohio nominated him for governor. He was elected and then re-elected in 1869. His two terms were marked by careful and honest administration, the partial application of civil service in appointments, support for education, prison reform, and improvement of institutions for the insane and other unfortunates. At the end of his second term Hayes could have had his pick of a number of offices—possibly another term as governor or a seat in the national Senate. He refused all offers. There is some mystery about his motives. Supposedly he felt bound by the tradition of two terms for a governor, but shortly he would show that this was not a compelling restriction. It is possible that he thought he had gone as high as he could or that he simply desired to return to the quiet of private life. The most likely explanation is that he was playing smart politics. He chose a good time to step temporarily aside. The Republican party nationally was rent by serious division that would burst forth in 1872 in the Liberal Republican revolt; and this division reached down into the state organizations. A politician with an eye to the future might well want to remove himself for the moment from the front lines. In 1872 Hayes remained regular, supporting U. S. Grant against the Liberal Republican Horace Greeley and suffering defeat as a Congressional candidate. More theoretical reformers might not like his adherence to an administration associated with corruption, but he had shown respect for one of the basic rules of politics—stay with the party. Politicians all over the country would now look with new interest on this man from a key state who had made a national name as governor, who was enough of a reformer to command a following among the shouters for good government and yet enough of a politician to realize the need for organization.

In 1873 Hayes retired to the lovely estate of Spiegel Grove that Sardis Birchard had founded at Fremont. Here, two years later, he heard again a plea from his party that he run for governor, backed by the argument that he was the only man who could wrest the state from the Democrats. He listened with interest, intrigued—as he confessed—by the distinction of a third term; but he dutifully declined in favor of his friend Alphonso Taft, an announced aspirant. But the state convention, rightly concerned with victory and knowing a good thing, nominated Hayes by acclamation. He pitched his campaign on a high level, speaking out for civil service and efficient administration; but when the Democrats put themselves in the position of apparently favoring state aid for religious schools, he was not above grabbing hold of what he called "the Catholic issue." With an eye cocked to the national scene, he discussed the money question, coming out roundly against greenbacks and for a return to specie payments. Some people were telling him that if he won the governorship, he would be a formidable candidate for the Republican presidential nomination. He affected not to take this talk seriously, but quite naturally he was influenced by it. He was elected by a narrow margin of some five thousand votes.

Hayes's third term as governor was peculiar. Inaugurated in January, 1876, he tried to devote his attention to the job, but increasingly he was drawn into the speculation and the maneuverings surrounding the Republican presidential nomination. In effect, as governor of Ohio, he was, whether he liked it or not, running for President. He liked it, as any politician conscious of his abilities would have. Hayes knew he was not a front-runner, but he also knew enough about the party situation to realize that the fortunes of politics could conceivably catapult him into the first ranks. The Republicans came up to the campaign of 1876 with uncertain prospects. Factionalism developing in the second Grant administration sapped the party's unity and turned its aggressions inward instead of outward against the Democratic foe. Three groupings were apparent within the organization. The Stalwarts, captained by New York's ornate Roscoe Conkling, were frank professionals, machine politicians who believed the end-all of the game was to win power and spoils; they accepted corruption as a necessary part of politics and relished the allocation of the awards. The Half-Breeds, led by Maine's magnetic James G. Blaine, were also professionals; but they were more circumspect in pursuing their goals, and they paid at least lip tribute to civil service and reform. In part, the rivalry between the two factions revolved around the personal enmity between Conkling and Blaine, who devoted their best forensic power to crucifying each other. Still a third faction consisted of the Liberals who had bolted the party in 1872 and of the genuine reformers; this group formed a minority and was usually referred to as the Independents.

The Republican problem was to find a candidate who could unite the various discordant factions and their aspirations. The party managers, alarmed by the recent upsurge of Democratic strength that had delivered the House of Representatives to the Democrats, knew that it could not be a man associated with the Grant scandals or any unethical episode or one who was too openly a machine operator. This ruled out Blaine, Conkling, and Senator Oliver P. Morton of Indiana, the three leading contenders. Nor could it be a man known primarily as a reformer, because he could not arouse the enthusiasm of the professionals. This disqualified Kentucky's Benjamin H. Bristow, the fourth runner. The ideal nominee was a figure from a big state who had a reputation as a reformer and yet was trusted by the professionals. Whether Hayes understood it or not, the specifications fit him like a glove, and it was almost inevitable that the party would choose him. The national convention met in June in friendly territory at Cincinnati. Hayes began with a respectable vote figure, climbed steadily on every roll call, and was nominated on the seventh ballot. In his letter of acceptance he stressed the importance of civil service, upheld a "sound" gold currency over cheap money, advocated national aid for public education, and spoke vaguely, yet assuringly, to the South about his concern with the problem of reconstruction. The Democrats nominated Samuel J. Tilden of New York, and between Hayes and Tilden there were only subtle differences on such issues as reform, money, and the South. The campaign, like others of the period, was fought over personal questions. The Democrats flung the charge of corruption against their opponents, but against Hayes and his record the charge did not stick.

When the votes were counted in November, a strange and dangerous result was disclosed. Tilden led in popular votes and apparently had an electoral majority. But it developed that three southern states, Louisiana, South Carolina, and Florida, with a total of nineteen votes, had sent in double returns—both parties claimed to have carried these states. Another complicating factor arose in Oregon, where one of the three successful Republican electors was declared ineligible because he held a federal office. The Democrats argued that the place should go to the highest Democratic elector, and the Republicans answered that the remaining electors should fill the vacancy. With state law to back them up, the Republicans had the best case, and the one disputed Oregon vote was not a serious issue in the controversy. But the nineteen Southern votes were crucial. Without them Tilden had 184 votes, just one short of a majority. Hayes with 166 certain votes would need all of them to grasp the prize. The question was: Who had won the disputed states? Or more specifically: Who determined who had won them?

The country, already shaken by the news of the dual returns, was further shocked to learn that no procedure existed to determine the correctness of the disputed votes. The Constitution stated that the president of the Senate should in the presence of both houses of Congress open the electoral certificates and that the votes should then be counted. But who was to do the counting? The Senate was Republican and the House Democratic. If the Republican president of the Senate did it, Hayes would be declared the victor. The Democrats would not accept such a solution. No other seemed feasible. If the houses balloted jointly, the numerical Democratic majority of the lower chamber would swing the decision to Tilden, and this the Republicans would not accept. If the houses voted separately, they would checkmate each other, and the country would be without a President, a result which the public would not want to accept. Some seemingly bipartisan way out of the difficulty had to be found, and late in January Congress acted to meet the crisis. A bill was passed creating an Electoral Commission to pass on the disputed votes. It was to consist of five senators, five representatives, and five justices of the Supreme Court. Because of the division of the houses, the congressional delegation would contain five Republicans and five Democrats. The law named four of the judicial members, two Republicans and two Democrats. The four justices were to choose the fifth, and it was expected that he would be David Davis, an independent who would cast a relatively unbiased vote. But at this juncture Davis accepted election to the Senate from Illinois, and refused to serve on the commission. The only remaining judges were Republicans, and of them the choice fell on Joseph P. Bradley. The commission would have a partisan basis after all. Hayes had favored having the president of the Senate count the votes and was brought to support the device of a special agency only by the arguments of Republican congressional leaders.

The commission sat throughout February and by a vote of eight to seven awarded all the disputed votes to Hayes. But its decision was not final. Both houses of Congress had to accept the results, and the Democrats could prevent reception by filibustering, which they immediately proceeded to do. At this stage one of the most unusual maneuvers in American politics was set in motion. Some of Hayes's newspaper friends, such as William Henry Smith of the Western Associated Press, and some of his political intimates, such as James A. Garfield of Ohio, perceived that many southern Democrats felt they had more to gain from a Republican than from a Democratic President and were willing to back Hayes—if the right concessions were made. These were concessions the southerners thought they were much more likely to get from the nationalistic Republicans than from their localistic northern colleagues—aid for internal improvements and for the Texas and Pacific Railroad to connect the South with the far western coast. Delicate negotiations between representatives of Hayes and the South ensued, the Republicans seeking to persuade the southerners to break the filibuster. The latter, realizing their power, raised their price: the appointment of a southerner to the Cabinet, a voice in the distribution of federal patronage in the South, generous internal improvements, and a subsidy for the Texas and Pacific. In return the southerners pledged to abstain from the filibuster, which would mean its failure, and, by enough of them absenting themselves, to let the Republicans organize the House.

Somewhere along the line the Republicans also agreed that Hayes would withdraw the federal troops from the South, thus abandoning the last Republican state governments in Louisiana, South Carolina, and Florida. But the compact about the troops was reached almost as an afterthought and was inserted largely to enable the southerners to explain to their people why they had permitted the accession of a Republican President. Hayes had said more than once that he did not like governments that had to be propped up by bayonets, and he had expressed the hope that a Republican party built on the support of native whites could be raised in the South. Hayes was certainly aware of the general nature of the negotiations, and he saw nothing wrong in them. He was convinced, as all historians have not been since, that the Republicans had carried the disputed states, and he suspected, correctly, that the Democrats were willing to make their own promises. He thought, with some justice, that a Republican President could most easily and durably deal with the problem of reconstruction. In the final settlement, the adjustment of 1877 was not completely honored, and Hayes was disappointed in some of the results. The South got its Cabinet representation and control of patronage and internal improvements. But Hayes backed away from the Texas and Pacific subsidy, and the Democrats did not let the Republicans organize the House. Hayes had to admit that his plans for a new kind of southern Republican party failed to materialize, and he saw with regret that the whites were not going to grant the Negroes the rights that he had hoped they would.

Hayes started for Washington before the final ratification of the commission's decision. En route, on March 2, he received word that he was President. When he was inaugurated, he was just short of fifty-five years of age. He was slightly over five feet eight inches tall and weighed about 170 pounds. In the White House he put on flesh and at one time reached 197 pounds. Lucy, as he ruefully noted, almost kept pace with him, going up to 170. He had blue eyes and a rather large head crowned by dark brown hair that silvered rapidly in the next four years. The features were sharp and regular, suggesting a keen intelligence behind them. And, in fact, as shows forth in the diary, Hayes had a good mind, analytical and, on occasion, deeply reflective. It was a mind fairly well stocked with knowledge derived from his early formal education and from reading. He liked to read and did so whenever he could. His own evaluation of his intellectual qualities was apt: he said he was not a student but had the instincts and aptitudes of one. Naturally his political activities restricted his literary ventures, and this was especially true during the presidential years. One gets the impression from the diary that here was a man who would have been a leader of broader stature if he had been able to read more—and to think about what he read.

In manner Hayes was dignified but not stuffy, and open and friendly. He worked hard and methodically, but he knew how to relax. He liked walks, drives, plays, good conversation, small White House socials, and the larger and more formidable formal receptions. From the diary a picture emerges of a man who found pleasure in his high office because it brought him in contact with all kinds of people—politicians of various vintages, religious leaders like Bishop Matthew Simpson of Mrs. Hayes's Methodist church, and literary figures like the venerable historian George Bancroft and the novelist William

Dean Howells. Perhaps Hayes enjoyed most of all the tours that took him to all parts of the country and before all classes of people. He described them with particular detail, and perhaps this once restrained man drew some strange comfort from the approval of his fellows in the mass. Social life in the Hayes administration was active and gay; there was always something going on at the White House. But it was in the beverage sense, dry. Mrs. Hayes had strong feelings about the use of liquor, and Hayes was willing to back her up. To the horror of Washington social lights, reporters, and diplomats, stimulants were barred at all official functions following the state dinner in honor of the Russian princes in April, 1877. According to newspaper gossip, some humane person saw to it that the oranges contained rum punch, and the consumption of fruit was tremendous. Hayes's humor shines through in a reference to this story in the diary after his Presidency. It was he who had directed that the oranges be flavored with a liquid similar to rum but containing no spirits. The deceived drinkers had quaffed them down with a smack of the lips and exclaimed, "Would they were hot!"

Like most American political leaders, Hayes did not have a conscious or systematic philosophy of government. But he had, although he did not fully realize it, a set of definite concepts about politics and economics. The thing that stands out in his thinking, and it stands out all through the diary, is that he was a nationalist of the nationalists. He believed in national aid for public schools. He supported national internal improvements. He fought for national supervision of state elections. In the railroad strikes of 1877 he unhesitatingly sent national troops into the states where disorder was greatest; although he acted at the request of the governors of those states, he indicated that if necessary he would uphold national power on his own authority. When a French company launched a scheme to build a canal across Panama, he ringingly declared that only the United States could control the isthmian waterway. He was also, and again he did not fully realize all the implications of his position, an advocate and an architect of an independent and strong executive branch. The power of the Presidency had sunk under Andrew Johnson whereas the prestige of Congress had risen, and the scales tilted more markedly in every succeeding administration. Hayes was the first President since 1865 to do something to reassert the authority of the office. In two important areas he swung the balance back. He insisted, against the opposition of Conkling and his own party, on the right of the President to make his own appointments, even at the expense of "senatorial courtesy." And against the opposition of the Democrats he defeated the assumption of Congress that it could attach to appropriation bills riders that had no substantive relation to the money measures.

In his economic thinking Hayes was a traditional nineteenth century conservative. It would be more accurate to say that he did not so much think about economic questions as take over prevailing notions without much analysis and make them his own. His basic biases were illustrated in his reconstruction policy. He did not like the carpetbag governments because he thought that they represented the lowest elements in society. Intelligence should rule, he said, and in his mind intelligence was related in some way to property—smart people were also people of economic standing. His hope was to call into being in the South a new Republican party, one that represented the white intelligence of the section. Surely southerners of property would recognize that their economic interests lay with the Republicans, and just as surely they would be equitable, as such men always were, to the poor Negroes in their midst. Before the end of his administration, Hayes had to admit sadly that his hopes had been largely illusory. Southerners remained Democrats, and they showed little disposition to observe Negro rights. In short, economic rationality failed to assert itself. Hayes's conservatism also came into play in his handling of the money question. In the Grant administration Congress had provided for the resumption of specie payments for greenbacks to take effect under Hayes. But the forces of inflation, which had strength among Republicans as well as Democrats, wanted to postpone resumption and to increase the currency with silver. Both objectives shocked Hayes's old-fashioned notions of finance, and he opposed them resolutely. He was able to put resumption through, but he could not stop, even with a veto, the Bland-Allison Act enlarging the amount of silver money. Given the economic knowledge of the time, Hayes acted naturally and perhaps wisely. But his grasp of the money issue was narrowly fiscal and not related to the economy as a whole. Significantly, in his years of retirement after the Presidency, when he had time to read and reflect about economics, Hayes arrived at entirely new concepts. He came to believe that the great corporations must be placed under rigid national supervision, and in some of his later ideas he antedated the Populism and the Progressivism of the modern era.

In ranking the Presidents, Hayes is usually placed somewhere around the middle. A poll of seventy-five historians in 1962 graded him "average," below "great" and "near great," and rated him fourteenth, just behind John Quincy Adams and ahead of his younger friend William McKinley. The allocation is probably accurate, but it needs to be said that the Presidents of Hayes's era, regardless of ability, were not able to make much of an impress on history. They were on the scene at the wrong time. The years between 1865 and 1900 were transitional. Great forces were changing the face of American society, but at that time few understood the nature of these forces or envisioned their ultimate impact. The national government was not as yet a positive actor in national life, and Presidents could not wield a positive influence. If, for example, Hayes had been Chief Executive in the early 1900s, it is entirely possible that with his fine intelligence and sensitive reactions he would have been a Progressive and, in a different situation, a very different and stronger President.

Another factor that helps to make Hayes and other Presidents of his time seem largely negative was the close division of party strength then prevailing. Every national election was decided by a thin margin, and no President had anything like a consistent control of Congress. In the first half of the Hayes administration the Democrats had a majority in the House, and in the second they took over the Senate also. All things considered, his record of accomplishment was impressive. He brought about an end to reconstruction. He completed the transition to a new monetary system. He withstood the efforts of Congress to dictate appointments and to form policy through riders to appropriations and re-restablished in some measure the independence of the executive branch. Finally, he gave the cause of civil service a big push forward. If he did not do everything that the reformers hoped for, if he made some political appointments and if he failed to make a real fight for a civil service law, yet he introduced the merit principle into the conduct of government. In the words of one reformer, he demonstrated that civil service was practical, and that was important. It was, in fact, a necessary prelude to the enactment of any civil service law.

Hayes, John Quincy Adams, and James K. Polk were the only Presidents who kept diaries. Obviously a presidential diary can be a very valuable and interesting document. The Hayes diary is both. It is written in a sprightly style and contains all kinds of information. Unfortunately it is not a full diary, that is, maintained from day to day. In periods of great activity, such as campaigns, Hayes wrote sparingly or not at all. The longest and most revealing entries were composed in stretches of comparative repose. Thus, the diary is only fair for the campaign of 1876 when Hayes was a very busy man, but it is excellent for the dispute after the election when he was largely a passive figure. It has full and revealing sections detailing his stand on such issues as reconstruction, money, civil service, the custom house appointments controversy, and the fight with Congress over the riders. It describes at length the social regime of the White House and the tours to all parts of the country; it is, in fact, one of the best accounts penned of the social and routine life of a President.

For some reason Hayes did not devote much space to members of his Cabinet or other political intimates. They appear in the pages but they are not sharply etched, and the diary is not a "gallery" of people. If this is a defect, it is more than compensated for by the rich portrait the diarist drew of himself. He was astonishingly frank and introspective in outlining his ideas of government and in depicting himself, the inner Hayes, his strengths and weaknesses. All this makes the diary a revealing and rewarding record of an American leader in a decisive moment of history.

THE HAYES ADMINISTRATION:
A CHRONOLOGY

I. The Nomination of a President

March 25, 1875.—A conference of Ohio Republican leaders at Columbus indicates a desire that Hayes should be the candidate for governor. He is attracted by the distinction of a third term but declines.

June 2, 1875.—The Republican state convention nominates Hayes to run against Governor William Allen. The issues in the campaign are separation of church and state (no financial aid for Catholic schools), and greenbacks against a "sound" gold currency. People tell Hayes that if elected he will be a contender for the presidential nomination.

October 12, 1875.—Hayes is elected governor by a margin of 5,500 votes.

January 10, 1876.—Hayes is inaugurated as governor. Now he hears increasingly from friends and would-be supporters that he may be named as the Republican presidential candidate. He doubts that he has much chance against the leading contenders, James G. Blaine, Roscoe Conkling, Oliver P. Morton, and Benjamin H. Bristow.

March 29, 1876.—The Ohio Republican convention instructs its delegates to vote for Hayes at the coming national convention in Cincinnati.

June 14–16, 1876.—The national convention meets and ballots seven times before choosing a candidate. On the first ballot Hayes has sixty-one votes and is in fifth place. But he climbs steadily and on the seventh and deciding ballot shows 384 votes to Blaine's 351. William A. Wheeler is his vice-presidential running mate. They will compete against the Democratic standard-bearers, Samuel J. Tilden and Thomas A. Hendricks.

July 8, 1876.—In his formal letter of acceptance Hayes announces support of civil service, a sound currency, and national aid for public schools. He assures the South of fair and sympathetic treatment and renounces a second term. As was the custom of the time, Hayes makes few speeches and public appearances and awaits the result in November.

II. THE DISPUTED ELECTION

November 7, 1876.—The election discloses a confused result. Tilden has 4,300,000 popular votes to Hayes's 4,036,000 and Tilden has also an apparent electoral majority. But the nineteen electoral votes of three southern states, South Carolina, Louisiana, and Florida, are in dispute. Without them Tilden has 184, just one short of a majority, and Hayes has 166. The country realizes there is no established method to settle disputed returns.

December, 1876–January, 1877.—Congress meets amid great popular excitement. The two houses appoint bipartisan committees to recommend a solution to the crisis, and these agencies suggest an Electoral Commission to consist of members from the Senate, the House of Representatives, and the Supreme Court.

February 1–March 2, 1877.—The Electoral Commission studies the returns and awards all the disputed votes to Hayes, who is declared elected with 185 votes. Hayes has started for

Washington on March 1 and receives the news while en route.

March 5, 1877.—Hayes is inaugurated as President a day late because the fourth falls on a Sunday. He has, however, to prevent an interregnum, taken a secret oath at the White House on Saturday, March 3. In his inaugural address he stresses the importance of settling the southern problem.

III. THE END OF RECONSTRUCTION

March, 1877.—As the Republican government in Florida has fallen, the only two southern states remaining under Republican control are Louisiana and South Carolina. Unofficial efforts by friends of Hayes to persuade the Republican claimants to the governorships of these states to resign fail.

March 10, 1877.—After a Cabinet discussion it is decided to send a commission to Louisiana to try to bring together in one government the conflicting parties. The commission is announced on March 21.

March 23, 1877.—Hayes invites the rival claimants in South Carolina, Democrat Wade Hampton and Republican Daniel H. Chamberlain, to Washington. Chamberlain learns that Hayes favors Hampton.

April 3–10, 1877.—By Hayes's order the federal troops are withdrawn from South Carolina.

April 19–24, 1877.—The Louisiana commission telegraphs that a legal government exists in the state under Democratic Governor Francis T. Nicholls and a largely Democratic legislature, and that the presence of the troops is unnecessary. Hayes orders the troops withdrawn.

IV. CIVIL SERVICE AND PRESIDENTIAL INDEPENDENCE

March, 1877.—Hayes's Cabinet appointments are coldly received by Republican congressional leaders. Hayes urges members of the Cabinet to employ the principle of civil service in making appointments to their departments.

May 26, 1877.—Hayes, in a letter to Secretary of the Treasury John Sherman, directs that in the administration of the New York Custom House some attention be given to appointment by merit. He forbids assessments on salaries for campaign funds and prohibits employees from engaging too openly in politics.

June 22, 1877.—In an executive order Hayes applies the rules of his letter to Sherman to all departments.

October 15, 1877.—Congress meets in a special session called by Hayes on May 5 to enact an army appropriation bill. The Democrats have a majority of thirteen in the House, and the Republicans a majority of two in the Senate. It is evident that many Republicans oppose Hayes on his southern and civil service policies.

October–November, 1877.—Two prominent officials of the New York Custom House, both henchmen of Senator Conkling, Chester A. Arthur, and Alonzo B. Cornell, defy Hayes's order for the conduct of their office. Hayes asks them to resign and when refused, removes them. As required by the Tenure of Office Act, he submits the names of his new appointees to the Senate, which buries the nominations in committee.

December 12, 1877.—In the regular session Conkling persuades the Senate to reject Hayes's nominations. The issue is joined: Can the President make appointments if a senator in the affected state opposes them?

July 11, 1878.—With Congress out of session, Hayes suspends Arthur and Cornell.

December 1878–February 3, 1879.—Hayes submits his appointments again, and they are finally confirmed.

V. The Defense of Conservative Economics

July–August, 1877.—The Hayes administration opens in conditions of business distress. Strikes in the railroad industry are accompanied by riots, and Hayes sends troops into the states where the disorders are greatest.

November, 1877.—In the special session, strong sentiment develops for an inflation of the currency. The House votes for repeal of the Resumption Act, passed in the Grant administration and providing for a return to specie payments for paper currency on January 1, 1879, and enacts the Bland-Allison Act for the free and unlimited coinage of silver.

December 3, 1877.—Hayes, in his annual message, takes strong ground against postponing resumption and against free silver. His influence helps to stop repeal of the Resumption Act in the Senate.

February, 1878.—The Bland-Allison Act, modified to provide for the purchase and coinage of a stipulated amount of silver, passes Congress.

February 28, 1878.—Hayes, against the advice of some party leaders and some members of his Cabinet, vetoes the Bland-Allison Act. It is immediately repassed.

January 2, 1879.—On this day (because the first fell on Sunday) resumption is accomplished smoothly. Prosperous conditions soon return, and Hayes credits the upswing to his sound currency policy.

December 6, 1880.—In his last annual message Hayes makes a final plea for a conservative monetary policy and warns against the dangers of tinkering with the currency supply.

VI. 1876 Revisited

May, 1878.—Rumors and charges circulate that the Republicans had used fraud to swing the votes of Louisiana and Florida to Hayes. The Democrats in the House sense an opportunity to discredit Hayes, and Clarkson N. Potter of New York offers a resolution to create an investigative committee. It passes, and the committee under Potter as chairman begins its work on June 1.

June 14, 1878.—Under criticism for raking up the past, the House Democrats pass a resolution stating that there is no purpose to deny Hayes's title to the Presidency or to oust him from the office.

October, 1878.—After the Potter committee has examined a number of witnesses hostile to Hayes, the New York *Tribune* obtains possession of some cipher dispatches sent by politicians in the 1876 crisis. Translation of them indicates that prominent Democrats had employed pressure to secure electoral votes and that possibly Tilden himself was implicated. Publication of the dispatches causes a terrific public uproar.

December, 1878–January, 1879.—The House Republicans demand that the Potter committee investigate the cipher dispatches, and the Democrats reluctantly agree to do so.

March 3, 1879.—The Potter committee makes its report, but much of the effect is blunted. The Republicans feel that the charge of fraud in 1876 will not be raised in future elections.

VII. The Battle of the Riders

February–March, 1879.—The Forty-fifth Congress adjourns without passing two of the most important appropriations bills, the one for the Army and the one for the legislative, executive, and judicial branches. To the army bill the Democratic House adds a rider repealing the law empowering the Army to maintain peace at the polls. To the other measure the House adds a rider repealing the federal election law authorizing the use of marshals in elections and the jurors' test-oath law which bars former Confederates from federal juries. The Republican Senate refuses to accept the riders, and the departments and the Army are without money. Hayes feels that the issues are vital—the Democrats are reviving the southern question and Congress is attempting to assert control over the executive branch. Congress adjourns March 4, and on the same day he calls a special session for March 18.

March 18–19, 1879.—In the new Congress the Democrats have a majority in both houses. Hayes, in a brief message, asks legislation appropriating money for the Army and the civil list.

April 25, 1879.—Congress passes the army bill with a rider, and Hayes vetoes it on April 29. The Democrats modify the bill to meet some of his objections, but on May 12 he vetoes the altered version.

May 29, 1879.—Congress passes the civil department bill with riders, and Hayes vetoes it. The Democrats, sensing that it is bad politics to withhold appropriations, decide to back down. They enact the army bill without a rider. They break the civil bill into two parts and pass appropriations for the executive and legislative branches with no restrictions. But to the bill for the judiciary they add riders repealing the test-oath law and forbidding payments to marshals enforcing federal elections laws.

June 23–25, 1879.—Hayes vetoes the judicial bill, although accepting the other measures. Congress then passes a bill providing for the expenses of the judiciary but repealing the test-oath and omitting payments for marshals. Hayes accepts this measure. But a separate bill for the marshals restricting their employment meets a veto on June 30.

June 31, 1879.—Congress adjourns. Hayes is almost completely victorious, and the contest draws him and his party closer together than ever before.

VIII. FOREIGN POLICY AND THE LAST DAYS

June 1, 1877.—Hayes authorizes the Army to follow Mexican marauders across the border. The Mexican incident is typical of the small but vexatious problems he has to deal with in foreign affairs.

February, 1879.—Congress passes a bill restricting Chinese immigration to the United States. Hayes vetoes it March 1 on the grounds it violates the Burlingame Treaty of 1868 providing for free migration between the two countries. But he sends a commission to China which in November, 1880, negotiates a treaty giving the United States permission to supervise and limit Chinese immigration.

March 8, 1880.—Hayes, taking note of the efforts of a French company to build an isthmian canal across Panama, sends a special message to Congress declaring that such a waterway must be under American control.

August 26–November 6, 1880.—Hayes leaves Washington for a trip that will carry him to the Pacific coast and back. He is the first President to visit this distant region.

November 2, 1880.—To Hayes's great satisfaction, the Republican candidate, James A. Garfield, wins the presidential election.

March 5, 1881.—Hayes departs from Washington for his home in Ohio. He takes pride in his record and in the increased respect and popularity which he has won in the closing years in the White House.

DRAMATIS PERSONAE

BLAINE, James G. 1830–1893. Brilliant and magnetic and not universally trusted, the senator from Maine was the leading contender for the nomination that Hayes received in 1876. An enemy to Hayes's enemy, Roscoe Conkling, he was yet scornful of Hayes. In turn, Hayes disliked Blaine, whom he characterized as "a scheming demagogue, selfish and reckless." Blaine, the head of the Republican faction known as the Half-Breeds, sniped continually at Hayes, yet felt constrained to defend the President against attacks by his hated rival of the Stalwart faction, Conkling.

BRISTOW, Benjamin H. 1832–1896. Appointed Secretary of the Treasury by President U. S. Grant, this Kentuckian made a reputation as a reformer by exposing the "Whiskey ring" scandals. He was a leading contender for the Republican nomination in 1876, but fell before Hayes. His failure marked the end of his political career.

BUTLER, Benjamin F. 1818–1893. At this stage in his checkered career Butler was a member of the House from Massachusetts. He had few contacts with Hayes and no influence. Hayes thought that Butler represented everything that was bad in politics and referred to his monetary theories as "Butlerism—cheap money schemes."

CONKLING, Roscoe. 1829–1888. Handsome, charming,

arrogant, and ruthless, the New York senator embodied all the elements of machine politics. The chief of the Stalwarts and a dominating figure in the Grant administration, he aspired to the Republican nomination in 1876. When Hayes named his Cabinet without consulting him, Conkling was furious and openly opposed the President thereafter. His contest with Hayes over the right to control appointments in the New York Custom House was one of the memorable controversies of the administration. Despite his real skill in the art of manipulation, he was too swayed by personal considerations to be a great politician. Hayes's summary of Conkling was apt: If he could not rule he would not play.

CURTIS, George William. 1824–1892. The crusading editor of *Harper's Weekly* was one of the leaders in the movement for civil service reform. He criticized Hayes severely for not pushing the cause harder, but conceded that the President had made a promising start in establishing a merit system. Hayes had shown, Curtis wrote, that civil service was practical.

DEVENS, Charles. 1820–1891. The Attorney General had been a judge on the Massachusetts Supreme Court. A good storyteller and an amiable companion, he was not a particularly strong member of the Cabinet. His appointment was viewed as a concession to Senator George F. Hoar of his state.

DOUGLASS, Frederick, 1817–1895. Under fire in his own party for being too lenient to the South, Hayes named this famous Negro leader as United States marshal of the District of Columbia. Southerners and segregationists cried out against the appointment, causing Hayes to observe that there was no pleasing the extremes.

EATON, Dorman B. 1823–1899. One of the reform leaders, Eaton was appointed by President Grant as chairman of the Civil Service Commission, whose funds were cut off by Congress in 1875. Hayes urged Congress without success to renew the funds and used Eaton's reports in composing his public statements on civil service. Hayes also encouraged Eaton to make a study of civil service in England. The result was a widely read book which stimulated the movement for a merit system. Eaton drafted the Pendleton Act of 1883, the first federal civil service law.

EDMUNDS, George F. 1828–1919. The Vermont senator was credited with breaking the impasse of 1876–1877 by offering the bill to create the Electoral Commission. Able, upright, and biting in debate, he was one of the most influential Republicans in the Senate. He agreed with Hayes on such issues as currency and civil service but doubted the President's southern policy and general political sagacity. After one interview with Hayes he reported that the Chief Executive's views were "more suggestive of a political dreamer than of the sober sense of a statesman."

EVARTS, William M. 1818–1901. In appointing Evarts as Secretary of State, Hayes challenged the boss leadership of his party. Evarts had been Andrew Johnson's counsel in the great impeachment case and then his Attorney General, and in New York he had opposed Conkling's ambitions. He had been the Republican counsel before the Electoral Commission. Tall and spare, witty and eloquent, Evarts was sometimes disposed to talk too much and too loosely. But he was a man of stature, perhaps the best-known lawyer in the country, and he added distinction to the Cabinet. He could also be, when the occasion demanded, an adroit political operator.

GARFIELD, James A. 1831–1881. The bearded, impressive Garfield was the Republican leader in the House. In 1877 he was one of the Republican members of the Electoral Commission. When John Sherman entered the Cabinet, Garfield prepared to try for his Senate seat. But Hayes urged him to remain where he was, on the understanding that the Democrats would let the Republicans organize the House and Garfield would be elected Speaker. If there was such an agreement, the Democrats did not observe it. Garfield was dubious about

Hayes's southern policy but continued to support the administration. In 1880 he received the Republican nomination and was elected.

HARLAN, John M. 1833–1911. Hayes was very proud of his nomination of this Kentuckian to the Supreme Court. Harlan's appointment might have been considered a reward for his support of Hayes in the disputed election, although originally he was a leader of the Bristow forces in the 1876 convention. He turned out to be an outstanding member of the highest tribunal. He dissented from the opinion of the Court which interpreted the Fourteenth Amendment to restrict Negro rights. Curiously, Hayes's second appointment to the Court was a northerner who supported the restrictions on the Negro. William B. Woods (1824–1887), appointed in 1880, was an Ohio Democrat converted to Republicanism. Serving as a Union soldier in the Civil War, he removed to Alabama after the conflict. His appointment was regarded as one of Hayes's several gestures to the South.

HAYES, Lucy Webb. 1831–1889. The President's wife was a plump and handsome woman, a busy White House hostess of good taste. But she had long believed in total abstinence from liquor and was prepared to enforce her views on official functions. Although Hayes had been known to drink occasionally before 1877 (and did after 1881), he gave up the practice during his Presidency. He agreed with Mrs. Hayes that the first family should set an example for temperate living. Liquor was served at a dinner for visiting members of the Russian royal household, but after that it was taboo at all functions, diplomatic or others. The dry regime aroused widespread ridicule and criticism, some of it rather savage; Mrs. Hayes was dubbed "Lemonade Lucy." Church and temperance people, however, applauded Mrs. Hayes's determination. Life at the White House was enlivened by the five Hayes children: Webb Cook, twenty-one years of age in 1877 and just out of Cornell University, who acted as an unofficial secretary to his father; Birchard, twenty-four and at Harvard Law School, and Rutherford, nineteen and at Cornell, both of whom were frequent visitors; and the two youngest, Fanny, ten, and Scott, six. Also a member of the family circle was Hayes's niece, Emily Platt, daughter of his deceased and beloved sister Fanny; her marriage to Russell Hastings was one of the big social events of the administration.

HOAR, George F. 1826–1904. Just beginning his long and distinguished career as a senator from Massachusetts, Hoar represented the same reform elements in the Republican party as Hayes. He was a frequent guest at White House social affairs.

KEY, David M. 1824–1900. The naming of Key as Postmaster General was Hayes's most unusual appointment. Key had been a Confederate soldier and a Democratic senator from Tennessee. Although Hayes referred in the diary to his bipartisan motives in appointing Key, his action had political overtones. In the election crisis the Republican negotiators had promised the southerners a Cabinet place, and Hayes had high hopes of being able through men like Key to build up a new kind of Republican party in the South. Key resigned in 1880 to become a federal judge and was succeeded by Horace Maynard, also of Tennessee.

McCRARY, George W. 1835–1890. For a time Hayes considered naming former Confederate General Joseph E. Johnston as Secretary of War. But he was told the appointment would never be confirmed. He then gave the post to McCrary, an Iowa congressman who was backed by the powerful railroad interests who had supported Hayes in the election crisis. In 1879 he resigned to become a federal judge; Alexander Ramsey of Minnesota succeeded him.

MATTHEWS, Stanley. 1824–1889. Matthews and Hayes had known each other since college days, had served in the same Ohio regiment in the Civil War, and were close political and personal associates. During the 1876–1877 crisis Matthews had acted as a representative for Hayes in the negotiations with the southerners. When John Sherman entered the Cabinet, Matthews succeeded him as senator. In the upper chamber he was viewed as Hayes's spokesman. But he deserted the President on the money issue, voting for the Bland-Allison Act and sponsoring a resolution to pay government bonds in silver. In 1881 Hayes nominated him to the Supreme Court. But the appointment aroused wide opposition, even from Republicans. It was charged that Matthews was connected with the Jay Gould railroad interests and was unfit for judicial service. His nomination was shelved in a Senate committee. Garfield, at Hayes's insistence, renominated Matthews, who was finally confirmed by one vote.

MORTON, Oliver P. 1823–1877. Thunderous and terrifying in debate, this Indiana senator was fully as much a machine politician as Conkling. Yet Hayes admired him and expected him to lead for the administration in the Senate. Morton's death in November, 1877, deprived Hayes of a potential strong supporter that he could have well used.

POTTER, Clarkson N. 1825–1882. This New York Democratic congressman sponsored an investigation of alleged Republican frauds in counting the electoral votes in the 1876–1877 crisis. The inquiry turned into a boomerang when cipher dispatches were discovered that also implicated the Democrats. Hayes scornfully referred to Potter's brand of politics as "Potterism."

SCHURZ, Carl. 1829–1906. The bespectacled, scholarly German-American leader was known as a maverick in politics. As a senator from Missouri he had opposed the Grant administration and supported the Liberal Republican revolt of 1872. He came back in the party in 1876 to work for Hayes's election. His appointment as Secretary of the Interior was particularly infuriating to the Stalwart leadership. He was one of the few Cabinet members who made a sincere effort to apply Hayes's rules of civil service in his appointments.

SHERMAN, John. 1823–1900. This veteran Ohio politician was the first man Hayes invited to join his Cabinet. A member of the Senate since 1861 and longtime chairman of its important Finance Committee, he was a logical choice for Secretary of the Treasury. In the crisis of 1876–1877 he had visited Louisiana to represent Republican interests, and Hayes leaned on him heavily. Yet he did not render an unqualified support to the President's financial program, being willing to make some compromise with the inflation forces. Competent but colorless, the grizzled Sherman attempted to secure the Republican nomination in 1880, but failed then as he would again in later years.

SMITH, William Henry. 1833–1896. Nobody could have admired Hayes more extravagantly than Smith, and no man could have worked longer and harder to promote an idol's career. As general agent of the Western Associated Press in Chicago, he played a key role in the scheme to secure southern acquiescence to the award of the disputed electoral votes to Hayes. He and Hayes corresponded constantly, and he was probably closer to the President than any other adviser. The references to him in the diary are, however, few and passing.

THOMPSON, Richard W. 1809–1900. "Uncle Dick," the Secretary of the Navy, was Hayes's most frankly political appointment. A noted stump orator and savage partisan, he had been the target of many charges of unethical conduct. From Indiana, he was appointed to please Senator Morton. Easily the most colorful figure in a staid Cabinet, he smoked an average of twenty cigars a day. In 1881 he saw nothing wrong in accepting a job with an American subsidiary of the Panama Canal Company at a salary of $25,000 a year. The shocked Hayes informed him that his resignation had been accepted.

TILDEN, Samuel J. 1814–1886. Prim and ascetic, the New York governor was Hayes's Democratic rival in the disputed election of 1876. His claims to the office kept rising like a ghost to haunt Hayes for the next four years.

WAITE, Morrison R. 1816–1888. The Chief Justice of the Supreme Court swore Hayes in as President twice, once secretly at the White House, and two days later publicly at the inaugural. He was an old friend of the Hayes family.

WHEELER, William A. 1819–1887. When Wheeler's name was first suggested as a possible running mate, Hayes asked who he was. The question was not surprising. Wheeler was an industrious and useful but relatively unknown congressman from New York. He was placed on the ticket with Hayes to give it a sectional balance. As Vice-President he was, as Hayes noted, one of the rare second officers to be on genuinely friendly terms with the President. One of his few pleasures was in visiting the Hayes family at the White House.

HAYES

The Diary of a President

Chapter I

MARCH 28, 1875—JAN. 13, 1876

Sunday, 28th March, 1875.—32° + Clear & fine. Yesterday we had good spring breezes with thawing weather all day. Snow all gone except a few small patches.

For some time I have made my Diary a mere weather record. We are living happily—never more so. Scott Russells promotion to pants has been the event of the last week. Little Fanny is healthy bright and good. She does not take to "book larnin." But that will come in time, no doubt. Birch takes more and more interest in the law. I think he will be a good lawyer. Ruddy, at Lansing, says he is homesick. He repeats it three times in the same letter. But his letters are cheerful. He says he works at chopping 3 hours daily. Webb writes good letters from Cornell. Lucy is healthy, and as she grows older preserves her beauty. She is large but not unwieldly. I think this paragraph cut from the last *Weekly State Journal* [Columbus, Ohio], describes her.

A Sunny Temper

What a blessing to a household is a merry, cheerful woman —one whose spirits are not affected by wet days, or little disappointments, or whose milk of human kindness does not sour in the sunshine of prosperity. Such a woman in the darkest house brightens the house like a little piece of sunshiny weather. The magnetism of her smiles and the electrical brightness of her looks and movements infect every one. The children go to school with a sense of something great to be achieved; her husband goes into the world in a conqueror's spirit. No matter how people annoy and worry him all day, far off her presence shines, and he whispers to himself, "At home I shall find rest." So day by day she literally renews his strength and energy, and if you know a man with a beaming face, a kind heart and a prosperous business, in nine cases out of ten you will find a wife of this kind.

The only drawback is her frequent attacks of sick headache. Perhaps twice a month she suffers for a day or two. I too am healthy. Getting a little too fat for comfort. The independence of all political and other bother is a happiness.

The Republican Caucus at Columbus last Thursday according to report was unanimously for me for Governor. A third term would be a distinction—a feather I would like to wear. No man ever had it in Ohio. Letters tell me I am really wanted. But the present condition of my money matters require attention. The chance of an election is not good. More important still, I do not sympathise with a large share of the party leaders. I hate the corruptionists of whom Butler is leader. I doubt the ultra measures relating to the South, and I am opposed to the course of Gen. Grant on the 3*d* term, the Civil Service, and the appointment of unfit men on partisan or personal ~~considerations~~ grounds.[1] I wouldn't hesitate to fight a losing battle, if the cause was wholly and clearly good, and important. I am not sure that it is in all respects what it should be, and as to its importance, I am more than in doubt. Hence I have said decidedly *no* to all who have approached me.

14*th April*, 1875.—30° + Ground frozen & white with over two inches of snow—bright & pleasant. Yesterday not less than four to six inches of snow fell. But it melted so fast that at no time was there more than two or three inches on the ground. The Grass green in & under the snow looks odd & pretty.

I am still importuned in all quarters to consent to run as Republican Candidate for Governor. Several suggest that if elected Governor now, I will stand well for the Presidency next year. How wild! What a queer lot we are becoming. No body is out of the reach of that mania.

*Sunday, 18th April, 1875.—*12° + (!) and the ground white with snow. Yesterday like the day before—a succession of snow squalls & calms—but colder than the 16*th* was. The mercury ranged in the shade from 23° to 25° + during the warmest part of the day, and by dark was down to 20°—no doubt below 10° + at the coldest part of last night. A bright clear morning today—

The talk about my candidacy for Governor rather grows in spite of my repeated refusals. I regret this, flattering as it is to my self esteem. I dont wish to say, against a general and urgent request, no with due emphasis. It looks like a lack of appreciation of the good opinion of the Party, and a want of gratitude for past favors. The prospect of an election seems to me to be not good. The third term talk, the Civil rights bill, the partisan appointments of the baser sort, in other wards the *Butlerism* of the Administration, are all bad, & weights on us.—

Transplanted a youngish pair of crab apple trees about 1½ inches in diameter and 10 feet high. Also the three little sickly Hemlocks just at s.w. corner of office [in Spiegel Grove]. Will any of these grow? No other plantings yesterday.

31st May, 1875.—Cool morning—bright.

I am still importuned to allow my name to be used for Governor. I am no less averse today than at the beginning. If Judge [Alphonso] Taft and others should withdraw, and the Convention generally should insist on my candidacy, I shall not refuse.[2] This is not likely to happen. A general demand by the party that has honored me so often, I regard as a Command which I must obey. If notwithstanding my declination and known preference the members of the Convention with substantial unanimity insist on my the use of my name, I shall regard this wish as a command, and obey it. If the friends of Judge Taft or of ~~the~~ other candidates still present their names, I ~~am~~ will under no circumstances ~~to~~ be a candidate against them. In that event my name must be unqualifiedly withdrawn.

3d June, 1875.—I was nominated for Governor yesterday at Columbus. I persisted in declining to the last. The leading other Candidate before the Convention, Judge Taft of Cincinnati, is an able and good man. But he had such a record on the Bible question in the Schools, that his nomination was impossible.[3] I did all I could to remove the predjudice against him, and to aid in his nomination. I sent to Richard Smith [of the *Cincinnati Gazette*], a leader in the struggle for Judge Taft the following dispatch: "I cannot allow my name to be used in opposition to Judge Taft. He became a candidate after I declined. He is an able and pure man and a sound Republican. I would not accept a nomination obtained by a contest with him." and another as follows to Chas Foster "I have stated to every body that I would not consent to go into a contest. I do not want it, and would not accept if nominated in opposition to Judge Taft."

I was nominated notwithstanding 396 for me 151 for Taft. The nomination on motion of a friend of Taft Maj. [W. D.] Bickham [editor of the *Dayton Journal*] was made unanimous. At first I wrote a dispatch declining. Then came a dispatch from the Sec'y of the Convention stating that on behalf of his father, Charles P. Taft had moved my nomination by acclamation, and that it was splendidly carried. I then sent the following

"In deference to the wish of the Convention, I yield my preference and accept the nomination."

The ~~meaning~~ substance of all this is that I did all I could to prevent my own nomination and to aid Taft. Taft being even then so far short of a nomination, and in view of the decided

4

wish of the Convention, and the injury my declination would do the party, I gave up my own preference and declared purpose, and accepted.

On pp near the end of this diary I propose to put down the points requiring attention in the Canvass.

[The following appears later in his diary, on page 59]:

Political "Mem[oranda]"

3d June, 1875.—Nominated yesterday for Governor—had declined in positive terms—had even gone so far as to say I would not accept against Judge Taft. After the nomination Taft and his friends relieved me from embarrassment, and for the sake of the friends and Party who have so greatly honored me I yielded and am now in for it. I think the interesting point is *to rebuke the Democracy by a defeat for subserviency to Roman Catholic demands.*

4th June, 1875.—Wrote to Gen C. H. Grosvenor requesting him to prepare an address on the objectionable features of the Last Legislature.

[Notes]

The Bible in the Public Schools—"A division of the school fund is agitated and demanded" by the same power and upon the same grounds, by which and on which the passage of the Geghan Bill [4] was demanded.

———

My topics chiefly drawn from State Affairs.

1. Conduct of Dem. Party in the investigation of grave charges of corruption in the Legislature.

2. Its measures as to the penal, reformatory, & Benevolent Institutions (Salaried Boards) (The benefit of unpaid service)

3. The Catholic question. Also *Independence of Party. The Doctrines of the Independents or Liberals.*

Gov. Allen [5]—*one Republican on each Board.*

The vacancy on the Centennial Board to be created by my election.

———

Bible in schools case p.105 Stallo.

We can say truly since the Supreme Court has decided the case, all men say to the Catholics

"Your complaints are groundless; the schools are open to all, & there is nothing done or taught in them at wh[ich] the most devout Cath[olic] can take offence. No sectarian flag floats over the school house, & no spirit enters there but that of peace & good will toward all men & creeds. ...We want to bring the children of Protestants, Cath, Jews & Unbelievers together in the common School room."

———

On the currency question either specie payments & Banks or unlimited Greenbacks without specie payment.

———

Where is the power in the Dem Party? In New York City. Draw a line from the eastern shore of Maryland to West Missouri, and every State north of it almost 2/3 of the Nation would be lost to them if the Catholic vote leaves them.

Instruction must be given in the Catholic faith or the public schools will be denounced as Godless, and they will be destroyed if the R. C. can destroy them—*See p 176 Archbishop J. B. Paroll*.

Our Constitution contains a provision on the right side of the question. Let us put that provision for its enforcement, interpolation, and practical exposition *in the hands of its friends not of its enemies*.

Dems oppose discussion, agitation of this topic. So they did of the Slavery question. But the enemies of the free schools discuss it. They in a solid body vote with reference to it

———

Learn of your adversary. Who is he for? Go against those he supports and you can't be far wrong.

———

Gen. Thos Mifflin a brave soldier of the Revolutionary Army—President of the Continental Congress which in 1783 or 4(?) received the resignation of Gen. Washington, was three times in succession elected Gov. Pa. from 1790 to 1799 and prior to that had [been] Prest of the Supreme Ex Council of Penna—as the successor of Benj. Franklin.[6]

Thos McKean, 1799–1808, a signer of the Declaration of Independence of whom Jefferson said   p. 306 "Govs of Penn"

Simon Snyder 1808–17.—the War Gov of *1812* [of Pennsylvania]. *Three terms of 3 years each.*

George Clinton—6 terms of 3 years each in New York.

Vice Prest on the Ticket with Jefferson in 1804 in the place of Burr & again V.P. with Madison in 1808.

D. D. Tomkins [Daniel D. Tompkins] *four* (4) times Gov of N.Y. & twice V.P. Gov, 1807–1810–1813–1816—elected with Monroe V.P., 1817–1825—

DeWitt Clinton—4 times.

~~M. Van Buren~~

Patrick Henry 3 terms of one year each—ineligible for a 4th term. During the Revolution—the first Republican Gov.

John Hancock Gov Mass 1780 to 1785—1787 to 1793—

Sam Adams three terms

———

Indiana 3 year terms formerly & many for 6 years.

I. *This is a Nation.*

Open with a general sweep showing the condition of things when the Repub Party came into power—and what it is now a solid Nation, free, debt paid—&c &c all people united and harmonious, to celebrate the 100" anniversary of our Independence—one flag, &c &c all which was accomplished in opposition to the great body of our adversaries—And now the past secure we approach the questions of the present & future.

They opposed every step of this great and beneficent progress—the Repub past is secure, the past of our adversaries . . .

But the people are not prepared for the issue. Gov [ernments] are not established to teach religion—to control conscience—very well, it is the Mission of the Republican Party to prepare them. If we go down in our election we will fight again—and sooner or later we shall be victors.

In the midst of the tremendous events of the last sixteen years there have been mistakes and errors in Civil and Military affairs. But the Rep party in dealing with the questions of the time did not make the great mistake on the debt, of opposing its honest payment, nor the mistake in reconstruction of opposing equal rights civil and political to all Citizens of the Republic—nor the mistake of opposing the measures of Lincoln which destroyed Slavery—nor the mistake of opposing the Measures wh[ich] saved the Union and made of this people one Nation.

And now the new questions

1. How to deal with Corruption in office and especially in Legislative bodies

2. How to secure a sound currency

3. How to preserve the School system

This (the School question) is one of the phases of the great question of our day. It interests in some form or other the people of all civilized Nations. It convulses Italy—it stirs Germany to its base—it fills England with its debates—Here we cant escape it. Think—deliberate—act. *What will Ohio do?*

The position of the two parties is: Democrats say, there is no danger. We are Sound; if there was danger—we are to *be* trusted if danger ever comes but all is safe, all is well. Do nothing. Act on other questions—*there is no danger!*

Republicans say, the demand is made now—the debate has begun—all is not safe unless the people act—unless they vote— Let them rebuke by their votes the first dawning of the attempt, &c.

———

Under our Constitution and decision—Schools have grown up in which all Protestants, all Jews, Unbelievers of every shade of Unbelief feel confidence.

When great questions are at Stake—and agitated, are debated —the party which says don't reply, dont debate, dont agitate there is no danger—all is well—dont reply— We are sound, but we deprecate discussion—the party that takes that position is ~~the Party~~ already at the half way house—they ~~will~~ are in route for the Camp of your adversary. They cant be trusted They must be voted down.

The same means used to pass the Geghan bill—the same motives operating—may ~~pass~~ in some form divide the school fund and destroy the schools. Look at it—the *threat—the result*.

5th June, 1875.—I am overwhelmed with correspondence by mail telegraph &c. &c., congratulating me on my nomination, and the manner of it. The newspapers show that it was done in a way never before seen in Ohio, and rarely if ever, anywhere. It is reading that would turn a head not *firm* and *level*. I have just written my competitor if it be proper to call a man my competitor with whom I in no way competed, & to whom I gave a hearty support from the beginning.

Private

Fremont O
5 June 1875

My Dear Sir:

I write to thank you in the sincerest and heartiest way for your action on my nomination. It gave me very great and much needed relief. On getting the Secretary's first dispatch

9

I was surely perplexed. To refuse would offend and disappoint friends to whom I was under many obligations. I wrote a dispatch declining, and was considering it with a friend when the second dispatch from the Secretary announcing the motion of Mr Ch. P. Taft came and decided the question. I am confident you would regard my course as fully justifying your friendly act and speech if all I have said and done since this affair arose were fully before you.

Sincerely yr friend

R. B. Hayes

Hon A. Taft
   Cinti

12th *October*, 1875.—Election day! The weather is perfect. Spiegel Grove—my home—never looked so beautiful before. I am as nearly indifferent, on personal grounds, to the result of this day as it is possible to be. I prefer success. But I anticipate defeat with very great equanimity. If victorious I am likely to be pushed for the Republican nomination for President. This would make my life a disturbed and troubled one until the nomination six or eight months hence. If nominated, the stir would last until November a year hence. Defeat in the next Presidential Election is almost a certainty. In any event defeat now returns me to the quiet life I sought in coming here.

The large considerations of country, patriotism & principle find little place in a deliberation on this question. The march of events will carry us safely beyond the dangers of the present ~~consid~~ questions.

17th *October*, 1875.—Elected—a pleasant serenade from my neighbors—a day of doubt and anxiety as to the result. It looked on Thursday as if the Dems were bent on counting me out. All right however. Now comes papers from all the country counties urging me for the Presidential nomination. Such as the following list—

Cinti Times
Toledo Blade
Dayton Journal
Springfield Republic
Ashtabula Sentinel
Fremont Journal
Kenton Rep
Bellefontaine Rep
Clinton „
Pickaway Herald & Union

Inaugural:

Shall repeal of Geghan
law be recommended?

[Notes]

Appointments must regard geography of the State—
Classes of Supporters as Germans, Liberals, Jews Welsh
&c &c

Men in Dem Counties to be preferred?

Col. Hayes of Trumbull—one arm.

Rodn[ey] Foos a clerkship

Jones a Comm. [L. C. Jones, of Warren, O.]

Taft a [   ]

Harrison a [   ]

For places—Private Secretary. x Geo. H. Ford, x Sharpe of
Delaware, ~~Barringer,~~ W. Claypoole Springfield, Capt A. E.
Lee, Cols. O.

Kennedy)
Nash   )
Wikoff   )
Stimson)

Curtis of Comm'l [Commercial]

Lee

Judges—*Herron*, Burns, Mason, *Whitman*, Hall of Lorain.
W. W. Johnston, *Rainey, Taft, Matthews, Harrison, Granger,
Page, Swan*, Mason.

Insurance, Capt. L. E. Bronson of Bryan, Barringer, [   ].

Librarian—[S. G.] Harbaugh, Stimson, S. W. Ely.

1st January, 1876.—70° + in shade!! Yesterday & today the warmest winter days remembered in this climate. 70° in the shade. Sun bright & clear & spring like. Lucy & Fan gone to Columbus to remain with Laura [Platt Mitchell, Hayes's niece, daughter of his sister Fanny]. Ruddy in Chillicothe—Birch in Cambridge. Webb & I clearing out trees in N. W. corner of fruit garden & making paths [in Spiegel Grove]. Swank, Jimmy & Edward our hands. I go to Columbus to assume the Govs office soon—leave here the *4th*.

Columbus, 13th January, 1876.—Inaugurated Gov 3d time on the 10*th*, Monday. Lucy came down to receive calls with our dear niece Laura on New Years. She brought Fanny with her. I came down & stopped with them at Mitchells on the *4th*. On Saturday 8*th* Webb, Scott & nurse Winnie [Monroe] came. Ruddy also from Chillicothe. The two large boys staid with their Uncle Wm. [Platt] & the rest here with Gen & Mrs M[itchell].

The weather cold & windy but bright. A handsome display of Military. I speak of Inauguration day. Gov Allen & I rode together. He is aged, but full of spirit & vim. Talked cheerfully & well. It all passed off pleasantly. Winnie, Rud, & Scott, returned today to Fremont.

NOTES

CHAPTER I

1 Hayes here indicates his strong dissent from the course of the national Republican party and his dislike of such leaders as Benjamin F. Butler. In a negative fashion, he outlined the exact policy he would follow after he became President. When he penned these first entries, he was living at his estate of Spiegel Grove, where he had also an office.

2 Taft had served briefly in President Grant's cabinet as Secretary of War and Attorney General. A man of solid if not brilliant attainments, he was the father of William Howard Taft.

3 What Hayes called the Bible question was often referred to in Ohio

politics as the Catholic question. It involved a whole complex of issues—
the right of Catholic priests to minister to inmates in state institutions, the
demand of Catholics for a share of public school funds for parochial
schools, and the use of the Bible in the public schools. The Catholics of
Cincinnati had persuaded the board of education to stop the use of the
King James Bible in the public institutions. Judge Taft, in a decision in
1870, supported the right of the board to ban the Bible. His position offended
his own party, which tended to equate Catholicism with the Democrats. The
Catholic issue would be a burning one in the coming gubernatorial
campaign.

[4] The Geghan Bill, passed by a Democratic legislature, permitted Catholic
priests to administer to inmates of state institutions.

[5] Governor William Allen, the incumbent Democrat, was Hayes's opponent in the campaign.

[6] These notes on eminent men who had held several terms as governors
of their states were evidently intended to be the basis of a defense against
Democratic attacks on Hayes for seeking a third term.

Chapter II

FEB. 1, 1876—OCT. 15, 1876

Columbus, 1st February, 1876.—1st [Senator John] Sherman in his letter on the Presidency says Hayes was not greatly distinguished in the Army.[1]

This is perfectly true in the sense in which S. intended it should be received. The rank of Gen Hayes was Major at the beginning of the war, and he never rose above the command of a Brigade and Division. But in his grade he was distinguished.

1. He commanded the Regiment which led the attack and successfully opened the battle of South Mountain.

2. He commanded the Brigade which led the assault & carried the works of the Enemy in the fierce battle of Cloyd Mt where the Rebel Genl Jenkins was defeated & killed.

3. He commanded one of the two Brigades which covered the retreat and saved Crooks ~~Com~~ Army after the defeat at Winchester 24 July, 1864

4. He commanded one of the two Brigades selected by Sheridan to ~~make~~ lead in repeated attacks on Early's lines in the Shenandoah Valley in Aug. 1864

5. He commanded one of the two Brigades which fought at Berryville Sept. 3*d*, & by great gallantry saved the day.

6. He commanded the Brigade which ~~turned~~ led in the flank attack which turned Early's left and defeated him

14

7. He commanded the Division which ~~passed~~ led up North Mt and routed Early in the Victory at Fishers Hill 22d Sept, 1864.

8. He commanded one of the Divisions which retained its organization, and ~~aided in~~ gained great distinction in the Battle of Cedar Creek, Oct. 19, 64.

9. In more than fifty engagements large & small he was always conspicuous for ~~reck~~ personal daring, ~~and~~ self possession and efficiency.

That is a piece of talk that looks like brag—but I think it does not overstate—quote Comly on several occasions [2]—the language of my promotion to Brig Genl & Brevet Maj Gen &c &c &c & refer to Crook, Sheridan &c &c.

Give the crossing of the Slough at Winchester Sept. 19, 64.

Urged to leave the Army in 1862 after his wound at So. Mt, but declined to go into politics.

In 1864 nominated for Congress & urged to come home to take the stump. Reply. (give it).

In 1865 nominated by Ohio soldiers in the Shenandoah Valley for Governor.

11th February, 1876.—My first school teacher, Mrs. Joan Murray of Delaware, is to be buried today. If I can I will go to the funeral. She was an excellent woman. Her letter congratulating me after the election, referring to my mother and sister touched me so, that I could scarcely see to read. A good woman gone. Another link broken, which connects me with the past in D[elaware].

Tuesday, 15th February, 1876.—Since I came to Columbus six weeks ago, there has been no day in which I have not had letters and visits on the subject of my nomination for the Presidency. Many days ~~it~~ there is a succession of callers at my office on this topic. I say very little. I have in no instance encouraged any one to work to that end. I have discountenanced all efforts at organization, or management in my interest. I have said the whole talk about me is on the score of availability. Let availability do the work then.

16th February, 1876.—Very cold again. A mild winter as a whole but in each month a few cold days. I look for Darling [Lucy] today.

20th February, 1876.—Lucy came as I expected, took part in the great affair at the City Hall, and in her pink or red silk looked her best. She went with me through the Dr. [W. B.] Hawkes house, & has now returned to Fremont to receive Dr. [Joseph T.] Webb & Aunt Anna [Matthews Webb, brother and sister-in-law of Mrs. Hayes], and to bring down such things as she may need here.

Friday I went with Judge [John M.] Pugh [of Columbus] to the Reform Farm near Lancaster. Charges made agst the gentleman in charge, Mr [George E.] Howe, made it necessary to investigate, & after some time spent in doing it, I have decided to reappoint Mr H.

It seems to me a plain duty to do so. I told Mr H. of the investigation & the result. He is somewhat sensitive about it, but on the whole was not much out of the way. Mrs Howe is acknowledged to be the right person for the place.

Some small matters in the Institution should be attended to.

1. Meterological tables should be kept. It is a lofty region said to be 600 feet above the Hocking.

2. A Telegraph line should be built to Lancaster & the boys taught Telegraphing

3. A narrow gauge R.R. should be run out there.

23d February 1876.—The first two months of this winter unusually mild weather prevailed. This month of Feb is probably about an average. Cold snaps about the *7th*, *17th* & *23d* —about as usual in this month.

Columbus, 2d March, 1876.—With Lucy, Fanny, & Scott came from Fremont yesterday. Found our man, the old soldier

Shermis in possession of the new home—Dr [W. B.] Hawkes house, no. 60 East Broad Street, off State House, on north side.

3d March, 1876.—When at home I sold by a trade of one acre of ground north of John street [now Hayes Avenue, Fremont, Ohio] for ten (10) acres in Wood County, i.e., 4 acres for 40 to Loudensleger.—We (Webb & I) measured the fence on Buckland [Avenue] & found 780 feet from B & Andrews to John Street—101½ from Buckl[and] Av to Lincoln St. over John—

Columbus, 19th March, 1876.—Three days of cold—Thermometer down to 6° +. High winds, snow & death to fruit!! Mch a wintry month.

Monday, 20th March, 1876.—Another wintry snow storm today!!

Columbus, 21st March, 1876.—The last week a large number of the counties have elected Delegates to the State Convention. Several counties have not expressed a preference on the Presidential [candidate] but the most of them have passed resolutions in favor of me. It is likely that all of the counties have sent delegates who are favorable. Certainly none are avowedly opposed. There is a sentiment for [Benjamin H.] Bristow as a second choice. His war on the whisky thieves gives him prestige as the Representative of Reform. I am not sure but he would be the best candidate we could nominate. I am sure I prefer him to any other man. It will be a small disappointment for me to give up my chances. With so general an expression in my favor in Ohio, and in fair degree of assent elsewhere, especially in States largely settled by Ohio people, I have supposed it was possible that I might be nominated. But with no opportunity, and no desire to make combinations, or to lay wires, I have not thought my chance worth much consideration. I feel less diffidence in thinking of this subject than perhaps I ought. It seems to me that good purposes, and the judgment experience and firmness I possess would enable me to execute the duties of the office well. I do not feel the least fear that I should fail! This all looks egotistical, but it is sincere. On the other hand I do not desire the place with any strong or uneasy feeling. I shall accept the result which now seems probable without any bitterness. If Bristow is nominated I shall give him hearty support in speeches and otherwise.

2d April, 1876.—On the 29*th* ult the Republican State Convention of 750 delegates was held. It declared by a unanimous vote that I was the choice of the Republicans of Ohio for President. They *instructed* the Senatorial delegates and requested the District delegates "to use their earnest efforts to secure his nomination." This is certainly very flattering. It was done with enthusiasm, and in earnest. From the beginning I have done nothing directly or indirectly to bring about this result. I have discouraged rather than encouraged "the Hayes Movement." And now for the future. I would be glad if now I could in some satisfactory way drop out of the candidacy. I do not at present see what I can do to relieve myself from the embarrassment of the position I am in. It does not greatly disturb me. My usual serenity carries me along. But I would like to be out of it. I will think of it.

11th April, 1876.—I have made the last appointments for this session of the Legislature. Some mistakes have been made, but on the whole I have been fortunate. One or two things I must bear in mind. No man should be finally determined on until the people where he resides have been heard from, *after he is seriously talked of, or nominated for the place.*

The saying that "no man knows what can be said against him until he is a candidate for office" has a wise side to it. I named a Democrat of excellent character for Trustee of Dayton Hospital for the Insane. Straight way it appeared he had been a bitter Copperhead during the War. Another, a gallant soldier and fine gentleman, was no sooner named than it was notorious that he was a shameless libertine. The pardon record makes a great deal of perplexing labor. Some rules

1. Grant no pardon & make no promises on the first presentation of a case. Take time before deciding, or even encouraging the party.

2. If two or more are concerned in the crime consider the cases of all together. One is often called the dupe until he is pardoned—then the other becomes dupe & the pardoned man the leader.

3. Pardon no man who is not provided with employment, or the means of subsistence.

4. Pardon no man unless some friend is ready to receive him as he comes from the prison.

5. Of course, the Judge, the Pros[ecuting] Att[orne]y, and some intelligent citizen of sound sense should be heard from in all cases.

These rules may be departed from in cases requiring it, but let them always be considered before the pardon is granted, or any Committal had.

In politics I am growing more indifferent. I would like it if I could now return to my planting and books at home. I wrote the following letter to one of the Delegates supposed to lean towards [James G.] Blaine in reply to his note on the subject.

Columbus 6 April 1876

My Dear Sir:

I am exceedingly obliged for your very satisfactory letter. A press of business has prevented an earlier reply. Having done absolutely nothing to make myself the candidate of Ohio I feel very little responsibility for future results. When the State Convention was called it seemed probable, that if I encouraged my friends to organize for the purpose, every District would elect my decided supporters. But to make such an effort in my own behalf, to use Paynes phrase on repudiation, "I abhorred."

Being now in the field without any act of my own, I have no uneasy ambition to remain a candidate. I think I have a right, however, to considerate treatment at the hands of the Ohio delegation. If I am to be voted for at all, and as long as I am to be voted for at all, may I not reasonably expect the solid vote of Ohio?

Whenever any considerable number of any [of] the delegation thinks the time has come to withdraw my name it ought to be promptly done. I can speak of this, I think, with a judgment as impartial as if it were the case of another man. I am not solicitous to be a candidate for nomination, nor for the nomination itself. I agree with you that Mr B[laine]'s course with you was very handsome.

You may show this note to Mr [Hiram] Garretson, but it is of course not for publication.

Sincerely

R B Hayes

P.S.

I am very glad the Asylum appointments are satisfactory.

7th May, 1876.—The Ohio friends think our prospect at Cincinnati grows daily better. Gen [James A.] Garfield writes me the following which I prize more than the prospect of success, if I can continue to deserve it.

I repeat with more emphasis than before what I said in my last letter to you that we are all delighted with the sensible and masterful way in which you are bearing yourself during the chaotic period of President-making. You are gaining strength every day with our most thoughtful people.

To which I reply,

I value the compliment in your closing paragraph. It has been my desire to deserve it. Not to lose my head, and to get through it without doing or saying anything unjust or even uncharitable towards competitors or their supporters has been my ambition in this business. If I am successful in this, the adverse result which I anticipate, will not give me a moments uneasiness.

19th May, 1876.—Nothing new in the political way of special personal interest. I still think Blaine is so far ahead in the number of Delegates he has secured and is securing that his nomination is not improbable. He has not been greatly damaged by the investigations. As a candidate before the people his newly acquired wealth, his schemes for getting the nomination, and his connection with money interests depending for success on legislation will damage him. But with two or three hundred delegates in his favor, will not all of the loose odds & ends gravitate to him? It so seems. If he fails, the next is a combination for selfish ends to make a candidate among the friends of the leading candidate. This would not be in my favor. My independent position, aloof from bargaining, puts me outside of the list from whom the managers will select. It is only in the contingency of a union between those who look for availability in the candidate, and those who are for purity and reform in administration, that I am a probable nominee.

I write to Sherman today as follows:

Columbus O
19 May 1876

My Dear Sir:

It would specially gratify me if you would attend the Cincinnati Convention. I do not mean to depart from the position I have taken to remain perfectly passive on the nomination. But it is fair to assume that the time may come when I ought to be withdrawn. To be able to act on this, and other possible questions, it is important for me that I have friends of experience & sound judgment on the ground by whom I can be advised of the exact condition of things, and of the proper course to be taken. I have consulted with the Delegate from my own District and Town, Gen [Ralph P.] Buckland, more freely than with any other member of the Delegation and regard him as a friend in whom I can confide unreservedly.

Sincerely

R B Hayes

Hon John Sherman.

21st *May*, 1876.—

I have a friendly note of the 18*th* from Secy of War Judge Taft in which he says:

I am no prophet in such confused elements of calculation but it really seems to me that your chances are stronger than those of any other man. I mean that taking into view such elements of calculation as exist and are appreciable the probabilities are in your favor. I should feel that it was another strong point gained for Ohio if it should come to you

Judge Dickson (W. M.) of Cinti asked me a question or two put him by an Eastern Correspondent. I replied. It turns out the correspondent was Geo. Wm Curtis. Judge D. now sends me the following reply of Curtis to his the judges', note sending my letter.

West New Brighton
Staten Island
N. Y.
17 May 1876

My Dear Sir

I am exceedingly obliged for your note and the letter of Governor Hayes which you have kindly sent me. I have read it, you will easily believe, with very great interest, and with equal satisfaction that I obeyed the impulse to ask you the questions. That it is the reply to a letter so frank as you state yours to have been is only the more agreeable, for it places him in a most manly and simple position.

His chances seem to me daily to improve for the feeling among the friends of other candidates is becoming so positive that I feel as if some compromise were probable. Yet the real compromise candidate is Blaine. The extremes are Bristow and Conkling. The friends of the latter however would very much prefer Hayes to Blaine, but might accept B. if they could do no better. I have never doubted that Conckling would be the final machine candidate, and very strong for that reason. But he would be so distasteful to all but the regulation Republicans that I can not but hope even his supporters will see it as you see. They are making great efforts to unite the N.Y. press upon him. But New England is strong against him. Excuse * * *

25th May, 1876.—I today received from Judge Dickson my letter to him, which he sent to Curtis & which was as follows.

My Dear Judge: Columbus 3 May 1876

Returning after a few days absence at Fremont I find your letters of the 27th & 29th. You evidently understand the situation as well as any one who is writing or talking on the subject. You are unquestionably ~~right~~ correct in assuming that your eastern correspondent is not personally acquainted with me. Having thus far avoided all complications, committals direct or indirect—having in short been a mere looker-on as you are, I do not now expect to change my course, or to give assurances of any sort. Your conjectures or views as given in the copy show plainly enough that you understand me so well that for your satisfaction nothing from me is required. You speak of management by my friends securing results. I think I can see that part of it impartially. If anything depends on management I suspect my chances may be put down at zero. The best I can look for is that the march of events may be allowed to go along undisturbed by friendly management either wise or otherwise.

In any event your letters interest me and oblige me. I class you, as a political writer, with our best men. With good health, you would, if you had chosen that path, ranked with Geo W*m* Curtis and our other great political writers—(if there are others abreast of Mr C.) but God disposes.

Sincerely

R B Hayes

Hon W. M. Dickson
&c &c

26th May, 1876.—Bought of young [E. O.] Randall at his bookstore on High Street, west side, South of State, this book and begin a new Diary volume. I am now living quietly as Governor at 60 East Broad Street opposite the State House square in a furnished house rented of Dr W. B. Hawkes. My family are Lucy, Fanny and Scott. Winnie [Monroe], assisted about half the time by Cora, does our housework. I rise between five and seven, write letters until breakfast at 8½ —am at my office until about 1 P.M. from 9 A.M.; dine about 2 P.M.—at office again until after 5 P.M. and evenings for calls and callers. Too little exercise is the only fault with it. I am in good health—weight about 180. My thoughts are on the political situation a good deal, and yet not anxiously or uneasily. It is certain that my own conduct and character are pretty well understood, and I see no reason to apprehend that I shall fail to pass creditably through the ordeal of candidacy. Whatever the event, my head is likely to remain level.

A few days ago I was interviewed by a [New York] Herald reporter. I said enough to induce him, as I hoped, not to publish as an interview what I was saying. But in this morning's [Ohio State] Journal I see extracts from his letter showing that with reasonable fidelity he has given my talk.— I received a letter from the Secretary [Gouverneur Carr] of the Republican Reform Club asking for publication my opinions on the Declaration of Principles issued by the Club. I could very heartily subscribe to them. But I do not think it consistent with the rule I have laid down for my conduct to write a letter for publication. Indeed I am in print fully and explicitly in favor of the coin resolution, and the resolution on civil service reform. As to the Economy talk, and the resolution about candidates, all parties profess the same thing. But not wishing to write a letter for publication I sent the following.

Columbus O.
25 May 1876

Private

Dear Sir:

I have the honor to acknowledge the receipt of your letter asking for publication my views on certain important political questions.

You are aware that my name has been mentioned in connection with the nominations to be made next month at Cincinnati. Having thus far done nothing with the purpose of promoting my own nomination by that Convention I prefer not to change my course of conduct either by the publication of letters on political questions, or otherwise. I must therefore respectfully decline to write to you anything for publication as requested in your esteemed favor of the 22*d* instant.

Sincerely

R. B. Hayes

Mr Gouverneur Carr
    Sec'y

10*th June*, 1876.—The members and others interested are assembling at Cincinnati preparatory for the Convention. Up to this time the course of the canvass, so far as I am concerned, has been agreeable. My friends have been quiet. Those of other candidates have generally treated me well. The Vice Presidency seems to be conceded to me on all sides, or nearly so. I have seen evidences of a desire to give me the 2*d* place on the ticket from Conkling, Blaine, and Bristow men. Morton is so near to us that, it would hardly do for his friends to suggest an Ohio candidate for Vice, and yet even they occasionally suggest [it]. The balloting among the readers of the N.Y. Witness, a Presbyterian paper of large circulation, puts me at the head of the ballot for V.P. This is all flattering and gratifying. However the thoughts of my friends are on the first place. My chances there are merely probabilities. Yet there are sound encouraging facts. I seem to be the second choice of many of the leading supporters of other candidates. Ex Vice Prest [Hannibal] Hamlin of Me, Prest White (A.D.) of N.Y. and others.[3]

Friday 8 A.M., *16th June*, 1876.—This is the third day of the Convention at Cinti. My friends were there a week ago tonight. One whole week of Convention work. At the adjournment last night, all was ready to begin the balloting. At ten this morning the decisive balloting begins. Early in the struggle my friends were very hopeful. But on the 13*th* Blaine became decidedly the prominent man—his prospects deemed almost a certainty. There has been a gradual change on the 14*th* and 15*th* and now it seems something more than a possibility that he will fail. If he fails my chance as a compromise candidate seems to be better than that of any other candidate. So we are now in suspense. I have kept cool and unconcerned to a degree that surprises me. The same may be said of Lucy. I feel that defeat will be a great relief—a setting free from bondage. The great responsibility overpowers me. That is too strong. It sobers me. It is a weight, but not overpowering. I shall try to do in all things, more than ever before, if nominated, precisely the thing that is right—to be natural, discreet, wise, moderate, and as firm in the right as it is possible for me to be. And in this Spirit I await the event!

Sunday, *18th June*, 1876.—I have had no time to write since my nomination on the 7*th* ballot about 4 P.M. on the 16*th* friday. Friday has been a lucky day for me before! My deepest

26

emotions were on receiving Blaines dispatch of congratulation. It for a few moments quite unmanned me. And then [R. M.] Shoemaker's dispatch wishing that Uncle [Sardis] Birchard was alive.

23d June, 1876.—The nomination has been well received. The best people, many of them heretofore dissatisfied with the Republican party, are especially hearty in my support. I must make it my constant effort to deserve this confidence.

8th July, 1876.—The nomination of Tilden [4] [at the Democratic National Convention in St. Louis] makes doubtful the State of N.Y., N.J. and Ct. [Conn.] I have prepared a bold and honest letter of acceptance. It will offend some, and cool the ardor of others, but it is sound and I believe will be strong with the people. At any rate it is the true course.

Our adversaries reckon on a *united South*. This is their hope. We must meet them on this.

They are under the same leadership which for fifteen years has been on the wrong side of every question.

Copy

Private

Columbus O.
29 July 1876

My Dear Major:

A slander has been started in West Virginia which you may be able to aid in putting down. It is said that I appropriated to *my* own use the money (about $300 or 400$) found on the Deserter who was shot at Monocacy the first week in August 1864. You remember the case no doubt. He was a rebel deserter—joined Co D 23d [Regiment, Ohio Volunteer Infantry]—deserted to the rebels—was taken prisoner at Cloyd Mt—escaped—became a bounty jumper and was sent to 23d (O.) at Monocacy early in August /64 tried as a deserter and executed; and it was decided. The money he had was received for bounties, and it was decided to take it and use it to get a man in his place. This (was no doubt done).

27

Certainly I didn't use the money. Tell me all you remember about it and oblige

Sincerely

R B Hayes

Maj. E. M. Carey
&c &c

(Also copy sent to Gen. H. F. Devol) Col Wm R Brown, Independence, Montgomery Co., Kansas.)

Columbus, 31st *July*, 1876.—The foregoing letter shows the sort of falsehoods which the partisan press gathers up, or fabricates. They are not believed however, and do not annoy me a great deal.

Sunday, 13th *August* 1876.—Last night with Atty Genl John Little I met Senator [Oliver P.] Morton at Bradford Junction on his request to talk over the political situation. We rode together to this place, having left here to meet him at 5:40 P.M. & reached here at 12:45 A.M. after an interview of three hours. Gov Morton regards the situation as grave, that if Indiana is Democratic in Oct our chance is not over one in ten (1/10) of success in the Country in November—that if we carry Indiana in Oct our chances of carrying the Country in Nov are 49 in 50 (49/50) in short that we lose the Presidency in November if we lose Indiana in October. He thought it his duty to state to me the condition and prospects—that we ought to face it. He detailed the figures of elections in Indiana since 1860. He showed the closeness of the State. Also referred to the Greenback party—its organization, growing strength, and the fact that it drew four fifths (4/5) of its voters from our side. I said "and now the remedy." He after some further talk said, *Money and speakers*. Money to pay men to travel and organize—to print and circulate Documents—&c &c To my question how much is needed to do the work required to carry the State he replied $1000 to a county will do it—or ninety four [actual number, ninety-two] Counties $100,000. I asked how much is generally used. He replied "four years ago we had from outside of the State $55 000." As to speakers he named Judge [William D.] Kelley, Robt G Ingersoll, Carl Schurz, [W. H.] Gibson, [George A.] Sheridan, and perhaps others. Others to be seen or written to on the money question are Gov [Edwin D.] Morgan, Mr.   of Boston and perhaps others.

On the whole his talk was not encouraging. The use of money I have little faith in, and I am confident no such large sums can be raised. I mean to go through cheerfully and firmly, and with clean hands. If defeated there will be no bitterness in the disappointment and I shall have my ~~own~~ self respect and an approving conscience.

Mem Write [William K.] Rogers on [William Dean] Howell book [5]—finance Committee business &c &c.

4 P.M. I just wrote Gen [Ralph P.] Buckland who is enjoying the Centennial the following honest words

> You are to be envied. Now that the flush of gratification upon the nomination is about at an end, I begin to prefer the independence of a private citizen. If the result leaves me so, I will be the most contented defeated Presidential candidate, having any prospects, that was ever voted for.

Columbus, 19th August, 1876.—Nothing during the canvass thus far has been said by adversaries against me that has given me much trouble. The attacks had been chiefly false statements as to the coal miners strike in the Tuscarawas Valley,[6] as to my being a salary grabber, as to joining a secret anti foreigners order in Philadelphia July *5th*, as to the [temperance] crusade, as to embezzling two cannon captured in West Va, as to neglecting to pay my board at Princeton, West Va during the war, [space left for additional sentences].

The only slander that has given me annoyance is the one referred to in my letter on page 6, ante,[7] addressed to Maj Carey, Col Brown, Gen Devol, Gen [Russell] Hastings.

It was printed in a Dem Paper at Pt Pleasant, and two publications have been made in the Cinti Enquirer in regard to it. It worries my friends in Pomeroy, Gallipolis, and the Kanawha Valley. I have not wished to make any denials of any falsehood over my own signature—[I have preferred] to leave my friends to deal with all such affairs. It now occurs to me to allow Loomis (B. J.) of the [Cincinnati] Commercial to interview me about it. Gov [Thomas A.] Hendricks has done this about some wench story, or other slander. I will now set down what can be said in an interview.

Reporter. I have called to ask if you object to an interview on the subject of the ~~subject~~ story of the Deserters [Isaac B. Whitlaw] money, said to have been appropriated by you to your own use?

Ans. I do not intend to discuss political questions during my candidacy—at least that is my present purpose about it, and I would decline to be interviewed on public affairs, but this charge ~~affects~~ aimed at my character for integrity, and as a soldier is of such a nature that I am glad to have an opportunity to reply to it publicly.

Reporter. Please give me the facts in regard to this charge.

Ans. The charge is that I appropriated to my own use $400 in money taken from a man who was shot as a deserter or spy (for he was both) at Monocacy Junction Maryland in General Sheridan's army of the Shenandoah in August 1864. The case was a remarkable one on account of the coincidences which led him to his fate. In the fall of 1863 he came in a rebel uniform into the Union lines in the Kanawha Valley claiming to be a Union man who had been forced into the rebel army. Subsequently, he ~~was~~ enlisted in Co D 23*d* Ohio. Soon after he became sick and was in Hospital a month or two. Next he deserted taking with him arms and equipments with watches and pistols that he stole from his comrades. Afterwards May 9, 1864 he was taken prisoner with arms in his hands fighting in the Rebel ranks at Cloyd Mt., was recognized by 23*d* men who were detailed to guard prisoners, and finding he was discovered managed to escape in the night. In August afterwards a squad of recruits and drafted men and substitutes was brought to the 23d Regiment from Ohio while the Regiment was camped at Monocacy Junction Aug 5, 1864. Among them this Rebel Deserter, Union Deserter, and Spy and Bounty Jumper was discovered. The ~~news~~ facts were reported to Gen [George] Crooks HdQuarters. His Adj. Genl Capt J. L. Botsford ordered a Drumhead Court Martial to meet immediately. The Court was probably mainly from my Brigade—~~probably all of the members—Perhaps all of the officers of the 23d Regt~~. But I was not on the Court and had nothing to do with it, as I now remember. The man was tried found guilty and sentenced to be shot. He confessed that after his escape in June 1864 he went down the Kanawha to Ohio and became a bounty jumper. That he had received a number of times ~~local~~ bounties from localities & perhaps individuals, and "had deserted—was prevented from doing it on this occasion by the recent order which required that recruits should be receipted for at their regiments before payment of bounties—that he had money about $400. received from bounties he had jumped and two watches—that he had no family ~~except~~ unless he had a mother living whom he had not seen in some years, and whose residence he couldn't tell. After the trial members of the Court Martial on talking it over concluded that as the bounty money of the rebel spy & Deserter was received from localities or individuals & the Govt to furnish a soldier for the 23d Regt that it ought to be used to get another recruit for the same Regt, and that it should be delivered to the ~~Judge Advocate, Quartermaster Provost Marshall or other officer~~ proper officer for that purpose. In all this I concurred. I have always supposed that this ~~is what~~ was accordingly done ~~with it~~ with the money. I have often told the story of this spy & Deserter it being interesting on account of its coincidences,

31

and have always spoken of the money as being used to get a recruit for the 23d in the place of the rebel deserter & spy.

[The following entry was marked out in the diary:] I have no recollection of ever seeing the money. I never receipted for it—I never took a receipt for it. I never pocketed it. I never had it in my custody and I know I never used it or appropriated it to my own use.   I have no recollection of Mr [W. W.] Harper [of Hartford City, West Virginia] in connection with it. But if he got the money from the deserter it is altogether natural and probable that I should have sent for him, and that he should have come to my Hd Qurs, and give up the money. If he did and it was ~~paid into~~ given into my hands it was at once then and there handed over to the proper officer for the purpose indicated. I know it never was retained in my custody—~~that~~ I could not forget *that*.

———

Mr Harper says ~~Col Comly~~ an orderly came from me after him, and that at my Hd Quarters he gave up the money in the presence of Gen Comly ~~and other officers~~. ~~This may be true but~~ I have no recollection of ~~any of this~~ it. But we were in the midst of the busiest year of the war—and were just entering on ~~the~~ one of the most exciting and absorbing campaigns of that year viz Sheridans Shenandoah Valley Campaign. Since hearing of ~~this affair~~ last month I have tried to find out all I could about it. this affair. I wrote the following letter and sent copies to surviving officers likely to know about it as ~~rapidly as~~ soon as I could learn their addresses.

(Copy of Letter to Maj Carey 29*th* July)

I sent [the letter] to Maj Carey of 23d who was President of the Court Martial and received a reply—to Gen Duvol who commanded 36*th* Ohio one of the Regiments of my Brigade, and a reply. To Col. Brown ditto & a reply—to Gen [W. H.] Enochs, to Capt Jas L Bottsford [Botsford] Gen Crooks Adj Gen & reply. [To] my Adj. Genl. [Russell Hastings], and others I hear of none who recollect the payment of the money by Harper. ~~Col.~~ But it might have occurred. My orderly who was most likely to have carried the word to Mr. Harper if he was sent for was Geo Brigdon my color bearer. He was killed in battle within four weeks after the execution of this deserter at Berryville. The most probable person to have been Judge Advocate was Capt [Amos F.] Gillis, 23d who was killed at the same battle. Capt [Andrew J.] Austin 23d another possible member killed in same battle. Capt afterwards Maj [Harry] Thompson of 23d is now dead. Gen Hastings my Adj. Genl. was absent the evening of the execution ~~also Maj [William] McKinley my Quarter Master.~~ Lt [S. S.] Mather[s], 13th Va one of my aids is confident Mr Harper never gave up the money—is ready to swear to ~~a~~ conversations with Harper in which he (H.) admitted having the money long after the trial. My other aid Lt O. J. Wood 36th Ohio, I have not heard from. ~~Many~~ A number of recruits came to the regiment after this affair at Monocacy.

Let the Reporter ask What became of the watches.

Ans. I understand that Mr. Harper has never been able to find the mother of the Deserter, and he therefore still has the watches in his possession.

Reporter What does Harper refer to when he says that both himself and you (Hayes) have been "maligned" and slandered about this money? Ans. I do not know. I never heard an intimation that ~~I was~~ there was a charge against me until since my nomination. Maj Carey says he never &c &c Col Devol &c &c

I have always believed that one of them [the recruits] was obtained with this money. ~~My opinion~~ While I have no recollection ~~as to the facts stated by Mr Harper,~~ of receiving the money as stated by Mr Harper, but if I did I believe his statement is substantially correct. At the same time I know that I never retained the money in my custody—I never used it—or appropriated it to my own use. If handed to me it was immediately there and then given over to the proper officer to get another recruit "So help me God!"

R. B. Hayes

Underhill my other orderly was driving cattle from Texas the last I heard of him.[8]

Columbus, 1st September, 1876.—Photographs since my nomination by all in Columbus—the best by Geo R. Elliott cabinet size—full figure by Elliott & Amisted the best.

Oil Paintings by   Adams of Cleveland, [John H.] Witt of Columbus, 1/2 length; [James H.] Moser [Mosure] of Cols, profile head; [E. F.] Andrews of Steubenville; Antrobus of Detroit, and many others.

Bust by [Olin Levi] Warner of N.Y. Various medallions.

––––––––

Columbus O 9 Sept 1876

My Dear S.

Your letter of the *6th* [reporting promising Republican outlook in New York] is very encouraging, and most interesting. I wish to make a suggestion—which I deem important. If you agree with me, you may see a way to do what is requisite. It is common to say "if *Indiana* & Ohio go right in Oct." "If *Indiana* is for us" &c &c thus hinging all on Indiana. Now Indiana is a Democratic State. Emigration of Republicans west & the Greenback heresy have made it so. Until within a fortnight I have seen small chance of carrying it. The chances are still greatly against us. The true pivot is New York. Let us therefore prepare our friends and the public not to be disheartened if Indiana is wrong—especially our friends in the East. *October will not decide the Election*

34

unless BOTH *Ohio & Indiana go the same way*. This is the truth. We ought to see that it is so understood everywhere.

Sincerely

R B Hayes

Hon Wm H Smith
&c &c

Columbus, 13*th September*, 1876.—Returned from Fremont with Lucy last night. Had a good time Sat. Sund. Mond. & Tuesday.

Maine Election shows a handsome Republican gain and is certainly encouraging.

14*th September*, 1876.—As an offsett to what is said of Gov Tildens income returns mine have been examined. It appears that in 1868 & 1869 I made none at all. No doubt all I made are substantially accurate. If none were made in the two years named it was because my attention was not called to the matter—a mere oversight. My taxable income in those years did not exceed 1500$ or 2500$. If no return can be found and no payments made, there is due from me the tax on that amount, and it will be paid. If no returns were made in the two years 1868 & 1869 it was because no returns were called for. I had left Cinti Dec 1867, and had my domicil at Columbus, my permanent residence still remaining at Cinti.

Columbus O.
8 Sept 1876

Private

My Dear Sir.

I send you a slip cut from an Eastern newspaper on the subject of Assessments upon official salaries for political purposes. It is charged that this is done by authority of the National Committee.

My views as to what ought to be ~~done~~ required of office

35

holders are set forth in my letter of acceptance and are no doubt sufficiently well known. But I think it is proper to say to the committee that if assessments are made as charged it is a plain departure from correct principles, and ought not to be allowed. I ~~think~~ trust the committee will have nothing to do with it.

Sincerely

R B Hayes

Hon R. C. McCormick
  &c &c &c

Columbus, O.
16 Sept 1876

My Dear Sir:

I have yours of 31st. At this time the tide is with us— at least this is the opinion of our friends generally. I think it is so. In Ohio the contest in October will be close.

The Greenback Democracy made the State ticket of the party, and will support it heartily. The Tilden Democracy will support it for the effect on November.

In November Greenback Dem's in considerable numbers will vote for Cooper and others for Hayes. They hate Tilden because he tried to beat Allen last year.

Indiana leans to the Democracy. It is owing to emigration West that Ohio and Indiana are not Republican. Catholics are taking the places of Republican farmers and soldiers. But if the tide is as our friends think we shall pull through.

The point you made as ~~to~~ the controlling idea of the canvass is rapidly becoming the one topic of the press and of speakers. It *does* tell. Excuse haste.

Sincerely

R B Hayes

Hon Edwards Pierrepont
  &c &c

Copy of a letter written by W. K. Rogers to Gen A. G. McCook—13 Sept 1876. (not sent)

"If the Gov. wrote to Mr Tyler it was in reference to a platform of principles which said nothing against the naturalization of foreigners or against naturalized citizens holding office. The principles of the Alliance which he might have approved denounces (as we understand) Catholic interference with the schools, and with legislation. If you find there is a letter from him, see if it is in his handwriting or in that of his private Sec. Capt. [A. E.] Lee—if his—get possession of it if you can—at all events a copy. Maintain a friendly spirit with Mr Tyler. We think him a sincere friend. I add this P.S. at the Govs suggestion. W. K. R.[9]

Columbus, 18th September, 1876.—This afternoon about three, Seth Kinman [of California] (and his son and others present) presented me at the Office a chair made by him of Elks horns—the feet those of a yearling elk—the seat Elk skin, and a robe of fox skins.

A few watchwords of this sort might be useful if well circulated.

Are you for a United South or are you against it?
"   "   "   the United South, or are you for the United States?
Are you for the Rebel South, or are you for the loyal North?
Who do you wish should rule—the South or the Nation?
Are you for the Nation, or for the Solid South?
Are you for the United States, or are you for the United South?
Are you for the Nation, or are you for the Rebels?
Has the time come when it is safe to let the rebels rule the Nation?
Should we give the Government to the men who tried to destroy it?

37

Rebel rule or Loyal rule? that is the question.
Are you for the Rebellion, or are you for the Union?
Are you for the United South, or are you the United States?
That is the question.
Are you for the men who wore the gray, or are you for the
men who wore the blue?

Columbus, 23d September, 1876.—I yesterday was called on
at my office by Ch[ief] Justice [Morrison R.] Waite. Among
other things we talked of Tilden. I asked him if the tax return
charges were believed. He said yes. That Tilden was a miser,
very exacting—"exacting to the last degree." That he could
in confidence give me an incident. He W[aite] was foreclosing
a mortgage on a R.R. (perhaps, A[tlantic] & Gr[eat] W[est-
ern]) Tilden represented the first mortage bond holders.
W[aite] on behalf of his clients was very anxious to enter a
decree. It was also in the interest of Tildens clients. But it
couldn't be done without T's consent. Time was of such importance that Waite spent several hours trying to get Tildens
consent. T. had no right to ask any money for his consent.
Neither the interests of his clients required it, nor had he rendered any services that entitled him to it. But he had the power.
"To get his consent I had to pay him $30,000." He probably
divided with others. But that is Tilden.

24th September, 1876.—I am looking anxiously forward to
the end of the contest. It is now almost one hundred days since
the nomination, and only about forty five to the election. The
general drift of the campaign has been rather favorable to our
side for some weeks past. The Greenback heresy in Indiana
and Ohio is likely to cause those States to do badly in October.
If there was no election before the final vote in November I
should feel very confident of a favorable result. But our friends
East, and elsewhere count on more favorable results in Ohio
and Indiana than are likely to occur. We shall be much
stronger at the Presidential elections in both States. But the

discouraging effect of defeats in Oct is sure to hurt us. Our adversaries are to be correspondingly encouraged. The truth is, time and money would be saved if all elections in Presidential years were fixed for the same day. It should be done.

"I am prepared for either event"—I can again repeat. To go into the great office will be a sore trial. Health comfort happiness all imperilled if not sacrificed. I shall find reasons enough for satisfaction with the result if I am defeated. If elected, the firmest adherence to principle against all opposition and temptations is my purpose. I shall show a *grit* that will astonish those who predict weakness.

Columbus, 4th October, 1876.—Birthday   fifty four years of age. The good omen of the day is that Colorado the first State to elect electors (or rather a Legislature that will elect electors) has been carried by the Republicans. "First Gun for Hayes" is the headline of the Journal.   I called on [James G.] Blaine at Ewing Millers. He looks well—is clear headed prompt and quick witted with no trace that I detect of his great calamity. He is hopeful and friendly. I called with him on Mrs Ben Smith, on Lucy, and at my office. We met Wayne McVeigh. He [Blaine] has almost precisely my views and hopes as to the South. By conciliating southern whites on the basis of obedience to law and equal rights he hopes we may divide the southern whites, and so protect the colored people.

Columbus O
5 Oct 1876

My Dear S.

Touching Lee's letter to the Sec'y of the Am[erican] Alliance I write these observations.

1. It was written without my knowledge before or after. I never heard of it until now—Lee had a general authority to reply to letters of congratulation and tenders of support—"suitable acknowledgements" merely.

2. I see nothing damaging, specially, in the letter if *we* dont write it into importance. It approves and endorses nothing.

3. The resolutions it replies to, in acknowledging are eight (8) in number, adopted at Phil'a July 4 and 5 and are all such as Republican foreigners, not Catholics, approve. You have seen the resolutions.

4. The whole affair is to put us on the defensive, and will fail if we are not led off by it. Three of our most intelligent Germans speaking of it (Cin'ti Germans) say it will not hurt a particle. That Republican Germans do not mind such Roarbacks &c &c.

5. The drift of the canvass is plain. The people *do dread* a victory for the United South. They see in it continued trouble—nullification of the amendments—Rebel claims and schemes &c &c &c and I think anything which withdraws attention from this issue to merely personal matters is a mistake. The school issue, the civil service issue, the currency issue &c are all in point and good, but merely personal issues may well be dropped with a few words of denunciation—

We see encouragement here and it increases daily.

Sincerely, ·

R B Hayes

Wm H. Smith

7th October, 1876.—Benj B. Redfield a grandson of my gr[ea]t Grandf[ather] Israel Smith called this morning. Resides in Lapeer, Mich. Israel S. served throughout the Revolution. Cyrus McMaster of Afton, N.Y. has his powder horn used in the Revolution.

12th October, 1876.—The elections have gone precisely as I expected. For three months I have predicted that New York would ~~have to~~ decide the result—that Ohio in October would go Republican, and Indiana Democratic. At this writing Ohio on the test candidate seems to be 8000 for us, and Indiana against us.

Columbus O 14 Oct 1876

Personal

My Dear Sir:

The elections have gone just about as I anticipated in these two States. Our majority in Ohio on the true test is ~~a trifle over~~ about 9000. It is made up by handsome gains in the rural districts which overcome losses in the cities. The reliable Republican counties have given their full high tide majorities. The cities like Springfield where business and manufacturing are prosperous have done well. Our losses are in Cities and Towns where the hard times pinch. All of the non-Catholic foreigners, Germans, Welsh, &c &c have stood by us except the trading classes in Cinti, who feared a loss of Southern trade —and even there I doubt if we lost in the foreign Republican vote. I infer from this that a full vote makes Wisconsin ours beyond ~~doubt~~ all question. We shall double our majority here in Nov without effort.

Indiana is surely now a doubtful state. We have a fair fighting chance to carry it. A much better chance, than we had to carry it in Oct. I do not write of the East. You understand about the situation there. In the South, if we have a prospect to carry any states, we must look after North and South Carolina, Florida, Miss, and La.

Another matter I would like to hear from you about. Ohio Republicans, interested in the Centennial, want an Ohio day, and wish me to be present—next week or the week after— Should it be encouraged?

Know Nothing charges made by the Dem's, the people here care nothing about. It is perfectly well known that I do not favor the exclusion of foreigners from the ballot or from office, and that I do oppose Catholic interference and all sectarian interference with political affairs—and especially with the schools. This last point is influential—particularly with non-Catholic foreigners. It has not, I suspect been sufficiently urged in the canvass. But I need not take up your time

41

with these rambling speculations. The contest is now with the East. The inflation states have done better for the hard-money candidates than you had a right to expect. Now let the hard-money states do as well, and we are safe.

Sincerely

R B Hayes

Columbus, 15th October, 1876.—The Oct elections leave the result of the Presidential contest still in doubt, and to be decided by New York in November. That Ohio has done so well is a great satisfaction. My friends urged as one of their strongest arguments for my nomination that Ohio was a doubtful State—that its loss in October would be fatal—that no man named except myself could surely carry it in October—that with me as the candidate success in Ohio in October was assured—that I always had carried it, and would do so again. After all this, the loss of Ohio in October would have been a sore mortification. We had at the head of our ticket a good soldier and citizen [Milton F. Barnes, candidate for the office of Secretary of State of Ohio] but one who was mixed up with the temperance crusade which was so hateful to all Germans, and to many others. He was a load—a heavy load to carry. But our prominent Germans, brewers and others behaved admirably, nobly, and we are safe! I can bear defeat in November far more philosophically than I could have borne the loss of Ohio in October. My own ward, Town, County, and Congr[essional] Dist. did well—indeed very handsomely. This is gratifying. Endorsed by my State and home, I feel gratified by the result.

NOTES

CHAPTER II

[1] Senator Sherman had, in a public letter of January 21, suggested Hayes as a Republican presidential possibility. Although Hayes welcomed the support of Sherman, whose own name had been advanced, he evidently feared that the reference to his Civil War record might be seized on and misrepresented. Hayes was extremely proud of his war service. Most of it was spent in West Virginia, but in 1864, the West Virginia army, under General George Crooke, moved to the Shenandoah Valley to join Philip Sheridan. Hayes participated in the campaign against Jubal Early that broke Confederate strength in the Valley.

[2] James M. Comly had served with Hayes during the war, following Hayes as colonel commanding the 23rd Regiment of Ohio Volunteers, and was now editor of the Columbus *Ohio State Journal*.

[3] The references are to Hannibal Hamlin, Vice President in Lincoln's first term, and Andrew D. White, president of Cornell University.

[4] The Democrats, meeting in convention at St. Louis in late June, had nominated Samuel J. Tilden on the second ballot.

[5] Howells, editor of the *Atlantic Monthly* and the famous novelist, was related to Hayes through marriage to a cousin. He had written a campaign biography of Hayes.

[6] In April, 1876, Hayes had dispatched militia troops to the strike area and kept them there until what he termed "lawless violence" ceased.

[7] This is the letter reproduced in the entry of July 8 referring to the charge that Hayes had during the war appropriated the money of a deserter.

[8] The proposed interview did not appear in the Cincinnati *Commercial*. It was published in the Columbus *Ohio State Journal*, in August, 1876, and was republished in the Fremont *Journal*, September 1.

[9] The American Alliance was an organization supposedly opposed to granting the suffrage to foreign-born citizens. Whatever the case, it had adopted resolutions that among other things, denounced Catholic influence in politics and approved Hayes's candidacy. Hayes's secretary, Alfred E. Lee, had acknowledged reception of the resolutions. His action would later cause Hayes some embarrassment. See entry of October 4.

Chapter III

OCT. 22, 1876—DEC. 31, 1876

Columbus, Sunday 22d October, 1876.—Only two Sundays more before the Presidential election. I am surprised whenever I think of it to find myself so cool—so, almost, indifferent about it. It would be a calamity, I am sure, to give the Democrats the Government. But public opinion, the press, the march of events will compel them to do better than their character and principles indicate. Here is our safety. Public opinion, the fear of losing the public confidence, apprehension of censure by the press, make all men in power conservative and safe. On personal grounds I find many reasons for thinking defeat a blessing. I should stand by my letter, I should hew to the line, but what conflicts, and annoyances would follow. I do not fear my pluck, or constancy a particle. But to be deceived by the rogues—to find many a trusted reformer no better than he should be, here would be humiliations and troubles without end.—The huge registration in New York City looks sinister. It seems to look to our defeat in that State.

Another danger is imminent. A contested result. And we have no such means for its decision as ought to be provided by law. This must be ~~looked~~ attended to hereafter. We should not allow another Presidential election to occur before a means for settling a contest is provided. If a contest comes now it may lead to a conflict of arms. I can only try to do my

44

duty to my countrymen in that case. I shall let no personal ambition turn me from the path of duty. Blood shed and civil war must be averted if possible. If forced to fight I have no fears of failure from lack of courage or firmness.

Sunday, 29th October, 1876.—Returned last night from Ohio Day at the Centennial. It was an enthusiastic and prodigious crowd which greeted me. I managed to shake some four thousand people by the hand and to make half a dozen speeches from steps, windows, & roof of the Ohio Building, without saying anything that I regret—without "slopping over." Lucy Birch, Webb, Fanny & Scott with our Colored servants were with me. The party was a good one Gen & Laura Mitchell, Col [L. C.] Weir—and (going on), Mrs Gov [E. F.] Noyes, Mrs Harry R Smith, Mr [William A.] Platt & Emily, and returning we had (instead of Platt & Emily, & Mrs Noyes & Mrs S.) Gen Benj[amin] Harrison & his wife of Indiana, ~~and from~~ to Pittsburgh, & from Pittsburg to Cols Mr Green & Gen Wilcox. A happy journey.

I return feeling that with the probabilities of fraud and violence—fraud North, violence South— ~~that~~ the chances are that we shall lose the election. My *luck* is the other way. But I have made a good fight—sound letter to stand on—a judicious course of conduct throughout—my head steady and level up to this time. Let me keep it so ten days longer.

1st November, 1876.—The contest is close and yet doubtful with the chances, as I see them, rather against us. So small a loss as the defeat in Hamilton County ~~may~~ in October may have made the difference between victory and defeat. A few hundred votes improvement there would have given our friends ~~there~~ the prestige of victory in Ohio and throughout the Country. Our loss was due to bribery and repeating. The hard times if we are beaten, may be assigned as the great and sufficient cause. All crimes are increased by hard times. It is especially so with crimes against the ballott box. It is easy to hire men desperate with want to vote contrary to their con-

45

victions, and even to become repeaters. Hard times then is the ultimate cause of our danger. We shall be beaten if at all by crime—by bribery, & repeating North and Violence and intimidation in the South.

Sunday, 5th November, 1876.—The election is only a day or two off, and I find myself strangely calm and indifferent about it. I shall read Mr   Andrews address, and other matters, as much interested in what I am doing as usual. It now looks as if the chance of my election was improving, and as if a Republican success was not improbable.

I make a list of states to be counted certain for us as follows,

Necessary to a choice 185

Maine	7	[votes]		[136]
N.H.	5		Kansas	5
Vt	5		Colorado	3
Mass	13			144
R.I.	4			
Penn	29	*Probably Republican,* Wisc		10
Ohio	22		California	6
Mich	11		S.C.	7 23
Ill	21			167
Minn	5			
Iowa	11	This leaves 18 required to		
Nebraska	3	elect out of the following		
	[136]	doubtful States.		

New Jersey	9			66
Nevada	3		N.C.	10
Florida	4		La	8
N.Y.	35		Ct	6
Ind.	15		Oregon	3
	66			93

Columbus 7th November, 1876.—Dies irae! A cold but dry day. Good enough here for election work. I still think Democratic chances the best—But it is not possible to form a confident opinion. If we lose the South will be the greatest sufferer. This misfortune will be far greater than ours. I do not think a revival of business will be greatly postponed by Tildens election. Business prosperity does not in my judgment depend on Government so much as ~~it is com~~ men commonly think. But we shall have no improvement in Civil Service—Deterioration rather, and the South will drift towards chaos again.

Saturday, 11 th November, 1876.—The election has resulted in the defeat of the Republicans after a very close contest. Tuesday evening a small party assembled in our parlor to hear the news. Gen [John Grant] Mitchell and Laura, our boys Birch and Webb, Gov [William] Dennison, a reporter of the Chicago Tribune, Mr Huntley, W. K. Rogers Rutherford Platt, and a few others at times—Emily Platt, Dr Fullerton and Fanny. The first dispatch was from Rutherford [his third son, at Cornell University], showing a majority of   in Ithaca N.Y. and a gain of   over Grant in 1872. We all felt that the State of New York would decide the contest. Our last dispatches from our Committee in N.Y. were very encouraging—full of confidence. Mr A. B. Cornell Chairman N.Y. State Committee said in an experience of ten years he had never seen prospects brighter on the eve of an election. But we all knew—warned by the enormous registration in the Cities of N.Y. and Brooklyn and other facts that we must not count confidently on carrying the State. The good omen from Ithaca was accepted with a quiet cheerfulness. Almost at the same instant came a gain of 36 in Ballville [Sandusky County, Ohio] the Township nearest my own home. This was good. Then came, one at a time, towns and precints in Ohio. The comparison was made with the vote in 1875 instead of with the vote of October last. This was confusing. But soon we began to feel that Ohio was not doing as well as we had hoped. The effect was depressing. I commanded without much effort my usual composure and cheerfulness. Lucy felt it more keenly. Without showing it, she busied herself about refreshments for our guests, and soon disappeared. I found her soon after abed with a head ache. I comforted her by consoling talk. She was cheerful and resigned, but did not return to the parlor. Without difficulty, or much effort, I became the most composed, and cheerful of the party. At   P.M. or thereabouts I̶ we heard that in some 200 districts of N.Y. City Tilden had about 20,000 majority which indicated 50,000 in the City. The returns received from the rural districts did not warrant the belief that they would overcome such a large City majority. From that time I never supposed there was a chance for Republican success. I went to bed at 12 to 1 o'clock. Talked with Lucy a̶b̶o̶u̶t̶ ̶t̶h̶e̶ consoling her with such topics as readily occurred of a nature to make us feel satisfied p̶e̶r̶-̶ s̶o̶n̶a̶l̶l̶y̶ on merely personal grounds with the result. We soon fell into a refreshing sleep and the affair seemed over. Both of us felt more anxiety about the South—about the colored people especially than about anything else sinister in the result. My hope of a sound currency will somehow be realized. Civil Service reform will be delayed, but the great e̶v̶i̶l̶ injury is in the South. There the amendments will be nullified, disorder will continue, prosperity to both whites and colored people, will be pushed b̶a̶c̶k̶ off for years. But I took my way to my office as usual, Wed morning, and was master of myself and contented and cheerful. During the day the news indicated that we carried California—soon after other Pacific States, all New England except Connecticut, all of the free States west except Indiana, and it dawned on us that with a few Republican States in the South to which we were fairly entitled, we would yet be victors. From Wednesday afternoon the City and the whole country has been full of excitement and anxiety. People have been up and down several times a day with the varying rumors. Wednesday evening on a false rumor

48

about N.Y. a shouting multitude rushed to my house, and called me out with rousing cheers. I made a short talk.

[clipping]

Speech by Hayes

Last evening a telegram came that the Republicans had carried New York. But very few people believed it. Governor Hayes had no confidence in it. It was submitted to him, and he expressed himself to the effect above stated. He had not received private advices confirming the story, which came via Chicago as a special to the *Tribune* from Washington. Nevertheless, a crowd of Republicans who had been watching bulletin boards rushed pell mell to the residence of the Governor, hurrahing for Hayes as they ran, and called him out. He said:

FRIENDS: If you will keep order for one half minute I will say all that is proper to say at this time. In the very close political contest, which is just drawing to a close, it is impossible, at so early a time, to obtain the result, owing to the incomplete telegraph communications through some of the Southern and Western States.

I accept your call as a desire on your part for the success of the Republican party; if it should not be successful, I will surely have the pleasure of living for the next year and a half among some of my most ardent and enthusiastic friends, as you have demonstrated tonight.

From that time the news has fluctuated just enough to prolong the suspense and to enhance the interest. At this time the Republicans are claiming the election by one Electoral vote. With La S.C. and Fla we have carried 185 [electoral votes]. This creates great uneasiness. Both sides are sending to Louisiana prominent men to watch the canvassing of the votes. All thoughtful people are brought to consider the imperfect machinery provided for electing the President. No doubt we shall, warned by this danger, provide by amendments of the

Constitution, or by proper legislation against a recurrence of the danger.

Sunday, 12th November, 1876.—The news this morning is not conclusive. The headlines of the morning papers are as follows. The News "Nip and Tuck", "Tuck has it", "The Mammoth National doubt," and the Herald heads its news column, "Which". But to my mind the figures indicate that Florida has been carried by the Democrats. No doubt both fraud and violence intervened to produce the result. But the same is true in many Southern States. We shall—the fair minded men of the country will—history will hold that the Republicans were by fraud violence and intimidation, by a nullification of the 15*th* amendment, deprived of the victory which they fairly won. But we must, I now think, prepare ourselves to accept the inevitable. I do it with composure and cheerfulness. To me the result is no personal calamity. I would like the opportunity to improve the Civil Service. It seems to me I could do more than any Democrat to put Southern affairs on a sound basis. I do not apprehend any great or permanent injury to the Financial affairs of the country by the victory of the Democrats. The hard money wing of the party is at the helm. Supported as they should be, and will be in all wise measures by the great body of the Republican party, nothing can be done to impair the national credit or debase the National currency. On this as on all important subjects the Republicans will still hold a commanding position. We are in a minority in the electoral Colleges—we lose the Administration. But in the ~~old~~ former free States—the States that were always loyal we are still in a majority. We carry eighteen of the twenty two and have two hundred thousand majority of the popular vote. In the old slave States, if the recent amendments were cheerfully obeyed, if there had been neither violence nor intimidation, nor other improper interference with the rights of the colored people, we should have carried enough

Southern States to have ~~carried~~ held the country, and to have secured a decided popular majority in the Nation. Our adversaries are in power but they ~~are in a decided~~ are supported by a minority only of the lawful voters of the country. A fair election in the South would undoubtedly have given us a large majority of the electoral votes, and a decided preponderance of the popular vote.   I went to church and heard a good strong sensible sermon by   Critchfield's son-in-law. After church and dinner I rode with Gen Mitchell and his children out to Alum Creek and around past the place of my old friend Albert Buttles. We talked of the Presidential question as settled, and found it in all respects well for me personally that I was not elected. On reaching home at Mitchells we found my son Webb with the following dispatch from Gov Dennison, a prudent and cautious gentleman, which seems to open it all up again.

Washington D.C. Nov 12, 1876 Recd at Cols 205 P.M.

To Gov R. B. Hayes

You are undoubtedly elected next President of the U.S. Desperate attempts ~~will be made~~ are being made to defeat you in Louisiana South Carolina & Florida but they will not succeed.

W. Dennison

(In the evening I asked if there were objections to publishing this dispatch. About 10 P.M. reply came *"No objections."*

Columbus, Thanksgiving, 30th November, 1876.—The Presidential question is still undecided. For more than two weeks it has seemed almost certain ~~that~~ that the three doubtful States would be carried by the Republicans. South Carolina is surely Republican. Florida is in nearly the same condition— both States being for the Republicans on the face of the returns, with the probability of increased majorities by corrections. Louisiana is the State which will decide. There is no doubt that a very large majority of the lawful voters are Republicans. But the Democrats have endeavored to defeat the will of the lawful voters by the perpetration of crimes whose magnitude and atrocity has no parallel in our history. By murder, and hellish cruelties ~~Bot hellish~~ they at many polls drove the colored people away, or forced them to vote the Democratic ticket. It now seems probable that the Returning Board will have before them evidence which will justify the throwing out of enough to secure the State to those who are lawfully entitled to it.

30th November, 1876.—Thanksgiving dinner and evening at Laura's. A happy time. Present W. A. P[latt] & Mrs. P. Dr & Mrs[Erskind Boies] Fullerton Emily P[latt], Ruddy P[latt] (a head ache kept him from dinner but he was with us afterwards), Frank Hickok, Webb C. Hayes, Lucy and I, and a merry crowd of little folks viz Susie, Lucy & Sarah Platt; Lilly, Fanny, Jeannie Andrews, & John G. Mitchell Jr, Laura Fullerton, and Fanny & Scott Russell Hayes—All under eleven and over three!

1st December, 1876.—Cold winter day—with snow & bluster. First snow fell on the *25th* Nov.

Col [W. H.] Roberts of N[ew] O[rleans] Times wanted an interview with me. Had lunch at [James M.] Comlys. After lunch he said he called on me to give me the views of [L. Q. C.] Lamar of Miss., Gen [Edward Cary] Walthall, Do., [that is, of Miss.] Wade Hampton of S. C. & probably [General John B.] Gordon of Ga. You will be President. We will not make trouble. We want peace. We want the color line abolished. We will not oppose an Administration which will favor an honest administration and honest officers in the South. We will favor measures to secure the colored people all of their rights. We may not, and probably will not leave the party of opposition, but such an Administration as you ~~will perhaps~~ can have we will support as men of the opposite party can. We want nothing of you in the way of promise or pledge. This was the substance

I replied by saying I was gratified to know it. That my letter of acceptance covered the whole ground. That it meant all it said and all that it implied. This was the substance.[1]

In case of my election there will be further conference, and I hope for good results.

Sunday, 3d December, 1876.—Various indications lead me to think that in Louisiana the report of the Returning Board will probably be unfavorable. No doubt a fair election would have carried the State for the Republicans. But it is possible that the wrong can not lawfully be corrected by the Returning Board. But suppose they do correct without sufficient warrant of law. The returns will be made to the President of the Senate, and on their face the Republicans will have a majority. Suppose a way is found to go behind those returns to the Senate. Should not in that event the whole case be gone into? Should not the equitable result be reached? Not only throw out the ~~Parishes~~ Democratic majorities where violence procured them, but count in fairly the honest Republican majorities which were prevented by lawlessness?

Today Scott [Hayes] was heard reading, as he pretended, to his sister very solemnly as follows viz

"R B Hayes is elected, and the Democrats will kill him. A monument will be built and on it will be

R. B. Hayes
Killed by the Democrats.

And they will kill all of the Republicans. If Tilden is elected the State will go to ruin."

This shows how a six year old looks at the crisis.

53

Columbus, 5th December, 1876.—Yesterday Elwood E Thorne & Francis A Stout of the Republican Reform Club of N.Y. came here and had an interview with me. The purport of their communication written and oral was that New York was lost by coldness and neglect, (perhaps treachery) on the part of the New York managers of the canvass—meaning Cornell, some of the Federal officers, generally I suppose friends of Conkling. Their facts were not very conclusive, but tended to show a lack of hearty support.

In the afternoon a number of Republicans who have been in New Orleans to witness the proceedings of the Returning Board, on the invitation of the President, or of the Nat. Rep. Com. stopped here on their return East. Senator [John] Sherman, Gen [James A.] Garfield, Eugene Hale of Me, Mr [Edwin Wallace] Stoughton & Gen [James H.] Van Alen of N.Y., & Gen [Harry] White of Indiana Co Pa constituted the party. Courtland Parker did not stop, but returned with this party. They called on me at my office about 3 P.M. Gen [James M.] Comly and Webb being present. They spread before me very fully the condition of things in Louisiana, and the action of the Returning Board. They emphatically endorsed the general fairness and honesty of the Boards conduct. They said it was the opinion of all of the Republicans who went down to N[ew] O[rleans] that the Republican ticket was lawfully and honestly entitled to be declared elected. That largely more Parishes and Polls ought to be thrown out for violence and intimidation, than was necessary to elect the whole Rep ticket State and National; that a fair election would have given the Republicans not less than thirteen to fifteen thousand majority; that the intimidation was deliberately planned, and systematically executed by means of rifle clubs organized in the Parishes selected for the process of intimidation known as 'bull dozing'. I asked each of the gentlemen for his individual views. All concurred in saying in the strongest terms that the evidence and law entitled the Republican ticket to the certificate of election, and that the result would in their opinion be accordingly. They spoke highly of [J. Madison] Wells and [Thomas C.] Anderson, and favorably of the two colored men [G. Casenave and Louis M. Kenner, of the Louisiana Returning Board].

Thanks to Laura and Webb they were all entertained with Hon. A. F. Perry at our house last evening. It was a jovial little gathering. Lucy and Laura the only ladies. Lucy and I before they came took tea with Mrs Price at Mr John L. Gills.

Columbus, 6th December, 1876.—Last evening we gave a reception to the Ohio Electoral College, all present. Gen [Allen T.] Wikoff & [the] State Rep Committee. My neighbors   Patterson, Wm G. Deshler, & John L. Gill, Denny Rogers and a very few others. During the evening we got dispatches from Gov [W. P.] Kellogg, Mr [S. B.] Packard, & Mr [John] Ray of La showing Hayes electors chosen by over 3000. This *entitles* us to 181 electoral votes without Florida. Wires down in Florida! Mrs [John W.] Herron, Laura, & Emily P[latt] with Lucy did the honors, and the affair was successful.

[Pasted in the diary at this point, showing attendance of the electoral college members at the reception, is a copy of the National Union Republican Ticket:] Senatorial Electors, of Ohio, Aaron F. Perry, Edward H. Bohm; District Electors, *1st* Dist., John W. Herron; *2d*, John W. Warrington; *3d*, George W. Hulick; *4th*, John C. Williamson; *5th*, Isaac N. Alexander; *6th*, James B. Luckey; *7th*, Orange Edwards; *8th*, Anson P. Howard; *9th*, John J. Hane; *10th*, John S. Davis; *11th* John L. Jones; *12th*, Augustus R. Keller; *13th*, Edward M. Downer; *14th*, Andrew M. Burns; *15th*, Columbia Downing; *16th*, David Cunningham; *17th*, John H. Whitcraft; *18th*, Samuel G. Barnard; *19th*, Benjamin F. Wade; *20th*, Worthy S. Streator.

Columbus, 7th December, 1876.—The Electoral College of Ohio met yesterday. Mr [Aaron F.] Perry presided. A unanimous vote for H[ayes] & W[heeler]. All passed off pleasantly. During the day I rec'd dispatches from Penn., Ill & S.C. showing that in these States the Colleges voted for H. & W. In the evening Platt Laura Emily & Fanny, ~~Mitchell~~ came in with ~~the~~ Gen M[itchell]. Dr Fullerton, and Ruddy Platt, and later Mr John W Andrews and Mrs A. and Miss   Grayson. We received dispatches during the evening from all of the Republican States except Florida, Iowa, Nebraska, Colorado and Oregon. We all felt doubts about Oregon. The vote of the State was indisputable Republican by 1100 majority; and over; But one of the Republican Electors, it has been charged, is ineligible being a postmaster. The Democratic Governor ~~has~~ heard argument on his right to refuse to give him a certificate. All this we knew. It led me to think there was a probability that the Governor would commission the highest Democrat on the defeated ticket and thus give Tilden the 185 votes required to elect. We retired after our visitors left, having had a lively happy little gathering, but with this doubt and solicitude about Oregon on our minds. This morning Isaiah, our colored man, when he came in to build the fire, laid the [Ohio] State Journal on our bed. He lighted the gass and I read the telegraphic accounts showing how Gov [La Fayette] Grover of Oregon had refused to commission [John W.] Watts the Republican elector, an ex-postmaster, and had given the certificate of election to [E. A.] Cronin the highest Dem elector, and how he Cronin had *met* as the College, and elected two Republicans to fill the two vacancies created by the refusal of the Republicans, two of whom were commissioned, to act or meet with him, and how this College met and cast two (2) votes for H & W and one (1) for T[ilden] & H[endricks], thus giving in the Nation to H & W 184 electoral votes and to T. & H 185 votes, and in this way electing the latter Pres & V. Pres. The two regularly commissioned Rep electors met

56

—[John W.] Watts the P. M. resigned, was re-elected *this* College gave H & W ~~185 votes~~ the three (3) Votes of Oregon, making their aggregate 185, and thus electing them, if this vote is treated as the true one.   Here is the danger. A contest ruinous to the country—dangerous, perhaps fatal to free government may grow out of it. I would gladly give up all claim to the place, if this would avert the evil, without bringing on us a greater calamity. I am determined that no selfish ambition or interest shall influence my conduct in the face of these tremendous events. Whatever, on the whole is best for the country, that I will do if I can know it, regardless of consequences to myself. I shall keep cool—master all tendencies that may lead me astray, and endeavor to act as Washington would have acted under similar circumstances. My wife feels some disappointment—is unhappy on account of the consequences of our defeat to the poor colored people of the South, but on personal grounds is contented, and will without effort show her usual cheerfulness. We shall both bear this new responsibility with composure. Our friends will suffer more than we shall, whatever the suspense or the final result.

8th December, 1876.—The Oregon fraud appears to have been carried out in so bungling a way that it is not likely to do more than complicate matters. Indeed it now looks as if it would damage our adversaries in the public judgment without in any manner injuring us. The fraud is so transparent palpable and disgraceful ~~that~~ that it is not impossible that it will be thrown aside without dissent from any quarter.

Columbus, 16th *December,* 1876.—We returned last night from Dayton. Our visits with John W. Herron at C[incinnati] and Richard C Anderson at D. were most happy. Lucy was in excellent spirits. Webb (who left us at Cin'ti) picked up a knowledge of Cin'ti public men, which he wanted, and had a good time generally. At Dayton I made an off hand talk which seemed to be successful. Several hundred people

57

shook hands with a gushing sort of enthusiasm, and I was visited by many of the best people. The ladies were very civil to Lucy. At Springfield the people especially the working-men turned out in great force. I spoke from the rear of the car until the train moved on. The weather has been favorable—rather cold but bright and clear.

17th December 1876.—Yesterday Col Albert D. Shaw consul at Toronto came from Washington to talk with me about affairs there, and my purposes as to persons and policies. He is a friend of Senator [Roscoe] Conkling, and seemed to be on intimate terms with the Secy of War [James Donald Cameron] and others in high places. He talked forcibly and with much feeling. He fears that the apprehension that I am in the hands of the Reform element of the Rep party will lose me in the Senate the friendship and support of enough Senators on the approaching struggle in the Senate to change the result of the Presidential election, and bring in Mr Tilden. Mr Conkling has been committed against our present views on some of the legal questions now before the Country—notably, as I infer, on the right of the Senate and house to pass on the returns of the Electoral Colleges. The Southern Republican Senators, are afraid they will be ignored, as "carpet baggers" or otherwise objectionable under the Hayes policy of conciliation. Names were not mentioned, but [George E.] Spencer, of Alabama, [Stephen W.] Dorsey of Ark, [Powell] Clayton and [Simon B.] Conover seemed to be the Senators Col S. was thinking of. I told Col S I had concluded that I ought to take no part in the pending contest in Washington —that I should probably make no declaration of policies, and no committal as to members of my Cabinet until the result was announced in February. That I stood on my letter [of acceptance]. That as to Southern affairs it plainly indicated what I thought desirable. That the Southern people must obey the new amendments, and give the colored men all of their

58

rights—that peace in that country could only be had in this way—that prosperity would come to the South with immigration from the North and from Europe—that to get this, people must feel as free to go to the South as they now do to go to Kansas or Nebraska—that I had no private views or pledges to give—that what I said to him I said publicly, and to all who called on me and desired to know my views.

He showed the reasons why Mr Conkling took no active part in the canvass—that his health was broken—and his eyes required that he should remain in a dark room. He explained the bad faith of [George William] Curtiss toward C[onkling] of Bristow towards C & Grant—of Morton towards C., &c &c &c He urged the appointment of C, (or rather of his being offered the appt) as Secy of State. Spoke well of [Thomas Collier] Platt—of [Justin S.] Morrill of Me—of Secy of War [James Donald Cameron]—and in disparagement of [William E.] Chandler, Blaine, and [Postmaster General Marshall] Jewell.

Although I gave him no pledges, and merely said as to appointments I would try to give first consideration to the claims of all sections of the Rep. party, he seemed to be pleased with what I told him. He evidently came with a desire to be pleased, and left professing to think he could overcome difficulties at Washington.

I found in Dayton a very respectable family of blood relations—descended from my G[reat] G[rand] father Ezekiel Hayes. David H. Morrison is my 2d cousin. His mother was a Humphries, and her mother was a daughter (Elizabeth) of E[zekial] H[ayes]. He is a successful bridge builder.

Rev Charles W Hayes 135 Portland, Me., is a genealogist, and descended from my Gr[eat] Gr[eat] Grandfather Daniel Hayes.

Robert P. Hayes of U.S. Express office, Buffalo, N.Y. sent me a copy of Rev C. W. H[ayes]'s pleasant story of Daniel

Hayes [*A Long Journey. The Story of Daniel Hayes* (Portland, Me., 1876)]

Copy

Columbus O
17 Dec 1876

My Dear Gov:

I am exceedingly obliged for your valuable letters. It seems to me desirable, that I should remain quietly in Ohio, committing myself to no person or policy beyond that which the public may fairly infer from my letter and other published and authorized utterances. Believing firmly that I have been honestly and legally elected, I propose to wait contentedly for the issue. If the result is changed by violence, fraud or treachery I shall suffer less than my friends—less than the country and I may ~~say~~ truly say I shall suffer chiefly on their account.

Sincerely

R B Hayes

Hon Wm Dennison

———

Columbus O
29 Dec 1876

Private

My Dear Sir:

I wish in strict confidence to say that in case our adversaries go to law with us I shall want you to assist the Att'y Gen'l. Let your thoughts dwell on the points that may be raised either to question our rights or simply to perplex and annoy us.

One other matter, my judgment is that neither House of Congress, nor both combined, have any right to interfere in the count. It is for the V.P. to do it all. His action is final.

There should be no compromise of our constitutional rights. We should firmly insist upon them.

Again allow me to assure you that I am in no way committed as to persons or policies—no one is authorized to commit me.—I shall remain free to the end.

Sincerely

R B Hayes

Hon S. Shellabarger
    &c &c

———

Columbus O

29 Dec 1876

Confidential

My Dear Sir:

I am exceedingly obliged for your interesting note of the *25th*. Without expressing any opinion on the points you state so clearly, I may suggest a query. Can an Act of Congress take from the V.P. the authority (the duty) the constitution has vested in him?

Sincerely

R B Hayes

Hon H. N. Conger
    &c &c

———

Columbus, 30th December, 1876.—Twenty four years ago today we married! A happy event for me—for us both. We look back with satisfaction. Our children are good.   We have had cold weather this month. The Ohio frozen over—navigation closed. Yesterday a deep snow fell on the well prepared ground.

The political event of the week is the visit made me by Judge T[homas] J. Mackey of Chester S.C. with a letter from Gen Wade Hampton.[2] Mackey is a fluent and florid talker. His ~~professions~~ representations are such as lead me to hope for good results by a wise policy in the South. The letter is not of much importance except as it indicates Gen Hamptons views of duty in case of armed resistance by the Democrats. I have a dispatch from C. P. Leslie as follows. "I warn you to beware of Tom Mackey.*** He is a first class fraud *** &c &c!." This is a specimen of the Southern complications!

Columbus O
31 Dec 1876

My Dear Sir.

I still think I ought to leave W[ashington] well alone. I have many friends in that city who can of their own motion speak confidently of my ways of thinking and acting. An authorized representative could remove some troubles that you now see, but only think of yet greater troubles he might create.

I like to get your suggestions, and am interested in the facts you give. Do not misconstrue my silence if in the hurry of the time I fail to reply.

Sincerely

R B Hayes

Hon J. A. Kasson
  &c &c

––––––

Columbus O
31 Dec 1876

My Dear Governor:

I have your letter of the 30*th*. I have not looked into the question you suggest. With the aid of [John A.] Little I will be able to get at the trouble. I am glad you mentioned it. It did not occur to me as a question.—The grand demonstration I had not heard of. Such affairs need judicious looking after by somebody, but of course I can not interfere with them.— Something like your views as to a friend, or friends at W[ashington] has been mentioned by a good many. There are two sides to it. It seems to me that Comly and Shellabarger and Dennison can give such facts about my general ways of thinking and action as will accomplish all that is right and practicable. I am in the habit of saying that we can better afford defeat by the knavery of the adversary or the crotchets or treachery of friends than success by intrigues. Of course I understand you to mean that we must have men at W. prepared to defeat the corrupt practices of our adversaries. For this purpose the gentlemen I name can be useful, and other of our friends who may be in W. can lend a helping hand. This must be left to volunteers. For me to select and send to W. a *representative* would in my judgment be a mistake. Think of it. I will *hear* and *heed*, but you have my decided impression.

Sincerely

R B Hayes

Gen E. F. Noyes
&c &c

Columbus O
31 Dec 1876

Private

My Dear Sir:

I recognise the friendliness and sincerity of your purpose but it seems to me it would be a mistake for me to send a representative to W[ashington].—There are several Ohio men in W. who know my methods of thinking and acting in public affairs. They can of their own motion speak confidently—Such men as Shellabarger, Comly, Noyes, Little &c &c not in official positions at W. and various Senators and Representatives can perhaps do and say all that can properly be said and done. All this must, I am confident, be left to volunteers such as the men I name or allude to. Don't misunderstand me. I am ready to hear and to heed the suggestions of friends, but I see this business today as above indicated.

Sincerely

R B Hayes

"Wm E Chandler"

P.S.

You now see the troubles which an authorized friend could remove. If you had such a friend in W. what other and greater troubles might you not then see?

H.

NOTES

CHAPTER III

[1] The conference Hayes describes lasted three hours. Roberts came at the suggestion of Ohio intimates of Hayes who recognized the importance of trying to break into the Southern front for Tilden. Both the Republicans and the Democrats claimed to have won control of the government of Louisiana, and two rival governments were in existence. Roberts wanted to know which of the contenders Hayes would support if President and what he would do about South Carolina, where the same situation prevailed. According to Roberts, Hayes said that he would want to consult with conservative whites; and that, while desiring to preserve Negro rights, he thought that intelligence should rule in politics. See Harry Barnard, *Rutherford B. Hayes and His America* (Indianapolis, 1954), 357-58; C. Vann Woodward, *Reunion and Reaction* (Boston, 1951), 24-26.

[2] Hampton was the Democratic claimant of the governorship of South Carolina.

Chapter IV

JAN. 1, 1877—MARCH 14, 1877

Columbus, 1st January, 1877.—A deep snow—six to ten inches on a good solid and smooth foundation has given us good sleighing for the last two or three days. Cold and cloudy this morning.

Our family are all enjoying good health, and fair fortune. Rutherford is at home from Cornell. Webb is our standby. Birch remains at the law school [at Harvard University] during the vacation. Lucy receives New Years callers today at home, 60 Broad St.

List of callers on Lucy about 10½ A.M.

Gen A. T. Wikoff, Frank Hickok, Mr Blaine, Mr Cowen, Judge Bates, Brock Walcutt, Young Hanford [and] Lane, Dr. Loring, Dr. Tooley, Mr. Huntington, Wm Deshler, Mr Gill, Broad 7, Mr J. E. Patterson, Mr. Patterson, Mr. Patterson, Mr Nevins Young [and] Friend, President Orton, Prof Tuttle, Gen Walcutt, Mr Stevenson, Mr Cook, Joe Loring, Bryan Collins, Mr. Gill, Mr. Huston, Mr Denmead, Mr. Monypenny, Mr Gill, Mr Tallmadge, 3—Olmsted, Monypeny, Aiken, Ed Taylor, Mr Taylor, Mr. Nash, Mr. Field, Mr. Lanman, Mr Fitch, Mr Faris, Mr Huston, Mr. Hutchison [and] 5 others, Mr Coolidge [and] son, Mr Kingman, Mr Swan, Mr. Black, Mr. Harvy, Mr. Manly, Mr. Holly, Rud Platt, Frank Hicock Rud Hayes, Webb Hayes, Mr Smead and Jorjy [George]

Smead, Mr Hanford Dr. Fulerton, Mr Lord, Mr Smith, Mr Potter, Mr Kilbourne, Mr Williamson and his sons, Mr. Parsons, Mr. Hanford and son.

Capt Ch C Chadwick, Frank L Fisher, Will H. Lott, Benj E. Orr, D. Henry Taft, Will H. Todd, H. R. Kingman, Frank Merion, J. H. Beebe, C. E. Freeman, M. N. Danshule, Wm Moneypenny, John C. English, Ch Parrott, Walter D Nicholas, James Watson,   Watson [and]   Watson; Willis H Wiggins, Clifton L. M. Stark, W. H. H. Wilcox, L L Stark, E. K. Stewart, Archie E Woods, Col. J. C. Donaldson, Rev. Jos M. Trible, Wm L. Jameson, Frank Jameson, Walter A. Dunn, Wilson L Gill, Herbert R Gill, John L. Gill—50th year of calling; J. V. Ramsden, John C L Pugh, L. G. Curtiss, Geo C. Mather, James H. Anderson, E. J. Blount, S. S. Rickley, R. Kingman, C. A. Wikoff, F. R. Shinn, J. T. Rodgers, J. C. English, Jr., Clifford Perin, Wm Moneypenny, Jr., J. B. Potts, W. F. Black, C.P.T. Butler, Wm Jamison, A. Gardner, J. M. Park, Rob Patterson, A. M. Greiner, E. F. Jamison, R. W. Grange, C. J. Wetmore, C. W. Simonton, W. S. Wagenhals, R. W. Manly, I. R. Sherwood, N. H. Young, C. T. Brent, USA, S. C. Thomas, F. C. Burt, H. J. Cox, G. J. Atkinson, A. W. Green, E. F. Beckwith, E. C. Beckwith, John Joyce, A. W. Thurman, Tom D. Huntington, Fred Shedd, Joe Hutcheson, Sollace B. Collidge, F. W. Hubbard, C. B. Coolidge, George Monypenny, C. O. Hunter, M. C. Blain, F. M. Brooks, R. H. Gardner, R. Nevins, Jr., H. H. Gibson, T. D. Duncan, C. T. Read, F. A. Layman, Will. Akin.

Harry Olmstead, W. P. Little, Luigi Lomai, USA, D. K. Watson, C. G. Lord, L. J. Critchfield, T. H. Hibbard, B. H. Brooks, J. Kilborne, W. C. Quincy, W. A. Hershiser, Theo Tallmadge, R. A. Whyte, T. E. Glenn, W. K. Field, G. A. Lyle, W. G. Benham, John Field, M. O. Price, B. F. Payne, F. J. Shedd,   Cowen, Ed. Denmead, C. Claypoole, W. A. Neil, T. B. Galloway, D. J. Smith, J. H. Geiger, W. A.

Mahony, T. Longstreth, G. W. Bright, J. A. Jeffry, J. G. Bull, E. A. Cole, T. C. Jones, E. C. Beach, A. Watson, Handford and Hunter.

The large handwriting is by Fanny. At this time the visitors came in such crowds that it was impossible to keep the names in order. Two hundred & sixteen (216) called.

Columbus, 2d January, 1877.—Our Cousin Mary Birchard of Fayetteville Vt was lost in the fearful R.R. accident at Ashtabula Friday evening. We have learned none of the particulars as to her fate beyond the general facts of the catastrophe. The accident was the most dreadful that has ever occurred on any Railroad in Ohio—and has rarely been equalled in the number of victims, and other circumstances of horror anywhere. Poor dear Mary. She was a kind hearted lovable woman! When I last met her, Ohio day at Philadelphia she was one of the happiest in that great throng of people!

Columbus O
3 Jan'y 1877

My Dear Uncle

We have been in an agony of suspense about our dear Mary [Birchard] for several days. After hoping against all reasonable probabilities we are now compelled to yield to the evidence and admit that she is among the unfortunate victims. You have our deepest sympathy and prayers. We pray that you and Aunt Birchard may have grace under the merciful goodness of God to bear up, and to receive in full measure consolation from the only Power that can sustain you in your great sorrow

Affectionately

R B Hayes

Hon A. Birchard

Columbus, 5th January, 1877.—My advices are that the result of the action of the Senate will depend on the Report the

Committee of the Senate makes on the election in Louisiana. This seems not to be in much doubt, but there is enough to leave ~~my~~ me in a state of suspense. I must therefore prepare for either event. The Cabinet is the chief work, next the Inaugural. As to the address I wish to repeat my letter of acceptance on *1st* currency and National faith, *2d* on Civil Service reform *3d* on the South. I must urge a liberal policy towards the South especially in affording facilities for education, and encouraging business and emigration, by internal improvements of a National character.

Columbus O.
5 Jan 1877

Confidential

My Dear Sir.

I have your note of the *3rd*. I do not wish to influence the action of our friends, and do not volunteer opinions. But *you* have a right to my opinion. I believe the V.P. alone has the constitutional power to count the votes and ~~to~~ declare the result. Everything in the nature of a contest as to electoral votes is an affair of the States. The rest is a merely ministerial duty. Therefore it is not right in my judgment for Congress to interfere.

Sincerely

R B Hayes

Hon John Sherman
U.S.S.

P.S. I would like your opinion and Senator Morton's on resigning as Governor before the count in February.

It would be a decided announcement of my own opinions as to the result of the election. I can do it with great satisfaction whatever the probable action of the two Houses if it is thought advisable.

H.

Columbus, 17th January, 1877.—[William A.] Wheeler, Chandler (Wm E) and others write that Conkling is decidedly hostile, and that he has enough followers to pass through the Senate a Compromise measure. The effect of this is to change the result in all probability. Well, I am personally content. I must go on to the end, and in the meanwhile prepare for either event. For the office I must have a private Secretary and Cabinet, and an inaugural address. My friend Gen [Manning F.] Force is my preference for Pri[vate] Secy. He declines, and almost feels hurt that I suggested it to him. Gen [Robert P.] Kennedy is my next choice.[1] On the subject of Cabinet, I have talked with Mr. Wheeler, Gen [Jacob D.] Cox, Gen [Ralph P.] Buckland and a few others. I am inclined to say that I must not take either of the leading competitors for the Presidential nomination—nor any member of the present Cabinet. My thoughts rest on [William M.] Evarts for the first place. On Gov [Alexander Hamilton] Rice or [John Murray] Forbes of Mass., or [John] Sherman   for treasury; on Gen [John M.] Harlan of Ky for Atty Genl. I think well of Gen [Benjamin] Harrison of Ind., and [Thomas] Settle of N. C. for places. Gov. [John Frederick] Hartranft [Penn.] has a democratic Lt. Governor, or he might be favorably considered. [George W.] McCrary of Iowa for a place. [Newton] Booth of Calif., (but his seat in the Senate would be filled by a Democrat).

Friday, 19th January 1877.—Three weeks ago today the great snow fell which gives us still good sleighing. Three weeks of good sleighing is a rare thing in Columbus. One very cold day; thermometer down at 9 A.M. to 20°—[minus zero]! 29°— at Agricultural College [Ohio State University]. This was I think Jany 9th.

Sunday, 21st January, 1877.—The compromise reported by the joint Committee seems to be a surrender, at least ~~partially~~ in part, of our case. The leading constitutional objection to it, perhaps, is that the appointment of the Commission by Act of

69

Congress violates that part of the Constitution which gives the appointment of all other officers "to the President. To this it will possibly be replied that the members of the Commission are not officers—that they are analogous to referees & master commissioners, to advisory boards, or committees. But is this true? Their decisions stand unless both Houses of Congress concur in overruling them. If the Commission decides to throw out the vote of Mississippi, the vote of that state will be lost if *one* House concurs. If the Commission decides that [E. A.] Cronin's vote for Tilden shall be counted, it will be counted if the House alone concurs. The commission is analogous to inferior tribunals. Its decisions are binding unless the superior tribunal overrules them by a concurrent vote of both houses.[2]

The President of the Senate, and the Senate may be overruled by the Commission and the House. Surely the members of such a Commission are officers. Their appointment by Congress is a usurpation of the Presidential authority. If the bill has not a two thirds vote in both Houses the President's veto ought to prevent it from becoming a law.

The next most important objection to the Bill is that if passed it ~~will~~ may turn out to be an Act to *prevent* the counting of the Electoral vote. There can be no count if the Commission refuses or fails to act. This power to prevent a decision is a power far above any power belonging to Referees, Master Commissioners, advisory boards or Committees.

Friday, 26th January, 1877.—The Compromise bill for counting the Presidential Vote passed the Senate by 47 to 17. More Republicans supported it than voted against it. The Dem's all voted aye except [William W.] Eaton of C[onnecticu]t. Its passage by a like majority in the House is probable. What Congress and the popular sentiment approve is rarely defeated by reason of Constitutional objections. I trust the measure will turn out well. It is a great relief to me. Defeat in this way after a full and public hearing before this Commission is not mortifying in any degree, and success will be in all respects more satisfactory. I have not tried to influence the opinions or actions of anybody on the Bill. Before another Presidential Election this whole subject of the Presidential Election ought to be thoroughly considered, and a radical change made. It is probable that no wise measure can be devised which does not require an amendment of the Constitution. Let ~~the~~ proposed Amendments be maturely considered. Something ought to be done immediately.

———

Columbus, O.

26 Jan 1877

My Dear Judge:

I am obliged for your valued letter. The Bill in relation to the Election will become a law. Of course with so strong a vote in its favor, the President will promptly sign it. I have not attempted to influence the result, and shall not. If the principles of Mr [Frederick Theodore] Frelinghuysen's speech are adopted by the commission, our success is almost certain. I take it our friends will see that we are ably and wisely represented both *on* and *before* the commission. This is the next point of interest.

Sincerely

R B Hayes

Hon A Taft
&c &c

Columbus, 31st January, 1877.—The Commission seems to be a good one. At 2 P.M. Webb announced "the judge—it is [Joseph P.] Bradley—In Washington the bets are five to one that the next [President] will be Hayes!" [3]

But I am in no way elated. I prefer success. But I am clear that for our happiness failure is to be preferred. I shall therefore await the event with the utmost composure. If the result is adverse, I shall be cheerful, quiet, and serene. If successful may God give me grace to be firm and wise and just—clear in the great office—for the true interest of all the people of the United States!

At this time Lucy is suffering from a severe attack of her headache—a monthly.—

1st February, 1877.—Dr [Erskine Boies] Fullerton's mixture settled the stomach and gave Lucy relief by 8 or 9 o'clock last evening. She slept well. This morning she is over it.

2d February, 1877.—We have two of Lucy's agreeable young lady relatives with us. Parties and life follow. Their bright faces add a charm to the house—Lucy Cook and Lizzie McKel[l]. Lucy puts "What's the difference between a honey comb and the honey moon? A honey comb is full of little cells and a honey moon is one great big sell."

"What is the difference between a bride and the groom? The bride is generally given away—and the groom is always sold."

"What is worth the most—the man or the woman? The woman is double you o man—W.O.Man."

"Why is a stagnant pool like a lead image of satan? Ans. The one is a dead level—and the other is a lead devil."

———

The count began yesterday. All objections were withheld until the call of Florida. That State was sent to the Commission. Counsel were named, all appeared. The great law suit is now on trial. We have a good case, apparently a good Court, and certainly able Counsel. But law suits are proverbially uncertain.

6th February, 1877.—Mild weather for about two weeks. The two months sleighing in Central and Northern Ohio left us quietly—slowly thawing—a great deal of ice and good skating in the streets.

———

"Why did the Devil never learn to skate? [Answer] How in Hell could he?

The young preacher's one sermon

"We come into the world naked and bare,
We go through it with trouble and care,
We die and go, the Lord knows where,
If we do well here, we shall do well there."

Columbus, 8th February, 1877.—Yesterday the Electoral Commission decided not to go behind the papers filed with the VP in the case of Florida. The question was well argued on our side. Judge [Stanley] Matthews was notably able and successful. Mr [William M.] Evarts' argument was worthy of his fame. I read the arguments in the Congr Record, and can't see how lawyers held can differ on the question. But the decision is by a strictly party vote—eight Republicans against the seven Democrats! It shows the strength of party ties. The general situation is now regarded as much more favorable to us, and now our friends are very confident of success.

9th February 1877.—The Reception to the 62d General Assembly [of Ohio] at the City Hall last night was very well attended, and an enjoyable affair.

I hear from   of Steubenville that Eli T Sheppard being unwell kept his bed in a hotel in Washington while Jerry [Jeremiah] Black discussed with his callers, in a room separated from that of S[heppard] by a door, the loud talk in Black's room on the situation. Black said "God Dam them, they will beat us and elect Hayes, but we shall give them all the trouble we can!" [4]

I am not likely to get much time to prepare an inaugural address after the Commission decides in my favor, if it does so decide. I would like to get clearly in view the main points. Refer to the pacific solution of the disputed Presidential contest—to the necessity of peaceful relations with all nations, and an allusion to arbitration as a means of averting war—this with a complimentary allusion to Gen Grant.—the Return to

73

specie payments—the permanency of Civil Service tenures—purity—appointments for merit &c &c. The South to be made prosperous by a cheerful acquiescence in the results of the war —by peace—by education—by improvements. Profess a desire to so appoint as to aid in good local government.

We expect to go tomorrow to Cincinnati. Saturday eve. at the Bar Association supper. I will give if called on ~~the Su~~ [a toast to the] memory of [W. Y.] Gholson, [Oliver M.] Spencer, and [Bellamy] Storer, the judges ~~of the~~ elected in 1854—the best bench I ever saw.

Cincinnati, 14th February, 1877.—Yesterday W[illia]m & Susan McGill of Bellevue, Ky, gave Lucy and me each a hand glass of his own workmanship—also a paper weight to me. He works with Wm Coulter & Son, 102 & 104 East 2*d* Street, Cinti.—

Cincinnati, 10th–14th February.—Returned eve of 14*th*. A happy visit at Dr. [John] Davis'.

17th February.—Last evening Louisiana was decided by the Commission in our favor. There is still some doubt, but apparently very little, of the result. The inaugural and cabinet making are now in order. I would like to get support from good men of the South—late rebels. How to do it is the question. I have the best disposition towards the Southern people —rebels and all. I could appoint a Southern Democrat in the Cabinet. But who would take it among the capable and influential good men of those States? Gen Joseph E. Johnston occurs to me. I must think of this.[5]

Sunday 18th February.—The indications still are that I am to go to W[ashington]. I talked yesterday with Fred. Douglass and Mr [James] Poindexter both colored, on the Southern question. I told them my views. They approved. Mr Douglass gave me many useful hints about the whole subject. My course is a firm assertion and maintenance of the rights of the colored people of the South, ~~as~~ according to the 13*th*, 14*th* and 15*th* amendments—coupled with a readiness to recognice all Southern people, without regard to past political conduct, who will now go with me heartily and in good faith in support of these principles.

19 Feb.—For Cabinet
1. A *new* Cabinet—no member of the present.
2. No Presidential Candidates.
3. No appointment to "take care" of any body.

Confidential

Columbus O.
19 Feb 1877

My Dear Sir:

The more I think of it the more difficult it seems for me to get ready to come to W. before Wednesday or Thursday of next week. I must fix affairs at Fremont, and can't begin it until I know the result. Why can't ~~my~~ friends be sent or come here?

It seems to me proper now to say that I am extremely desirous that you should take the Treasury Department.

Aside from my own personal preference, there are many and controlling reasons why I should ask you to do this. It will satisfy friends here in Ohio. I understand Gov. Morton and our friends in Washington like it. The country will approve it. You are by all odds the best fitted for it of any man in the Nation. Your resignation from the Senate will be a great loss to that body, but it will cause no serious dissensions or difficulty in Ohio. Do not say no until I have had a full conference with you. There is no reason why you should not visit Ohio as soon as you can be spared from W. Of course the public will know of our meeting. But they will be gratified to know it. No possible harm can come of it. I should have said all this before, but I did not want to embarrass you in your action on Presidential questions.

Sincerely
R B Hayes

Hon John Sherman

———

My Dear General:

I am in receipt of your very kind note of the 20*th*. Sinister rumors from W. leave us in doubt as to the final issue. In case of success I expect to be in Washington next Thursday, 29*th*, and to go directly to Senator Sherman's. If after seeing you it seems best, I will be glad, to accept your hospitality on Saturday for myself and family. I will also be pleased to dine with you as proposed, on that day. I can not name all or perhaps any of my party except my own family, but I suppose that besides Mrs. Hayes and myself and son, Webb C., there will also be Gen and Mrs [John Grant] Mitchell and possibly four others. If you wish to invite others, may I suggest Mr Wheeler, Senator and Mrs. Sherman.

I noticed an item saying that you will would on leaving the Ex[ecutive] Mansion go to Mr [Hamilton] Fish's. I will be *particularly* gratified if you will remain where you are as long as it may be convenient for you to do so, and until your own residence is ready. Mrs. Hayes is now absent, but you may assure Mrs. Grant that my wife will feel obliged to her if she will remain at least a few days with us after the 5*th* of March.

As to my family coming to your house on Saturday—it occurs to me that with your dinner &c &c this may be inconvenient and that it is best for me to remain at Senator Sherman's until after inauguration. All this on the supposition that we are finally declared successful.

Sincerely

R B Hayes

Gen U. S. Grant
President

P.S. It is perhaps best that the date of my expected arrival in W. should not be made public.

———

25*th February*, 1877.—Yesterday the Commission decided Oregon to be for Hayes & Wheeler. This is the last of the disputed and doubtful States. The only apparent chance of defeating us now is the revolutionary conduct of the Dems in the House. The Southern members of that party who have hitherto been conservative and favorable are disturbed by an article in the Ohio State Journal unfriendly to them which is charged to have been inspired by me. The truth is I stand on my letter [of acceptance]. If I speak at Fremont or elsewhere during the next few days I may say

My letter expressed what I thought were just ~~and sound~~ sentiments on the leading questions which then interested the country. I thought its doctrines were sound before the election ~~in June last.~~ I think they are sound now that the election is over, and if the issue ~~now~~ pending in Congress shall be decided in our favor, those principles will be the standard by which my official conduct shall be guided. ~~in during the next four years.~~ If I were to write that letter now I would give that part on the Southern question ~~still~~ greater emphasis. The ~~people~~ great body of the people of this country earnestly desire a wise and just settlement of that question. They want peace—they long for repose. What is required is

First that for the protection and welfare of the colored people the 13th 14th, and 15th amendments shall be ~~faithfully~~ sacredly observed and faithfully enforced according to their ~~letter~~ true interest and meaning.

Second We all see ~~It is seen~~ that the tremendous revolution which has passed over the Southern people has left them impoverished and prostrate, and we all are deeply solicitous to do what may constitutionally be done to make them again prosperous and happy. They need economy, honesty, and intelligence in their local governments. They need ~~to have~~ to have such a policy ~~encouraged~~ adopted as will cause sectionalism to disappear, and that will tend to wipe out the color line. ~~They~~ They need to have encouraged immigration, education, and ~~the work of peace.~~ every description of legitimate business and industry. We do not want a ~~solid~~ united North, nor a ~~solid~~ united South. We want ~~a solid~~ a united country. And if

77

the great trust shall devolve upon me, I fervently pray, that the Divine Being who holds the destinies of the Nations in his hands ~~nearly~~ will give me Wisdom ~~and His grace~~ to perform its duties so as to promote the trust and best interests of the whole country.

Fremont, 26th February, 1877.—Why not adopt provisionally a rule that no application for office will be considered at present Papers will be filed with the proper officer, or in the proper department. Hereafter rules will be adopted and made public. Personal applications to the President will in no case be favorably considered.

Columbus, 27th February, 1877.—Mark Twain recommends Lt. Col. Richard Irwin Dodge, author of the Great Plains, &c for the head of Indian Department. "Knowledge of Indians & humanity."

M[oses] M. Granger wants a lawyer's office.

———

Mem[orandum] of [Proposed] Cabinet Feb 1877

Evarts	State	N. Y.
Sherman	Treasury	O.
Harlan	Atty Genl	Ky
Forbes	Navy	Mass
Schurz	Interior	Mo
	War	

Southern man [for] P[ost] M[aster] [General]

[For Secretary of War:]

Hale of Me		
McCormick	Arizona	California
McMichael	Pa	
Hartranft	Pa	
Harrison	Ind	
McCrary	Iowa	
~~Settle~~		

78

Failing a *Southern* man [for Postmaster General] *then*

x *Alcorn*	Miss.	
x *Settle*	N.C.	
Key		
Johnston		
Hilliard H W	Columbus	
State	Evarts	N. Y.
Tr[easury]	Sherman	O.
Navy	Hale	Me
Atty Gen	Harlan	Ky
War	McCrary	Iowa
Interior	Schurz	Mo
P.M.Genl	Johnston	Va

Washington 14th March, 1877.—Wc [(] William Henry Smith, Ex Gov [Edward F.] Noyes, Gov [Thomas L.] Young, Gen [Charles H.] Grosvenor [and] Col H[enry] C. Corbin [)] left Columbus soon after noon Thursday Mch 1st for Washington on a Special car—having in fact two cars of Col Tom [Thomas A.] Scott, attached to the regular passenger train.[6] The evening before we had a reception at the State House, given by the people of Columbus. A large crowd followed us to the Depot. We were escorted by the College Cadets. I made a short speech, which was well received. Crowds met us at Newark, Dennison, Steubenville and other points. The enthusiasm was greater than I have seen in Ohio before. At Marysville (?) near Harrisburg we were wakened to hear the news that the two Houses had counted the last State, and that I was declared elected! We reached W. about 9½ A.M.—Gen and Senator Sherman met us at the Depot, and we were driven directly to Senator Sherman's House. After breakfast I called with Senator Sherman on President Grant.

It was arranged that I should in the evening before the State dinner at ~~Gen Grants~~ the White House be sworn by the Ch[ief] Justice, to prevent an interregnum between Sunday noon (the 4th) & the inauguration Monday. I then drove This was the advice of Secy [Hamilton] Fish and the President.[7] I did not altogether approve but acquiesced. ~~I then drove~~ with Senator Sherman to the Capitol. The colored hack drivers and others cheered lustily. I went into the V. P.'s room, and many Senators and Reps were introduced to me. Several Northern men, S. S. Cox and other Dems, and still more Southern men.

Saturday and Sunday saw Senators and Reps and others, and [received] many suggestions on the Cabinet. Blaine urged [William Pierce] Fry[e]. [Hannibal] Hamlin much vexed and grieved when I told him I couldn't appoint F[rye]. Blaine seemed to claim it, as a condition of good relations with me. [James Donald] Cameron, & [John A.] Logan, greatly urged all day. I told C[ameron] I could not appoint him. Too many of the old Cabinet had good claims to remain, to recognize one, without appointing more than would be advisable. I accordingly nominated

Wm M Evarts	N Y	State
John Sherman	O	Treasury
Carl Schurz	Mo	Interior
Gen Ch[arles] Devens	Mass	Atty Genl
D. M. Key	Tenn	P. M. Genl
[George W.] McCrary	Iowa	War
R. W. Thompson	Ind	Navy

The chief disappointment among the influential men of the party was with Conkling, Blaine, Cameron, Logan, and their followers. They were very bitter. The opposition was chiefly to Evarts   Key and especially Schurz. Speeches were made, and an attempt to combine with ~~Northern~~ the Democrats to defeat the ~~ratification~~ confirmation of the nominations only failed to be formidable by [reason of] the resolute support of the Southern Senators like [John B.] Gordon, [Lucius Quintus Cincinnatus] Lamar, and [Benjamin H.] Hill. After a few days the public opinion of the Country was shown by the press to be strongly with me. All of the nominations were confirmed by almost an unanimous vote.

The expressions of satisfaction from all parts of the country are most gratifying. The press and the private correspondence of [William K.] Rogers and myself are full of it.

My policy is trust—peace, and to put aside the bayonet. I do not think the wise policy is to decide contested elections in the States, by the use of the National army.

NOTES

CHAPTER IV

[1] Force, fifty-two years old at this time, had attained distinction during the Civil War as a volunteer officer and presently was a judge. A scholar and author, he felt that the office of private secretary was not important enough for him. Kennedy, a younger man, had served with Hayes in the war and later would become lieutenant governor and Congressman. He too declined, and the choice fell on William K. Rogers, a long-time social, legal, and political friend. Although devoted to Hayes, Rogers was not an effective secretary. He was inept at handling reporters and callers. On one occasion he turned away Mark Twain, confusing the famous author with George Train, a colorful eccentric. Much of the secretarial burden was taken on by Webb Hayes, the first son.

[2] Hayes, in common with many Republicans, had misgivings about the appointment of the Electoral Commission. He contended that the Vice President should count the votes or that the dispute should be referred to the Supreme Court. Cronin was the contesting Democratic elector in Oregon.

[3] After David Davis declined to serve on the Commission, the choice of the fifth judicial member fell on a Republican, and it turned out to be Justice Bradley.

[4] Black was a noted Democratic lawyer who represented Tilden's case before the Commission.

[5] Hayes thought of naming the former Confederate general Secretary of

War. But after consulting with party leaders and W. T. Sherman, commanding general of the army, he decided regretfully that the appointment would be too offensive to Northern opinion and to the veterans of the Civil War armies.

6 There was a curious symbolism in Hayes riding to Washington in Scott's cars. Scott was president of the Pennsylvania Railroad and also of the Texas and Pacific Railroad. As a part of the negotiations that had made Hayes President, the Republicans had promised federal aid to extend the latter road to the Pacific coast.

7 Fish was Grant's Secretary of State.

Chapter V

MARCH 16, 1877—NOV. 29, 1877

16th March, 1877.—Stanley Matthews was yesterday night nominated for Senator at Columbus. This is an endorsement of the policy of peace and home rule—of local self government. A number of Southern Rep[ublican] members are reported ready to go over to the Democrats. On the other hand the bar of this District are in a state of mind because Fred. Douglass, the most distinguished and able colored man in the Nation, has been nominated Marshall for the District [of Columbia]. If a liberal policy towards late rebels is adopted, the ultra Republicans are opposed to it; if the colored people are honored, the extremists of the other wing cry out against it. I suspect I am right in both cases.

Different plans for La & S. C. are offered

1. A new election
2. Lawful action of Legislatures
3. Acknowledge [S. B.] Packard & [Daniel H.] Chamberlain [as Governors], and leave them to their own State remedies [1]
4. Withdraw troops and leave events to take care of themselves.

Here I am too crowded with business to give thought to these questions. Let me get a few outside opinions—Judge [William M.] Dickson [and others].

[Memoranda:] Cabinet Meeting at 10 A.M. 7½ P.M. [John D.] Defrees & [William Henry] Smith. Fred. Douglass? ~~Alfred E. Lee—Frankfort.~~ [Appoint Mike J.] Waldron, Marshall W[estern] Tenn.

20th March, 1877.—Webb was twenty one today. V. P. Wheeler, Arthur Stem [young Cincinnati lawyer], Emily Platt & Emma Foote, dined with us. An extra dinner got up by the new Steward—

Cabinet meeting at 10 A.M.—all present—Considered an extra session [of Congress]. Mr Evarts and others opposed it on grounds of expediency, but Sherman, McCrary and Devens found legal objections to all plans for raising and disbursing money without ~~new~~ appropriations. General opinion agst. attempt to get on without extra session. No decision—subject passed. Louisiana troubles discussed. All but Devens seem indisposed to use force to uphold Packard's Gov't, and he is not decidedly for it. All finally agreed to send a Commission to Louisiana. Mr V. P. Wheeler, Judge David Davis, and Hoar (E. R.) agreed upon and Gov [John C.] Brown, of Tenn., and [Blanche Kelso] Bruce and K[enneth] Rayner [of North Carolina] suggested for the other two. Mr Evarts is of opinion that the military can't be used to sustain one Gov't agst another in case of contested elections. The States must take care of those matters themselves.

I incline to think that the people will not now sustain the policy of upholding a State Gov't agst ~~the~~ a rival Gov't by the use of the forces of the U.S. If this leads to the overthrow of the de jure Govt in a State, the de facto Gov't must be recognized.

21st March, 1877.—Cabinet meeting full. Decided to call extra session of Congress 4 June. Mr Evarts will prepare proclamation. Talked over Commission to Louisiana. Decided to send Wheeler, [John C.] Brown, [E. R.] Hoar, [John Marshall] Harlan & [Charles B.] Lawrence. If Wheeler fails, then Pres[iden]t [Theodore Dwight] Woolsey [of Yale] or

84

Judge David Davis was preferred, but he declined. He [Davis] advised the Commission. Thought it would do good.[2]

23d March, 1877.—It is not the duty of the President of the United States to use the military power of the Nation to decide contested elections in the States. He will maintain the authority of the U.S. and keep the peace between the contending parties. But local self government means, the determination by ~~of~~ each State for itself of all questions as to its own local affairs.

The real thing to be achieved is safety and prosperity for the colored people. Both Houses of Congress and the public opinion of the Country are plainly against the use of the army to uphold either claimant to the State Government in case of contest. The wish is to restore harmony and good feeling between Sections and races. This can only be done by peaceful methods. We wish to adjust the difficulties in La and S. C. so as to make one government out of two in each State. But if this fails—if no adjustment can be made, we must then adopt the non intervention policy, except so far as may be necessary to keep the peace.

24th March, 1877.—The number of applications for office made to Mrs Hayes and other members of the family is so great that a rule has been adopted that such applications will not be considered.

No person connected with me by blood or marriage will be appointed to office.

25th March, 1877.—Francis A Stout [of New York] writes in favor of Hampton from S. C. He says a "benevolent neutrality" is the true policy.

26th March, 1877.—[Memoranda] Cabinet. 1. Courtesies to Gen Grant. Catalogue books of Ex[ecutive] Mansion— Xchange them, get Adams' Diary, &c. 2. Washington Monument.

28th March, 1877.—[Memorandum] Senator [Blanche K.] Bruce [of Mississippi] 8 P.M. Cabinet Meeting at 12 M. Senator [Aaron A.] Sargent [of California] as to seizure of "Montana." Chas. Lee Collins for West Point [Academy]. Gov [D. H.] Chamberlain 2 P.M.; Senator Bruce, 8 P.M.

29th March, 1877.—[Memoranda]. Cabinet Meeting. 1. To publish Wade Hampton's letters. 2. W. V. Turner a cl[er]k in Treasury Dept.—colored.

2d April, 1877.—Cabinet Meeting 10 A.M. [Memoranda:] Reappointment of [George H.] Sharpe, N.Y. [Surveyor of Customs]—*Secy of Treasy*. Maggie Ahren to be kept [in office]. Appt of Thos. J. Clay in Army—*McCrary*. Mrs Espy McCoy—*Schurz*. Gen Comly at Honolulu—*Evarts*. Ed Gause, P.M., Crocket, Texas—Judge Key. Fremont, [O.] Post Master, Geo. J. Krebs.

5th April, 1877.—Cabinet Meeting [Notes:] 1. ~~Evarts~~ Diplomatic State dinners. [George H.] Sharpe, Surveyor. 2. War—Gen J D Kurz, Report on Washington M[onumen]t. W[est] P[oint] *Graham M Fitch*. 3. P.M.Genl—Mansfield Ct.; *Fond du'Lac;* Delaware, O. [postmasters to be appointed]. 4. Secy Sherman. N.Y. affairs. Wells vice *Mahan*, an *Auditor*. (*Canton*). 5. Atty Gen Devens—Hamilton Dist Atty—get Commission.

$8000, & various acknowledgments promised (?) by Khedive—Cairo.

8th April, 1877.—Bishop [Edward Raymond?] Ames preached an old time entertaining sermon today.

I paid to the church my year's subscription, to the Foundry M.E. Ch[urch], viz $160, today.

22d April, 1877.—We have got through with the S C & La [problems]—at any rate, the troops are ordered away and I now hope for peace, and what is equally important, security and prosperity for the colored people.

The result of my plans is to get from those States by their Governors, Legislatures, Press and people, pledges that the *13th, 14th* & *15th* amendments shall be faithfully observed—

that the colored people shall have equal rights to labor, to education, and to the privileges of citizenship.

I am confident this is a good work. Time will tell.

Now for Civil Service Reform—Legislation must be prepared & Executive rules and Maxims. We must limit, and narrow the area of patronage—we must diminish the evils of office seeking—we must stop interference of federal officers with elections. We must be relieved of Congressional dictation as to appointments.

[Memorandum:] Send Photos: Willie J. Bryan, care Col James, Military Institute, Austin Co[unty], Texas.

15th May, 1877.—[Memorandum:] [New York City] 9½ A.M., Photos [taken]; 1 P.M., Gen [James Grant] Wilson's lunch; 2½ P.M. [Dedication of] Halleck's Statue [in Central Park, New York City]; 4 P.M., Mr [Theodore] Roosevelt—Nat[ural] Hist[ory] Museum]; 6 P.M., Col [A. D.] Shepard's dinner; 9 P.M., Gov [Edwin D.] Morgan's Reception.

16th May, 1877.—[Memorandum, New York City:] 2 P.M. Mr [John Jacob] Astor's breakfast. 7 P.M., Gov Morgan's dinner.[3]

24th July, 1877.—12:25 [P.M.]—Cabinet [Meeting]. Present   Ev[arts]—Sh[erman]—Th[ompson]—Key—Dev[ens]—Sch[urz]. Dispatches from Cleveland, Buffalo, St. Louis, Philadelphia. Strike still extending but violence diminishing. U.S. troops every where respected.—[Troops] wanted at N.Y. to guard 100,000,000 U.S. treasure in the city.—also in Cinti & St. Louis.—[4]

Naval officers & military disturbed about rank.

Gen [E. O. C.] Ord, 22d arrested [Gen. Mariano] Escobedo & other Mex[icans] recruiting on our side, about 15 in all.—[5]

Spanish Minister is ready to settle claims.—Secy Th[ompson] proposes to send Monitor to N.Y. to clear streets around Custom House. Sh[erman] thinks streets too crooked. Ev[arts] says the big guns will straighten them! Monitor *ordered*. Gov of Ohio wants arms. *Ordered*. An officer of militia wants blankets. Directed that on proper requisition they be furnished.

Mr [Frank] Gilbert apptd Ass[istant] Treas. at Chicago fails to make his bond—a new appointment to be made.

Shall the reports be prepared in full for Congress at Extra Session, or deferred to regular session in Dec? Message for Extra session to be limited to the reasons for the extra session.

Dispatches of quiet, &c &c.

Shall the troops of U.S. be used in St Louis until Gov. calls? *No.* Gen [John] Pope asks the question.—

Gen [J. M.] Schofield dispatches formally.—

Can an officer move his men agst the mob before Gov[ernor] calls? says Th[ompson]. Ev[arts] replies, "It will be given him in that hour what he shall do!"—Muskets sent to Treasurer in N.Y.—200 troops are to be sent to Reading if Gen [W. S.] Hancock thinks best.—

Adjourned to 12 tomorrow.—

Ev[arts] says I tell office seekers I cant see them until after Cabinet meeting—& after Cabinet meeting I have no time.

25th July, 1877.—Cabinet Meeting. Present Gen Schurz; Judge Key, Sherman, McCrary, Col Thompson, Gen Devens, Evarts.

A bitter feeling as to the riots. Col T[hompson] reports 1000 naval force—marines & sailors at N.Y.—probably 1100 if boys included. Guard increased at Brooklyn around Pub. property.

I read dispatches from Gen [E. B.] Tyler, Balt[im]o[re], Gen [J. R.] Hawley, Ct. and Gov [John F.] Hartranft, [Pa.] T[yler] suggests a committee to compromise; H[awley] says Ct. [Conn.] has 2000 reliable troops. Gov H[artranft] is for calling volunteers. Secy of War reads disp[atches] from Omaha, Chicago, Cinti, & Gen Schofield & others. Citizens enrolled at Indianapolis & Committee of Conciliation. Marshall of Ind. wants to appt deputies &c &c. Thos Scott advises U.S. to take hold of the affair, or "the greatest destruction of life"

&c. R.R.'s refuse to carry mails alone. Judge [Thomas] Drummond orders Marshall to go to St Louis. He reports no adequate force.—Meeting in Terre Haute between strikers & R.R.'s—good temper—no result.

N.Y. Asst. Treasurer feels safe—regulars & armed clerks & marines.— Pittsburg danger of a revival of riots.

Sherman reports "another little war breaking out in Sitka, [Alaska]." A Revenue Cutter to Sitka at once. Thompson says "your Rev Cutter out of coal, & I supplied you from the Navy." Sherman says "Thank you." Col T[hompson] reads letter from Tom Scott. He is much depressed, & gives a gloomy view. Wants Gov't to assume responsibility & act vigorously. Gen Hancock thinks Gov H[artranft] is doing good work at Pittsburg. Another letter calls attention to the relations between State & U.S. authorities.

Phila. Com[mercial] Exch[ange], John Welsh, et al, thinks U.S. should add to its forces—Balto. ditto. E[varts] suggests that the U.S. may put these rioters in the position of levying War agst the U.S.—I advise a proclamation to be issued soon. Proclamation to be [sic] The Proclamation is to be prepared, but as to its issue the decision is to be postponed. *Subject passed.*

Mexico complains of Escobedo & others.

Carter is recommended for Minister to Brazil.

26th July, 1877.—Cabinet [Meeting]. Present All members, also Gen Schofield.

Dispatch from Gen [Benjamin] Harrison et al. Several R.R.s at Ind'plis in hands of Receiver of U.S. Courts. Ordered that Marshall [Benjamin] Spooner use U.S. troops & open, or keep open, such R Rs.—Gen Hancock with 400 Regulars & Gov Hartranft with 2500 mil[itia] to go to Pittsburg to keep open R Rs for coal supplies & food. Regulars took Reading & coal traffic opened.—Gen Schofield gives full a/c of situation in Pa.—Indiana affairs left to the Marshall & regulars.—

S.C. [South Carolina] R.R.'s reported (some of them) stopped—strikers, it is suggested, are all Carpet baggers.

Illinois authorities ought to take care of that State, with aid of troops under the Marshalls.—Wisconsin Gov [Harrison Ludington] asks for old soldiers in [Soldiers'] Home! Evarts laughs. "Old Home men had better be called out to keep open the drives in the Park."

It was suggested that Gen Jeff C Davis be sent to take charge at Ind'polis. Evarts says "Dems will think it is Jeff Davis of the South."

California Gov. [William] Irwin asks aid. The Navy ordered to aid & co-operate with [the] Governor. "Hoodlums will take care of the Chinese."

Nebraska wants Omaha let alone. Gen S[chofield] says Hancock has found 3000 men this side of the Miss[issippi]. Ev[arts] says "well, as the rioters kill none of them, that may be enough."

Shall the U.S. forces be used to suppress riots in Chicago, before we issue a proclamation? No, says Ev[arts]. Gen Schofield to take command at W[ashington]. Gen [George Washington] Getty to have rank (according?) to brevet.

Adjourned to 12 Noon Friday.

27th July, 1877.—Cabinet Meeting. All present.

Riots diminishing. Discussing the propriety of allowing the U.S. forces to be used by local authorities in States where no President's proclamation has been issued. If the troops act we will justify it. Rules are made to be broken, Ev[arts] says, "the ten Commandments would not have been made if they were not to be broken."—He also says, "those philosophers ought to be sent to the Penitentiary to give them time to reflect." "The Cooper Institute or Tompkins Square meeting impeach Evarts and Schurz, and every body assails Sherman." Sherman says money must be plenty. I have $60,000,000 Greenbacks on Deposit without interest & $40,000,000, gold. This belongs to Citizens.—

After some discussion as to form of instructions to officers at Chicago, Secy War says Now, listen, I want it so if anybody is killed, all are responsible. "Yes, says Evarts, you want us all hanged." Schurz says we want more troops for the Indians in Dakotah. Ev says "the moral power of the U.S. army seems to be of no account against Indians."

28th July, 1877.—Cabinet [Meeting.] All Present, also Gen Schofield.

Reports from all quarters favorable. No action seems to be required.

Sherman calls attention to danger at Sitka. The Revenue cutter has 1500 miles of Coast to attend to. Evarts says, "the question is in that case how far the 'moral effect' will extend!" "Send our Communists to Sitka to reinforce the people. The Indians will help them redistribute property." The Cutter ordered to go to Sitka without delay.

On Ind[iana] R R's, a President said to his men striking that he would attempt to move no trains, & they agreed to protect the loaded cars from outside mobs. "Yes, says Evarts, they will maintain the Status quo."

———

Gov [B. F.] Potts [of Montana] writes about supplying arms to Indians. "There is no actual hostility on this subject, I hope, between the Int[erior] & War Dept. I am ready to treat the Indians as Indep[endent] Nations."—Mr. Plunket writes that $2000000 of British pork at Chicago was in danger. Evarts replies to P. that the late reports are favorable, and local authorities will take care of all property.—

Sherman says he is getting too much gold, & he wants to stop its deposit.—

31st July, 1877.—Cabinet [Meeting]. *All Present.*

All quiet, exc[ept] at Cleveland & a few points a peaceful blockade is kept up.

Sherman calls attention to the book as to R R traffic & its magnitude, as showing the need of National action.

Thompson suggests contract betw[een] R Rs.—Evarts says it is a case for Gov't, not contract.

Secy McC[rary] says the power to regulate Commerce covers it. Ev[arts] says the country is ready for an exertion of its power, but it is a difficult subject, "& men are not to be Court Martialed for a difference of opinion." "Wages, (says McC) is a part of it." "The war (says Ev) made water run up hill."—As to accepting Nashville invitation, Ev says "another Strike may come to our relief."

Should Diaz be recognized as Prest. of Mexico? Shall we determine it now or let Mexico hang by the eyelids during August? There is no good reason why we should not recognize M. when we are ready.

Lerdo has no force; Escobedo is under bonds not to make war—this gives him a moral reason for not going on.

It is said by Mr. Key that a gentleman named plays cards for money but he is not a gambler. Evarts says it is "not his sole occupation."—

Changeing old for new is objected to—but it is my only way to rid of a horse. I cant sell him, but I can swap. I want better horses in the State Department, but if I sell I must turn it in to the treasury.—The Marshall of Ala. has got a man to go into the M[oun]t[ain] Dists. to get subscribers to a book.— He got the stills into his hands & made arrests. It would not be well for a man to get book subscriptions in that Country now!

2d August, 1877.—Soldiers Home. On our return from our Boston & Harvard trip the last of June, we came out to the Soldiers Home for our summer residence. It is an agreeable abode for the hot weather. Our month here has passed away swiftly. ~~The~~ Ruddy [Rutherford P. Hayes, his third son] and Fanny [his daughter] went with Emily and Ruddy Platt to Ohio just as the strike was breaking out about the 18*th* of July. They passed through Pittsburg only about twenty four hours before the dreadful events of that awful Sunday. Fanny will stay with Laura [Platt Mitchell] during the hot weather, either at Columbus or Gambier.

Sunday, 5th August, 1877.—Sol. Home [W. Garl] Brown[e], a good artist [of Washington, D.C.] who painted Gen [Thomas Lanier] Clingman [of North Carolina] for the Corcoran gallery, finished a bust portrait of me Friday. It is perhaps the best yet painted. He painted [it] as a study for a full length portrait for the Corcoran gallery. Thus far the best portraits have been painted by [John H.] Witt, (several), by

(three), [Eliphalet Frazer] Andrews of Steubenville, one full length, and now this, perhaps the best by Brown[e].

The strikes have been put down by *force*, but now for the *real* remedy. Cant something [be] done by education of the strikers, by judicious control of the capitalists, by wise general policy to end or diminish the evil? The R.R. strikers, as a rule are good men sober intelligent and industrious.

The mischiefs are

1. Strikers prevent men willing to work from doing so.
2. They sieze and hold the property of their employers.
3. The consequent excitement furnishes opportunity for the dangerous criminal classes to destroy life and property.

Now, "every man has a right if he sees fit to to quarrel with his own bread and butter, but he has no right to quarrel with the bread and butter of other people." Every man has a right to determine for himself the value of his own labor, but he has no right to determine for other men the value of their labor. (not good).

Every man has a right to refuse to work if the wages dont suit him, but he has no right to prevent others from working if they are suited with the wages.

Every man has a right to refuse to work, but no man has a right to prevent others from working.

Every man has a right to decide for himself the question of wages, but no man has a right to decide that question for other men.

I grow more conservative every day on the question of removals. On ex parte statements, I have made mistakes in removing men who perhaps ought to have been retained, and in appointing wrong men. Not many removals have been made. Less than by any new Administration since John Q. Adams. But I shall be more cautious in future.—Make removals only in clear cases—and appoint men only on the best and fullest evidence of fitness.

[Memoranda for an address:]

There are some points on which good men North and South are agreed—*generally* are agreed, for it is not given to men that *all* good men should be agreed on any question relating to public affairs.

1. We agree that it is not well that political parties should be formed on sectional lines

2. That it is not well that parties should divide on color lines.

3. That we should not divide on any line or principle of division which inevitably leads to (contest) conflict which can only be settled by the bayonet.

4.

It is very gratifying to receive such a (greeting) welcome as this by citizenss of the State of Virginia.

8th August, 1877.—Soldiers Home. A common slang word is *"polafox"*—to deceive, to swindle or the like. In the Hayne Debate [the Webster–Hayne Debate over the nature of the Union, January, 1830] I see that [John] Holmes and [David] Barton speak of Polafox (perhaps a character in Don Quixotte). Is not this the origin of the word?

26th August, 1877.—Sol. Home. After four days in Vermont and four in New Hampshire, and a rousing evening in Worcester, we are home again in good health and spirits. The people seemed pleased. My speeches were wholly unpremeditated—not therefore very satisfactory to myself—rather slovenly and ill constructed. I tried to impress the people with the

94

importance of harmony between different sections, States, classes and races, and to discourage sectionalism and race and class predjudice. ~~But~~ I must in future take more pains with my little addresses. I get tired of the ceaseless iteration of phrases of thanks for receptions, welcomes—I speak of "hearty," "kind," "cordial," "generous," "warm" and "flattering" receptions and welcomes—"enthusiastic" and "spontaneous" also "unexpected", "unmerited" "undeserved"—"entertainment," "demonstration." I must also speak of "salutations," "greetings," being all qualified by the foregoing adjectives—also kind, friendly, courteous.

My next tour is to Ohio, Kentucky, Tennessee, and Virginia. First I shall meet the 36th Ohio, at Marietta. With them I can speak of our common hardships, dangers, and services—of the once strong long line of a thousand men—now shortened and growing shorter.

Instead of hostility and strife, we desire friendly feeling and peace between the late belligerent sections. Our aspiration is for the reign of peace and good will over the whole of our recently agitated (disturbed) and afflicted land.

The people wish to show respect and courtesy due to the office which for the time being I happen to fill—occupy.—

How would it do at Fremont to talk freely of life and occupation at Washington?

A reception by my friends and comrades of the 36th Ohio will be very gratifying. We served together during almost three years of the four years war for the Union. We first met, 1861, in the Mountains of W. Va. on the upper waters of the Kanawa, and we fought together our last battles in the Shen[andoah] Val[ley] under Sheridan. It is a common remark that with good material a good Colonel always makes a good regiment. Your regiment was ~~fortunate~~ signally fortunate. Its men were largely volunteers from the Ohio Company's purchase. Many of you were descendants from that

95

colony of patriotic revolutionary soldiers who first settled Ohio.

6th September, 1877.—Left W[ashington] on a tour through Ohio, Ky, Tenn. Georgia & Va & returned Tuesday at 8:30 P.M. *25th* Sept. Absent nineteen days (19). Received everywhere heartily. The country is again one and united! I am very happy to be able to feel that the course taken has turned out so well.[6]

At Charlottesville Va Col [Charles S.] Venable made the address at the Hotel [Farish House]. Dr. [James F.] Harrison, at the head of the University, received me there. The general committee was Col [Thomas Lewis] Preston, Judge [John L.] Cochran, who married a James of Chill[icothe], Mr——Fishburn,——Woods &——Brown. This was 25 Sept.

3th October, 1877.—Lucy went last night to New York with Mr Evarts. Webb, Birch & Emily P[latt] [went] to Ohio. We are at the Home, viz Fanny, Scott and myself.

I am to go to Fairs at Frederick City Md 10*th* Oct & at Richmond Va two weeks later. I must prepare to say a few words at each. Congress meets in Extra Session 15*th* Oct.[7] I must have a short message ready.

4th October, 1877.—Fifty five years old today! Lucy absent —gone to New York. My official life in the Presidency has so far been successful in the main, and happy. The country does seem to be coming back to the ancient concord, and good people approve what I am trying to do. My family affairs are satisfactory. The three grown boys are truthful, honest, moral and gentlemanly. Birchard is conscientious, scholarly, but not so practical yet as I hope he will become. Webb is full of sense of the practical sort. Ruddy not yet quite equal to the others, but improving, and is like both. Fanny, now ten years old, is very sensible, does not take jokes, defends her absent friends, is like Mother Hayes. Scott is a handsome little fellow of six—seven in February.

I must resolve on this birthday to do better in the future than ever before. With good health & great opportunities, may I not hope to ~~render a lasting services that will~~ confer great and lasting benefits on my Country! I mean to try. Let me be kind and considerate in treatment of the unfortunate who crowd my doorway, and firm and conscientious in dealing with the tempters. The Southern question seems to be on a good footing. The Currency also. The Mexican question is perplexing. The improvement of the Civil Service I must constantly labor for.

The men in the Executive Office are as follows
Maj C. C. Sniffen, with Grant. Leaves Oct 10
O. L. Pruden, with Grant & Johnson. Asst. Secy
Col [W. H.] Crook, with Grant. Disbursing Cl[er]k
Charlie [L.] Chapman, with Grant. Records Clerk
[W. R.] Price, detailed War Dept., Hayes
[Henry C.] Morton, detailed Treasury Dept., Hayes
Chas. [M.] Hendley, detailed Interior Dept., Hayes' Aman-
uensis
Benj[amin] F. Montgomery, detailed Signal Corps
[George A.] Gustin, detailed P. O. Stenographer.

Sunday, 7th October, 1877.—Sols. Home—Lucy returned yesterday morning from N.Y. The nomination by the Southern members of the Peabody [Education Fund] Trustees, and the unanimous election by the whole board are agreeable things. They prove that the pacification measures are approved by the whole country. It is also an exceedingly honorable and pleasant employment.

White House, 13th *October,* 1877.—During my busy hours with the Cabinet Webb and Lucy began to move to the White House and we shall sleep here tonight. We return after an absence from this House of over three months. We entered "the Home" June 30.

18th *October,* 1877.—My message, for the Extra session was sent in Tuesday. The joint Committee, Messrs. [Thomas F.] Bayard, Garfield, [Milton] Saylor [and others] called on me

Tuesday morning to inform me that the two Houses were ready to receive communications.

I must now take up the subject of my annual Message and prepare for it thoroughly. I propose one general paragraph on the prosperous condition of the Country—then the matters pertaining to each department in their proper order—and here I must inquire as to the proper order—examine for this J. Q. Adams & Van Buren and others who would be likely to be correct and careful about this.

I must remember the Indians, the [Washington] Monument, the Civil Service, the South, Education,   .

Congratulate the country on the fact that the pacification on the basis of the amendments has gone forward so well. No brag, but refer it to the excellence of our system and the character of our people.

In reforming the Civil Service the following points are to be observed

1. Remove the officers from political management—Let officers attend to the business of their places and have nothing to do with the manipulation of politics

2. Divorce the appointments from Legislative control except the power of confirmation by the Senate

3. Rules for appointments—methods

4. Removals by what methods and under what rules.

Let me ascertain the names, without regard to party, of members of Congress who are sincere friends of the reform. I think I may count on the following Senators

[Isaac P.] Christiancy	Mich	Rep
[Benjamin H.] Hill	Ga	Dem
[Stanley] Matthews	O	R
[Theodore F.] Randolph	N.J.	D.

In the House

[Jacob D.] Cox	O	R
[James] Monroe	O	R
[William J.] Bacon	N.Y.	R

White House, 19th October, 1877.— A committee of in-vitation from Richmond, Va., arranged for our visit to that city. We are to leave Washington Oct. 30, Tuesday A.M. so as to arrive at R. about 3 P.M.—To be received that day by the Mayor. Wed 31*st* to go out with the Gov. to be received by the State on the Fair Ground. To return Nov 1. in the evening.

[Memorandum]. [Consult] Gen [Salmon P.] Chase on Ordinance of '87

21*st October*, 1877.—Is it practicable to obtain an expression of opinion from Congress, or from either House, that it is not proper for M.C.'s to take part in appointments except on the request of the Executive for information? Or, that Federal Officers should not interfere in politics except to write, or talk, or vote?

I go to Richmond next Tuesday week. In the few remarks I shall make in reply to the Mayor, may I properly refere to the interest I felt in knowing the response the people would make to my efforts for a permanent pacification on the basis of the amendments? and then to refer to the support and en-couragement which came to me by letters, and conversations, and the press of R[ichmond]?

1. · To take the offices out of Politics.
2. To relieve M[embers of] C[ongress] from responsi-bility.
3. Rules as to original appointments.
4. Rules as to removals.

[Memoranda:] "A Nation divided against itself cannot stand."

A distinguished Virginian has said

"Geographical Union, the Union of political parties, the Union of the States is not enough. What we need is Union of hearts and union of hands, union of interests and union of hopes."

Insist that the Constitution of the Country shall be respected and obeyed—insist that the laws shall be enforced. Insist that

99

every Citizen however humble he may be and wherever he may be shall be secure in his right to life liberty and the pursuit of happiness.

24th October, 1877.—It is now obvious that there is a very decided opposition to the Administration in both Houses of Congress, among the Republican members. There seems ~~to me~~ not to be any considerable personal hostility to me. But a conference of about twenty members of the House at Mr Sherman's developed a decided hostility to my measures on the part of ~~many~~ members, respectable both in character and number. The objections extend to all of my principal acts. ~~and~~ The opposition is directed against

1. The Cabinet. It is said there are only four Rep members viz Sherman, Devens, McCrary & Thompson. That Evarts and Schurz are disorganizers, doctrinaires, and Liberals, and Key is a Democrat.

2. The attempt to make the Civil Service non-partisan ~~is~~ is ruinous to the Party, unjust and offensive to office holders, and is an attempt to accomplish the impossible viz a non-partisan Civil Service.

3. The Pacification of the South is a total departure from the principles, traditions, and wishes of the party.

A majority of members probably favor some part of these measures. Only a small number support all of them. The adversary points to the results of elections as showing that the people condemn the administration, and that it is destroying the party. The most bitter opposition arises from the apprehension that the course of the Administration will

4. Deprive Congressmen of all control and share of the patronage of the Government.

How to meet and overcome this opposition is the question. I am clear that I am right. I believe that a large majority of the best people are in full accord with me. Now my purpose is to keep cool—to treat all adversaries considerately respectfully and kindly but at the same time in a way to satisfy them of my sincerity and firmness. In all parts of my official conduct to strive conscientiously and unselfishly to do what is wise. In my anxiety to complete the great work of pacification I have neglected to give due attention to the Civil Service—to the ~~duty of~~ appointments and removals. The result is some bad appointments have been made. Some removals have been mistakes. There have been delays in action. All this I must try now to correct

Gen Grant in his messages takes strong ground in favor of a reform of the Civil Service. See Dec 1870 p 17

[Memorandum:] [In address at] Richmond Va—[stress] Education, Immigration, Agriculture, Union vs. Sectionalism.

3d November, 1877.—Our trip to Richmond & return Oct 30, 31 & Nov 1. was altogether a happy and successful one. There are thousands of intelligent people who are not Democrats, & who would like to unite with the Conservative Republicans of the North.

5th November, 1877.—Topics for regular Message

1. A general paragraph—cheerful in its views—a suitable expression of gratitude to God.

2. The condition of the country in connection with the several departments in their proper order, (?) say with Foreign relations first & Interior last—in the order in which members of Cabinet sit at the Cabinet table

3. Miscellaneous topics such as—The District of Col[umbia]—

Washington Monument
Southern question
Indian question   See [James] Monroe p 218
Currency question   Resumption & Silver—
The army, if not fully treated as part of topics (2)
Education National University
The mode of determining the result of Presidential Elections.
Education. See Wash'n pp 3-4

Improvement of Miss[issippi] River & improvements
gen[erally]
Census of 1880
The riots in July '77
Improvements—R.R.s & Levees?
Department of Agriculture.

Recommend repeal of test oath as to veterans of War of
[18]12—Pensions to Vet[eran]s of Mex[ican] War (?)
Amnesty for all past political offenses (see Grant).—

[George] Washington delivered no inaugural address on
his second election. The allusion to his re-election in his
Dec[ember] Message, 1793 shows this.

John Adams in his first In[augural] Ad[dress] speaks of
an "overruling Providence."—In a special Message he calls
God "the Supreme Dispenser of national blessings," & again
"dispensations of Divine Providence," "the Supreme Ruler
of the Universe."

[Thomas] Jeff[erson] in his In[augural] Ad[dress] says
"let us restore to social intercourse that harmony and affection
without which liberty and even life itself are but dreary
things." He speaks also of an "overruling Providence," again
"and may that infinite Power which rules the destinies of
~~nations~~ the Universe lead our Councils to what is best & give
them a favorable issue" &c &c.

Jeff[erson] says Fellow Citizens of the Senate & House of
Rep &c See opening of Jeff's 2d Message, p 70. Jeff no 2d In.
Ad. see p 84.

J. Q. A[dams] in his In. Ad. talks well of Party Spirit,
Union—230–1.

[As to civil service reform:]

1. Give permanency, security, to official life by removing
nobody during their official term except for cause.

2. Take them out of politics. Separate the civil service
from the active work of party management.

3. Remove patronage from Congress.
4. Limit the area of patronage.
5. Let the terms be for a different period—longer than the Presidential term—say six years.

———

Silver was demonitized by the act of 1873. When was the first movement in Congress to remonitise it? Was there any until silver had lost its value?

———

Message—Pensions to Soldiers of 1812—test oath &c &c

———

To attempt to pay the public debt in depreciated silver coin is a violation of the public credit and public faith, and thereby add to the burden of the debt.

For the re-establishment of silver coinage, with every legitimate advantage belonging to it, can be had without injustice to creditors either public or private & without impairing ~~the~~ public ~~credit~~ or private credit.

We think with Hamilton that it is a mistake to abridge the quantity of circulating medium—we want a "full" and not "a scanty circulation"—but we want it all to be coin, or redeemable in coin—to have intrinsic value—to be money, & not a mere promise.—

———

[*Memorandum*:] This mem shows that Dr [Joseph T.] Webb rents to Hayes his third of the Duluth, [Minnesota], block from Mch 1, '77 to Mch 1./81, and Hayes agrees to pay therefor $600. a year semi annually.—

Nov 26, 1877.—

R B Hayes
J. T. Webb

29*th November*, 1877.—We had a charming Thanksgiving dinner in the State dining room. All the executive clerks and their wives & little folks were our guests. One roast pig, and three turkies (one a monster from R.I., Gov[Charles Collins] Van Zandt). After a happy dinner from 2½ to 5 P.M., blindman's buff gave entertainment to the little folks, [George A.] Gustin the hero of it. The list at table as follows, viz

[Omitted here by Hayes, but given in the White House social register: The President and Mrs. Hayes, B. A. Hayes, Webb C. Hayes, Fanny and Scott R. Hayes; Private Secretary and Mrs. W. K. Rogers, Willie, Phoebe, and Andrews Rogers; Assistant Secretary and Mrs. O. L. Pruden, Willie Pruden; Mr. and Mrs. W. H. Crook, Harry and Carrie Crook; Mr. and Mrs. C. L. Chapman, Stella and Charley Chapman; Mr. and Mrs. G. A. Gustin; Mr. and Mrs. C. M. Hendley; Mr. H. C. Morton; Mr W. R. Price; and Mr. B. F. Montgomery.]

NOTES

CHAPTER V

1 Packard was the Republican claimant to the governorship of Louisiana, and Chamberlain to the same office in South Carolina.

2 The Louisiana commission as eventually constituted contained Brown, Harlan, and Lawrence of the names proposed. Its chairman was Wayne MacVeigh of Pennsylvania.

3 There is no apparent reason for the gap between this and the next entry. In the spring of 1877, Hayes was engaged in his effort to establish the merit principle in appointments, especially in those to the New York Custom House. On June 25, he left Washington for Boston and did not return until the thirtieth. On June 27, he received an honorary LL.D. from Harvard University.

4 The summer saw the beginning of what amounted to a general railroad strike that affected most sections of the country. Hayes, at the request of several governors, unhesitatingly dispatched troops to the strike areas.

5 For years Mexican marauders had, without interference from their government, conducted forays into Texas. Hayes ordered General Ord to pursue the raiders over the border and if necessary into Mexico. Relations between the United States and Mexico were at this time complicated and strained. The American government did not recognize the government of strong man Porfirio Diaz. The Mexican dictator was willing to co-operate in suppressing the raids, but he also wanted to press the United States into granting certain concessions. Secretary Evarts, for his part, would extend recognition but demanded his own concessions as the price. The result was a

series of haggling negotiations that settled little. Escobeda was in rebellion against Diaz and supposedly represented the interests of a former president, Sebastian Lerdo.

6 The southern tour covered a circuit of three thousand miles, and its length accounts for the absence of more entries for September. Hayes was accompained by members of his cabinet and other friends. The purpose of the trip was to conciliate southern opinion and to appeal for support for Republicanism from conservative southerners.

7 Because the Forty-fourth Congress had adjourned without enacting an army appropriation bill, Hayes had in May called a special session. At first he had fixed May as the meeting date but then had postponed it to October, when it was hoped Republican objections to the southern policy would have subsided and the party would be more united. Actually Hayes would have little control over this session. The Democrats had a majority in the House, and the slim Republican majority in the Senate was not united in support of the administration. Almost immediately Hayes provoked Roscoe Conkling and other Senators by removing two of Conkling's men in the New York Custom House, Chester A. Arthur and Alonzo B. Cornell.

Chapter VI

DEC. 6, 1877—MARCH 18, 1878

6th December, 1877.—The Message has been well received
—encouragingly so. It has but little on the reform of the Civil
Service. I must now prepare a special message. Let me say

1. There should be legislation [which] will relieve Congressmen from all responsibility for the appointments.—They
must neither seek to control, nor even to influence appointments.

If Congress fails to legislate for this end, I must adopt &
publish rules

2. Divorce office holders from the active management of
politics.

3. Admit to subordinate places on examinations.

4. Retain all good officers during their terms & establish
rules

Judge M L Bundy of Indiana says "the last time I saw Gov
Morton he paid you a very high compliment. He said I have
read all of the President's speeches on his Southern tour. He
has always talked good sense—he ~~has~~ never said a foolish
thing." This was good from such a judge.

9th December, 1877.—I am now in a contest on the question
of the right of Senators to dictate or control nominations. Mr
Conkling insists that no officer shall be appointed in New York

106

without his consent obtained previously to the nomination. This is the first and most important step in the effort to reform the Civil Service. It now becomes a question whether I should not insist that all who receive important places should be on the right side of this vital question. None who are opposed to the Cincinnati platform on this important question are to be regarded as Republicans in good standing. How would this do? Rather radical, probably, but if the war goes on I must think of it.

I must look up the State platforms of 1876. Nothing broader can be found in support of the "Southern policy" than the New York Convention [resolution] of 1875.

For Southern question see
Resolutions N.Y. Sept. [18]75
Resolutions N.Y. Sept. [18]76
Letter of Acceptance
Grant's Message
Grant's Dispatch to Packard, 1877, Mch 3d.

13th December, 1877.—In the language of the press "Senator Conkling has won a great victory over the Administration." My N.Y. nominations were rejected 31. to 25. But the end is not yet. I am right, and shall not give up the contest.—

18th December, 1877.—I go to New York to attend the Union League reception Friday evening, and the New England dinner Saturday evening.

[Notes for a talk at the New England dinner:]

Mr President and Gentlemen: I trust I shall be excused if I adhere to the rule I have adopted on occasions like this, and refrain from altogether from the discussion of the topics interesting topics suggested by this anniversary. I therefore wish merely to make my acknowledgments for your kindness and to say that I am in the heartiest sympathy with this Society, and that among the recollections most dearly cherished by me are those connected with the lives and homes of my New England ancestors.—

There is much said as to plans for harmonising the friends and opponents of the Administration.~~on~~ It is desirable certainly that more friends should be found among Rep Congressmen. Why is not the best basis for harmony the Cincinnati platform? If differences exist as to its meaning consult the letter of acceptance, and the State platforms after the nomination and before the election.

26th December, 1877.—Our visit to New York 21*st* & 24*th* was a most happy one. The Union League reception 22*d*, the American Museum of Nat[ural] Hist[ory] opening, and the New England dinner, all enjoyable.

Xmas the presents to the children made them and their parents equally happy.

30th December, 1877.—The anniversary of our wedding day 25 years ago. Our friends from Ohio filled the house. Gen [Manning F.] Force & wife came ~~Saturday~~ Friday evening. Saturday we went with them, Webb, Scott & Fan, & Maria, to Mt Vernon. Saturday eve[ning] came Col L. C. Weir, Dr & Mrs [John] Davis, J[ohn] W. Herron & wife, dau[ghter] & nurse, Rev. Dr. L. D. McCabe, Laura & Lilly [Platt], &c &c.

Rainy day. Went to Foundry Ch[urch] with Lucy, [and] Dr & Mrs Davis.

After lunch ~~dinner~~ had a Christening in the Blue room of Mr & Mrs H[erron's] seven weeks baby—called her *Lucy Hayes Herron*. Also baptised & Christened Fanny & Scott. All [the] company in a circle around the blue room. Mr & Mrs Rogers also present and most if not all of the attendants and servants of the Mansion. Lucy in her wedding garments of twenty-five years ago. A fine dinner—Emily [Platt] rather the Adjutant of the affair. All cards at table were written full of names [of those] present. Twenty three (23) in all. Singing in the evening.

Before the Christening all gathered in our room. Gen Force read letters and poems sent by friends [in observance of the twenty-fifth wedding anniversary]. The presents were as follows viz

1. A poem beautifully illuminated with a silvered frame, gift of Dr & Mrs Davis

We had published that presents were not expected or desired—but a few friends felt at liberty to send them

2. Wm M Evarts gave us a very beautiful silver Pitcher.

3. Justice and Mrs N. H. Swayne: 2 handsome oxydised silver candlesticks and candles.

4. Emily Platt, a silver cream jug.

R. B. Hayes to Mrs R. B. H., a Cameo Medallion Likeness.
B. A. Hayes—a Silver Comb.
Webb C. Hayes—a Silver Vase.
R. P. Hayes—a Silver Portmonaie
Fannie & Scott Hayes—a Cut Glass Smelling bottle.
Gen & Mrs John G. Mitchell, a set of Berry Spoons (two).
Wm. A. Platt, a card case.
Emily Platt, a Cream ~~Jug~~ Pitcher.
R. H. Platt, a Silver paper Knife.
Maria McKell, a Cream Jug.
Mrs Dudley, a Silver Thistle Pepper Box.
Maj. & Mrs. Breckinridge, a Silver Portmonaie.
23rd Reg't Ohio Vol. Inf., A Silver Tablet, on velvet, in Ebony Frame. On the Tablet "To 'the Mother of Ours' " "from the 23rd O.V.I." At the top is engraved the "colors of the 23rd O.V.I." and at the bottom the Log Cabin occupied by Col & Mrs R. B. Hayes, Birch & Webb Hayes at Camp Reynolds, Kanawha Falls, W. Va., Jan to Mch 1863. The Winter Quarters of the 23rd O.V.I. and the following, written by Sergt. Major Wm E. Sweet, 23rd O.V.I. "To the
Wm T. Crump, a Silver Berry Spoon.
Capt [Joseph A.] Joel,—"Life Studies of the Great Army".

Larkin G. Mead—A Silver Tea Seive.

Mary Breckinridge—A Silver Match box.

General & Mrs Force—A Silver Butterfly for the Hair.

Dr & Mrs John Davis—An illustrated Poem—Silver frame.

Rev. Dr. [Lorenzo D.] McCabe—A Photograph of self.

Mr & Mrs Rogers—A Silver Jelly dish & spoon.

Secy & Mrs Evarts—A Chased Silver Pitcher.

Post Master General & Mrs Key—Silver Desert Set, 5 pieces.

Attorney General Devens—a large Silver Strawberry Dish.

Justice & Mrs [Noah H.] Swayne—Two oxydised Silver Candle sticks with candles.

The Clerks[of the] Executive Mansion. Set of after dinner coffee Spoons.

Col & Mrs T. L. Casey—a Silver Mustered Pot & Spoon.

Gen & Mrs J. H. Potter—a Silver comb.

Mr & Mrs Wm G. Deshler—A Salid Spoon & Fork

Gen W. A. Knapp—Helmet of Mother of Pearl.

Mr & Mrs L. Whitney—

~~Judge~~ Wm W. Worden— "Christmas Morning" in Silver frame.

Mr   Pond—Poem in Silver frame.

Mrs Adm[iral J. A. B.] Dahlgren—An American Lace Handkerchief in Japanese case.

A. S. Pratt—Portfolio of Sketches

Crafts J. & Mrs Wright—a Mss in Silver binding

Mr [Hart L.] Strasberger [Strassburger] (Shoe man) Silver Kid Slippers

Congratulatory Telegrams "To the Mother of the Regiment" were received from

The 23rd Reg't O.V.I. Association of Cleveland Ohio.

Gen'l & Mrs. R. P. Kennedy, Bellefontaine Ohio.

Capt & Mrs. John S. Ellen, Willoughby Ohio.

Capt S. B. Warren,   Kansas.

Capt J. L. Botsford, Surgeon [John] McCurdy Youngstown, O.
Capt A. B. Logan, Newark, Ohio.

Letters were received from Major & Mrs. Wm. McKinley, Canton, Ohio, and from Capt. Joseph A. Joel, New York City. The 23rd Reg't was represented by

Senator Stanley Matthews formerly Lt. Colonel.
General Russell Hastings formerly Lt. Colonel.
Col Wm. E. Sweet formerly Sergt. Major
Capt W. H. Nessle formerly 1st Lt.
Wm. T. Crump formerly Co I., 23rd O.V.I.

The whole celebration and the visit of our old friends were very enjoyable. Gen & Mrs Force never seemed so near to us before. Mrs F. was particularly happy in making all around her happy. I had not thought of her as beautiful before. But she is very beautiful.

Birch & Ruddy Platt returned to New York the evening of the 1st. Gen & Mrs F[orce] left Saturday evening. Herron & wife & child & nurse left the 2d with Col [L. C.] Weir. Dr and Mrs Davis left Wednesday 9th.

———

Silver [now] worth 53 3/4 pence—the equivalent of the gold dollar of 425.25. 8/10 grains would be 452.65 grains of silver. The average for 1877 equivalent of the gold dollar was 443.92 grains of silver.

———

I have a beautiful Epithalamium for our Silver wedding from Wm D. Gallagher.

A letter of congratulation on the Southern policy, from Washington McLean of Cin[cinna]ti.

[Seating at the] Dinner on the 30*th* Dec 1877—Wedding day—Silver day

<table>
<tr><td colspan="2" align="center">The President   Mrs. Hayes</td></tr>
<tr><td>Mrs. Gen Mitchell</td><td>Rev. Dr. L. D. McCabe</td></tr>
<tr><td>Hon John W. Herron</td><td>Mrs M. F. Force.</td></tr>
<tr><td>Mrs Dr John Davis</td><td>Dr John Davis</td></tr>
<tr><td>Mr W. K. Rogers</td><td>Mrs W. K. Rogers</td></tr>
<tr><td>Mrs John W. Herron</td><td>Judge M. F. Force</td></tr>
<tr><td>Rutherford H. Platt</td><td>Miss Maria McKell</td></tr>
<tr><td>Miss Emma Foote</td><td>Col. L. C. Weir</td></tr>
<tr><td>Lily Mitchell</td><td>Miss Emily Platt</td></tr>
<tr><td>Webb C. Hayes</td><td>B. A. Hayes</td></tr>
<tr><td>Fanny Hayes</td><td>R. P. Hayes</td></tr>
<tr><td colspan="2" align="center">Scott R. Hayes</td></tr>
</table>

————

Executive Mansion
Washington
Dec. 31, 1877.

My dear Sir:

I have your note of the 26*th*. It would gratify me and I think be useful to the cause, if we could have a good long talk over the situation. If you can write me your views, or rather, precisely what ought to be said in the message on reform, it would aid greatly. How to appoint? How to remove? How to divorce office holding from the active work of party politics? How to separate the legislative from the executive function of appointment—are the points. I am sorry to find in your note even a hint that you doubt my loyalty to the minority in this contest. Loss of confidence in those who lose a fight, or even a skirmish, is common; but I hope it will not be, in this case, permanent.

Sincerely
R. B. Hayes

Hon. Geo. Wm. Curtis

————

Washington, 12th January, 1878.—Last evening after dinner I received the following dispatch from Maj W. D. Bickham.

Dayton, O., Jan 12, 1878

Richard Anderson's dead body was found in his pasture lot this afternoon. Physician says apoplexy. Family thought he was in Cincinnati.

Wm D. Bickhan.

And so one of my dearest friends is gone! A friend of thirty years standing. A man of such warm affections, so unselfish, honorable, and true, that his friendship was to be counted as one of the greatest of blessings. His home in Dayton was my home. But why selfishly think of my loss, when it is so small compared with that of his wife and daughters, and sons. In his last letter to [W. K.] Rogers he says

"What a sad & bitter disappointment it is to me not to meet you & your wife at the Silver Wedding of our friends for whom we have so much love and respect and in whose happiness & good fortune we so heartily rejoice. Death however and so many misfortunes among our friends seemed absolutely to forbid. *** Express my, or rather, our most sincere regrets in your own honest sincere way to the President & Mrs Hayes & all other friends at the Silver Wedding that we cannot be with them on that joyous occasion." At the time of our Silver Wedding it was mentioned as remarkable that the friends with whom I was most intimate when I married in 1852 were all still my most intimate friends—all living as follows viz

Richard C Anderson, Manning F. Force, John W Herron, Geo W. Jones, Wm K. Rogers & R. H. Stephenson.

19th January, 1878.—Maj J. H. Mayborne of Geneva, Kane Co., Ill., yesterday wanted to talk over the situation. He began to find fault with what I had done. I took the same course with him, and attacked him for his doubts and suspicions as to my Republicanism. After getting him on the defensive, I went into an exposition of my views of the Republican party, its genius, mission and duty. Soon it became apparent that he thought as I did on all the points I touched, and he closed by saying he was satisfied of my Republicanism, and we parted in excellent temper with each other. "Mem"—it is better to attack than to defend.

[Clipping pasted in diary:]

Chicago Times: The Chandler's red glare, the Blairs' bursting in air, disclose through the night that R. B. is still there.

———

Dinner to Ex-Secretary [Benjamin H.] Bristow, Private Dining Room, 24 Jan. 1878 [Seating]

Senator [James B.] Beck
*

Senator [George F.] Hoar	* *	Mrs [David] Davis
Mrs. [William B.] Allison	* *	Sec'y [Carl] Schurz
Sec'y [John] Sherman	* *	Mrs. [John] Sherman
Mrs [William M.] Evarts	* *	Mr. [Benjamin H.] Bristow
THE PRESIDENT	* *	MRS HAYES
Mrs. [Morrison R.] Waite	* *	The Chief Justice [Morrison R. Waite]
Sec'y [William M.] Evarts	* *	Miss Schurz
Mrs. [George F.] Edmunds	* *	Senator [George F.] Edmunds
Senator [William B.] Allison	* *	Miss [Mary] Devens

*
Senator [David] Davis

———

Sunday, 27th January, 1878.—I have a dull headache at night. No severe pain. Nothing acute, but it leads me to ask what does it mean? The pains are in the back of the head for the most part, and leave me when I get up in the morning. They are not severe enough to prevent my sleeping quite well.

I usually am awake a few times during the night, but not uncomfortably so. I sleep as well as I ever did. The head pains are like those I have had when using quinine. They have rather increased the last few weeks.

———

29th January, 1878.—State Dinner, State Dining Room. [Seating arrangements]

Mr. McKell (J. S. of Chil[licothe])

*

Gen. [Randall L.] Gibson (M.C.) *	* Miss [Emily] Platt
Miss [Mary] Devens *	* Gen. [James A.] Garfield (M.C.)
Mr. Kelly *	* Mrs [Albert S.] Willis
Mrs. [Horatio C.] Burchard *	* Senator [George F.] Hoar
Senator [James G.] Blaine *	* Mrs. Kelly
Mrs. [Stanley] Matthews *	* Senator [Henry B.] Anthony
Sec'y [Carl] Schurz *	* Miss Schurz
Mrs. [Thomas F.] Bayard *	* Mr. Justice [Nathan] Clifford
Sec'y [William M.] Evarts *	* Mrs. [William M.] Evarts
MRS. HAYES *	* THE PRESIDENT
The Vice President *	* Mrs. [Nathan] Clifford
Mrs. [Noah H.] Swayne *	* Mr. Justice [Noah H.] Swayne
Atty. Gen. [Charles] Devens *	* Mrs. [James G.] Blaine
Mrs. [George F.] Hoar *	* Senator [Thomas F.] Bayard
Senator [Richard J.] Oglesby *	* Mrs. [James A.] Garfield
Mrs. [Omar D.] Conger *	* Senator [John T.] Morgan
Senator [Stanley] Matthews *	* Miss [Emma] Foote
Miss Smith *	* Mr. [Omar D.] Conger (M.C.)

Mr. [Horatio C.] Burchard M.C.) *   * Miss   Cook

*

Mr. [Albert S.] Willis (M.C.)

———

3d February, 1878.—It is now almost a certainty that the Silver bill will pass in such shape that I must withhold my signature.[1] I am not so opposed to silver coinage that I would veto a bill which guarded the rights of creditors, and operated only in futuro. But I cannot consent to a measure which stains our credit. We must keep that untainted. We are a debtor nation. Low rates of interest on the vast indebtedness we must carry for many years is the important end to be kept in view. Expediency and justice both demand honest coinage.

6th February, 1878.—The measure will contract the ~~currency~~ coin of the currency by expelling gold, which will not remain in the presence of the depreciated silver.

8th February, 1878.—Miss Mary Devens, niece of Atty Genl [Charles Devens], a sensible attractive girl of 22 or so, from Boston (or Cambridge) left us, after a visit we have enjoyed, this morning. Her three weeks has been a happiness to us.

Scott [Hayes] celebrated his birthday. A noisy happy party of thirty young folks. Gen [Clinton B.] Fisk, Gov [Henry P.] Baldwin of Mich., & Bishop [William Logan] Harris looked on. While we talked country and religion, we saw the blindman's buff and other sports in the East room and halls.

In the evening Lucy Scott dau[ghter] of Dr Isaac Scott ~~called~~ came for a visit with Mrs Mary McFarland a cousin of Lucy—*my* Lucy.

15th February, 1878.—The topic of interest now, ~~after~~ next to the Silver bill is the [Thomas C.] Anderson prosecution in New Orleans.[2]

I put it as a simple question of good faith—of honor on the part of Louisiana. Suppose all of the facts proved against A. to have existed—but suppose the Returning Board had counted the State for Tilden. Would there have been any prosecution? No body believes there would. Is it not a clear case then within the Resolutions of the Nicholls Legislature, and the letter of Gov Nichols Believing the affirmative I rely upon—I trust the honor of Gov Nichols.

To H. Clay Trumbull
 Editor of the Sunday School Times:

  Dear Sir:

  The only American whose birthday is generally known and widely celebrated is Washington. The Father of his Country is remembered and honored throughout the world for what he did, and what he was. None of my young friends who read this patriotic number of the Sunday School Times are likely to have an opportunity to do such great deeds as were done by Washington, but all of them will have an opportunity to be like him in character. They can have his love of country, his integrity, and his firmness in doing the right. To have such a character is better than rank, or wealth, or fame. It is a possession which can't be taken away. As Webster said so impressively of "a sense of duty," "it will be with us through this life, will be with us at its close; and in that scene of inconceivable solemnity which lies yet farther onward," it will still be with us.

Sincerely,
R B Hayes

————

17th February, 1878.—The Silver bill has passed the Senate with amendments that will send it back to the house. It will no doubt reach me during this week. I have given the subject some study and much anxious reflection. I shall veto the bill. It will probably become a law notwithstanding my veto. In my Message I ought to give a brief summary of the objections to it, and probably I ought to indicate what sort of a silver bill might receive my approval(?) but that is a question for consideration. I feel the importance and responsibility of my action. But I have no misgiving. The Nation must not have a stain on its honor. Its credit must not be tainted. This is the first, and great objection.

  1. It is a violation of the National faith. [not completed].

23d February, 1878.—Spent at home. [Charles] Foster and of N.Y. talked of Silver bill, just passed, my probable veto, and the course of the Administration. P.M., at three, a long procession of Temperance people passed in review (as it is called) before me under the portico. In the evening dined at Mr [George] Bancrofts with about 18 at table—a delightful dinner party.[3] Mr Bancroft spoke of Washington's love of the Union, his support of John Adams in preference to Jefferson because of his Union sentiments, and as apropos gave the toast, The President. Present, Ch[ief] J[ustice] Waite, Secy. Evarts, Bancroft Davis, Senator [George F.] Edmunds, Senator [George F.] Hoar, [list not completed].

[Memoranda]

Absences, 1877

21–24 Dec.	Union League & N.E. dinner	3	days
Oct 30–31 & Nov 1	Richmond Va	3	"
Sept 6–26	Ohio, Ky, Tenn, Ga & Va	19	"
Aug 14–22	Vt, N.H. & Mass	8	"
June	Boston & Harvard College	4	"
May	N.Y. Unveiling Halleck Statue & dinner with Chamber of Commerce	3	"
May	Phila. Opening of Exposition	2	"
		42	"

At Fremont

1. Get the large family scrap book.
2. [Get] Half of the cigars left by Uncle [Sardis Birchard]. Send Photos of Lucy [to] A. P. Miller   Toledo, O.

Falsehoods of the Campaign [of 1876]

That,

Hayes in the army said he wouldn't return the salute of a

private because there were no gentlemen in the ranks as privates!

Hayes converted to his own use $400 taken from a deserter and Bounty jumper who was executed at Monocacy Junction 5 Aug 1876 [1864].

He ordered two captured cannon to be hauled off and sold, and proceeds divided between himself and the men who sold them.

He kept $800 to $1000 deposited with him by Nelson LeRoy the evening before he (L.R[oy]) was killed in Sheridan's Victory of Winchester 19 Sept 1864.

He paid $500 to support the crusade in Fremont in 1873–4.

He left Princeton, West Va., in 1862 without paying his board-bill.

He was bribed with $10,000 to pardon Capt. [Lewis K.] McCoy [of Steubenville] in 1869.

He voted in the Ohio Legislature to allow no man the right to vote unless he owed at least $300. worth of property.

He promised in 1875 at Warren to appoint a man who lost his arm in firing a salute to an office if he (Hayes) was elected, and didn't do it.

He made false & fraudulent returns of property for taxation in Fremont in 1874, 5 & 6.

He is subject to dangerous attacks of insanity which give his friends great anxiety.

He had James Murphy executed at Dayton, Aug., 1876, for fear a commutation would injure his prospects politically.

He destroyed Democratic ballots sent for the Soldiers at his camp in 1864, near Winchester, Va.

He was taken prisoner near Petersburg in 1864 by a rebel soldier, James H. Price, his surrender being under circumstances very disgraceful to him.

He was taken prisoner by another rebel soldier at

He voted in the Centennial Board of Commissioners against keeping the exposition open on Sundays.

He caused the rebel spy to be executed to get his money.

He perjured himself to get rid of paying his just share of taxes.

He pocketed seventy-five bounties (see resolutions denying it of 23*d* [Regiment] at Cleve[land], 14 Sep 1876)

West Point

1. The young hero, 6 ft 4 [inches], by Senator [Bainbridge] Wadleigh of N. H.
2. Rev Dr N. H. Schenck's son.

Visitors at W[est] P[oint].

Gen James Grant Wilson, of N.Y.

[Possible appointments]

Wm D. Howells Minister to
Gov E. F. Noyes Minister to France
Gen James M Comly Minister to Sandwich Islands
L. P. Morton of Morton, Bliss, & Co
Maj D. W. Rhodes, promotion
Col John McDowell—Supt, Chicago
Capt A. E. Lee, Frankfort, [Germany].
Mrs Thurston P. M. at Cumberland, Md.
Coolidge of Columbus—Indian Agt, Mail Agency &c.
Smith (Hamilton Prof.), a consulate &c Egypt, Cairo.
Dr [C. A.] Cowgill of Fla, Gov [M.L.] Stearns, [S.B.] McLinn.
A. M. Stem, Cin[cinna]ti

20*th February*, 1878.—Dinner to General [W. T.] Sherman
and staff, State Dining Room. [Seating arrangements]

Mr. Dickinson

*

Mrs. [Joseph C.] Breckinridge	*	*	Miss [Emma] Foote
Lt. [Eric] Bergland, U.S.A.	*	*	Miss Platt
Miss [Lucy] Scott	*	*	Mr. [W. R.] Mead
Col. [John E.]Tourtellotte USA	*	*	Miss E. H. Evarts
Mrs [Orlando M.] Poe	*	*	Col. [John Mosly] Bacon, U.S.A.
Gen. [ ] Chrittenden, USA	*	*	Mrs. [ ] Chrittenden
Mrs. [Mary E.]McFarland	*	*	Gen. A. McD. McCook, U.S.A.
Governor[William] Dennison	*	*	Mrs. [William] Dennison
MRS. HAYES	*	*	THE PRESIDENT
Gen. [W. T.] Sherman, U.S.A.	*	*	Mrs. [William D] Whipple
Mrs.[ ] Forsythe	*	*	Gen. [ ] Forsythe, U.S.A.
Gen. [Orlando M.] Poe, U.S.A.	*	*	Mrs. [ ] Mc Cook
Mrs.[John Mosly] Bacon	*	*	Mr. [ ] Brown
Maj.[Joseph C]Breckinridge, U.S.A.	*	*	Miss [ ] Dickerson
Miss [ ] Sherman	*	*	Mr. [ ] Russell
Gen. A. G. McCook	*	*	Miss [ ] Ward
Gen[Russell] Hastings	*	*	Gen. [ ] Knapp

*

Miss [   ] Cook

———

Washington, 26th February, 1878.—My new book [of his
series of diaries] begins with exciting times. Today at Cabinet
meeting we considered the Silver bill passed last week. I had
prepared a Veto Message, and read it to the Cabinet. Col
Thompson opposed a Veto. He said he was an old Whig and
believed the old Whig doctrine was sound. He thought there
should be no veto on grounds of expediency or policy. There
must be a violation of the Constitution, or haste or mistake.
Here was was a measure long discussed—the people almost
unanimously for it—two thirds of each house for it—the measure a wise one, and demanded very earnestly by the Country.
I told him the message put the veto wholly on grounds of
principle. The faith of the nation was to be violated—the obligation of contracts was impaired by the law. Col T[homp-

son] replied that there was no provision denying to Congress the right to impair the obligation of contracts—that no obligation was in fact impaired—that contracts were made in view of the right of Congress to alter the legal tender.

Mr. Evarts differed totally from Mr T. as to the right of the Prest. to withhold his assent to measures which he did not approve. The Prest. under the Constitution is part of the law making power. The people have willed that no measure shall become law unless he approves until Congress a 2d time acts on the bill and by a 2/3 vote passes it again.

Sherman disliked the condition of things. [August] Belmont, the agent of the Rothschilds, fears the effect of a veto—prefers the bill should be approved, *bad* as he thinks it is. But S. sees no other course. McCrary also fears a veto. Would like it if the bill is to pass over the veto. But if the veto is successful in killing the bill, he regards with great apprehension the result. The Democrats with their worst elements in advance will come into power. Judge Key does not see how with the known principles of the Administration anything else can be done than to refuse assent to the bill. Judge Devens regards a veto as on all accounts the true course. Gen Schurz thinks a veto, if successful will save the country from an immoral and dangerous measure and if not successful the consequences will be less damaging than the effect of concurrence. For a veto decidedly Evarts, Key, Schurz, Devens—4. For a veto with some doubts Sherman and McCrary—2. Opposed to a veto, Thompson.

1st March, 1878.—I sent in my Message against the Silver bill yesterday. The message was short and I hope forcible. My objection to the bill is that it authorizes what I think is dishonest. I trust that in fact no actual dishonesty will ~~actually~~ be permitted under it.

A year ago today we left Columbus to come to Washington. The year, if I think of the scenes through which I have passed, seems an age. If I recall the farewell at Columbus, the throng at the State House—the procession to the Depot, the speech and farewell there, the lapse of time is but a day.

I have tried to do my duty. The crowd of business, the urgent misrepresentations poured into my ears by men who ought to be trustworthy have led to mistakes—serious mistakes, mainly in appointments, but the general course has been right. I have been firm and self possessed on the most difficult and trying occasions. I am not liked as a President by the politicians in office, in the press or in Congress. But I am content to abide the judgment—the sober second thought of the people.

Last night we had our second regular State dinner. The guests were congenial. Very little reserve or stiffness and it passed off satisfactorily.

State dinner, 28 Feb. 1878, State dining room, Executive Mansion [Seating order]

Mrs. [Mary E.] McFarland

*

The artist [Albert] Bierstadt	*	* Mr [Amos] Townsend (M.C.)
Mr. [Charles] Foster (M.C.)	*	* Mrs [Jay O.] Moss
Mrs. [Eugene] Hale	*	* Senator [John B.] Gordon
Senator [Theodore F.] Randolph	*	* Mrs. [Theodore F.] Randolph
Mrs. [Henry L.] Dawes	*	* Senator [William] Windom
Senator [Justin S.] Morrill	*	* Mrs. [Justin S.] Morrill
Mrs. [D. M.] Key	*	* Mr. Justice [S. F.] Miller
Speaker [Samuel J.]Randall	*	* Mrs. [Samuel J.] Randall
MRS. HAYES	*	* THE PRESIDENT
The Chief Justice [M. R. Waite]	*	* Mrs [S. F.] Miller
Mrs. [John] Sherman	*	* Sec'y [John] Sherman
The P.M.General [D. M.Key]	*	* Mrs. [William] Windom
Mrs. [John B.] Gordon	*	* Senator [Thomas W.] Ferry
Senator [Henry L.] Dawes	*	* Mrs. [Benjamin H.] Hill
Miss Waite	*	* Senator [Newton] Booth
Senator [Benjamin H.] Hill	*	* Mrs. [Charles] Foster
Mr. [Eugene] Hale	*	* Mr. [Thomas] Swann (M.C.)

*

Mrs. [Amos] Townsend

———

5th March, 1878.—Last evening Mr [Charles] O'Neal [O'Neill], M.C. from Phila[delphia] called with two young men of the Commercial Exchange to invite me to visit Phila. and their association at high [ex]change. I accepted ~~to take~~ for the first week in April. I must now arrange all of my engagements to visit Phil., as follows in the order of invitation

1. Union League, H. A. Brown
2. Industrial League, Gen [Robert] Patterson &c
3. Commercial Exchange, Mr [Francis Mark] Brooke
4. Launch at Chester ship yard, Mr [John Roach]

6th March, 1878.—H. C. Chauncey is now of Fabbre & Chauncey, N.Y., So. America &c.

9th March, 1878.—I will box and send to Fremont the following books not wanted here which now encumber the shelves of my private book case. They are mostly gift books, and not required here—

Hayden, [Fredrick Vandiveer:] Final Report [of the] U.S. Geological Survey of Nebraska and Adjacent Territories, 1867.
— [Annual Reports]. U.S. Geological and Geographical Survey of the Territories, 1867–68–69.
— U.S. Geological Survey of Wyoming and Adjacent Territories, 1870.
— U.S. Geological Survey of Montana and Adjacent Territories, 1871.
— U.S. Geological & Geographical Survey of Colorado . . . 1873.
— U.S. Geological Survey of the Territories, 1874.
Bulletin of the U.S. Geological & Geographical Survey of the Territories. Vol. I & II, 1874–75, 1876.
U.S. Geological Survey of the Territories . . . [Miscellaneous Publications, No. 3], F. V. Hayden in charge, "Birds of the North West." [by E.] "Coues." 1874.
Adams, [Sebastian C.] . . . Synchronological Chart or Map of History.

Photographs showing Geological and other features of the Western Territories, West of the 100*th* meridian, 1871,72, 73. Lt. [George M.] Wheeler.

International Exhibit[ion], 1876. General view [of] U.S. Gov't Building, "War Depart[ment]."

International Exhibit[ion], 1876. 2 copies.... Official Catalogue   British Section.

International Exhibit[ion], 1876.... Reports   on Education Department, Brit[ish] Section.

United States Centennial Welcome. Mrs C. F. Deihm.

Geology of New Hampshire, Vol. I and II. [Charles Henry] Hitchcock.

Geology of Wisconsin, Vol. II, 1875–77.

U.S. Geological Survey of the Territories, Vols. I, II, V, VI, IX, X, and XI, F. V. Hayden in charge.

Geology of the Uinta Mountains.... [John Wesley] Powell.

[Exploration] of the Colorado River of the West, 1869–72. Powell.

History of the First Troop Philadelphia City Cavalry. 1774–1874.

Instruments and Publications of the U.S. Naval Observatory, 1845–76.

The Heliotype Process, by Ernest Edwards, Boston, 1876.

Washington, [D.C.]. Astronomical and Meterorological Observations. 1874.

Contributions to the Centennial Exhibition, [by] John Ericsson, 1876.

Michigan and the Centennial, Edited by S. B. McCracken ... Officers and Men of New Jersey in the Revolutionary War.

Record of Officers and Men of New Jersey in the Civil War, Vol I and II.

Provincial [and State] Papers   New Hampshire, Vols. I–X inclusive.

12*th March*, 1878.—The end of the first year of my administration furnishes a topic for the press. There is enough of favorable comment from independent papers like the N.Y.

Post, the [Cincinnati] Gazette, the [Cincinnati] Commercial, the Boston Advertiser, the Phila. papers, and notably the religious newspapers, but the body of the party papers of both parties are the other way. The main point is that the President has so few supporters in Congress and among the newspapers.

It is to be remarked that a non partisan President or administration will of course be feebly supported, if at all, in Congress or by the Press. The party men do not like it, among the Republicans, and Democrats find no interest in ~~pleasing~~ heartily supporting an Adm. they did not elect. On the whole the Republican party has been strengthened rather than weakened by the ~~new~~ Administration. We are in a period when old questions are settled, and the new are not yet brought forward. Extreme party action if continued in such a time would ruin the Party. Moderation is its only chance. The party out of power gains by all partisan conduct of those in power. On the whole the years work has produced results

1. Peace, safety, order in the South to an extent not known for half a century.

2. The Riots—not a man shot but order promptly and firmly upheld.

3. A vigorous and successful Mexican policy.

4. Civil Service reforms.

    a. No nepotism in Executive appointments.
    b. No machine work by Federal office holders, in caucuses or elections.
    c. Congressional dictation resisted—for the most part successfully.
    d. Removals except for cause not made—fewer removals than under any Adm. in its first year since J. Q. Adam's.
    e. Officers secure in their terms, if conduct, official and private, is good.
    f.

5. The financial management has steadily adhered to the policy of a sound currency, untainted credit, and a faithful ~~performance~~ fulfillment of pecuniary obligations.

6. The pervading sense of responsibility for faithful and honest official conduct has given purity and efficiency to the service. Fewer scoundals than before in many years.

Cabinet

7. A list of foreign appointments, and officials retained, that will compare well with *any* previous period in our history. Look at our European representatives [John] Welsh, Eng— [Edward F.] Noyes, France—[Bayard] Taylor, Germany— [James Russell] Lowell, Spain—[George Perkins] Marsh, Italy —[John A.] Kasson, Austria—[Edwin Wallace] Stoughton, Russia—[Horace] Maynard [later Postmaster General under Hayes], Turkey—[John Meredith] Read, Greece—

8. The most important appointments are the judicial. They are for life, and the judiciary of the Country ~~touches~~ concerns all interests public and private. My appointments will bear examination [John M.] Harlan, Justice of the Supreme Court [John] Baxter & [Samuel] Blatchford, Circ[uit] Court; Bancroft Davis, Ct of Claims. District Judges in Vt., Wisc [onsin], N.Y.

9. ~~Cabinet~~ Bureau officers appointed [Richard C.] McCormick, [John D.] Defrees, [James N.] Tyner, Gen [William G.] Le Duc, [John B.] Hawley, [Edward] McPherson, [Albert Gallatin] Porter, [Robert M.] Reynolds, [Glenn] Schofield,

13th *March*, 1878.—The election of Gov [Benjamin F.] Prescott & the Administration ticket in New Hampshire, notwithstanding the defection of [William E.] Chandler and his followers is very gratifying. It encourages me to be more and more faithful in adhering to reform of the civil service. Let me disregard more and more "influence" of every sort, and be guided by a sense of duty alone. It is hard to have friends made sour because their wishes are not heeded. Newspaper and other abuse is not comforting to say the least. But the second thought of the best people is I believe with me.—Good for New Hampshire!

Friday, 15*th March*, 1878.—The past winter has been mild beyond precedent. Picnics in Berkshire Co. Mass Jan 1.—Sailing parties steaming on Lake Pepin.—Lake Erie open to navigation all winter—ploughing in Ohio every winter month—nothing like it "in the memory of the oldest inhabitant." In 1812–13 such a winter one says—another in 1816–17—and in the absence of statistics, this winter has no twin.

This morning, a lovely spring sunrise, Lucy goes for a fortnight's visit to Ohio. Chillicothe, Columbus, Delaware. Birch & Webb go with her, also Emily Platt; our niece, the two cousins, Lucy McFarland and Lucy Scott of N[ew] O[rleans] go to Lexington Ky—same car from here to Chil[licothe].

Fanny returned from her visit to New York last evening. The great city not so grand to her as Washington. "Broadway not near so Broad as Pennsylvania Avenue."

The picture painted, full length, by Garl Brown is now in the State dining room, and is a great favorite with Lucy, and generally regarded as the best ever taken of me.

I read few books—no time—J. Q. Adams' diary of Monroe's time shows M[onroe] had almost the same troubles that I have had.

16*th March*, 1878.—Lucy left for her native Town yesterday morning. Mr. J. O. Moss, of Sandusky, furnished his private car on the B. & O. RR. It was no doubt a merry ride. The party consisted of Birch, Webb, Emily Platt, Lucy McFarland, Lucy Scott [incomplete].

I found the White House lonely without them. Mr. Evarts lunched with me. Fanny presided at the tea pot. Scott filled up the table! At dinner I had a pleasant company [Charles] Foster and wife from my District, and [William] McKinley

& wife of Canton, O. In the evening enough to do. My afternoon ride was with Mr. [Thomas B.] Bryan, one of the Dist. Comm[issone]rs appointed by me.

Am told several of the Indiana delegation are offended, or made it a topic of remark, that Mr. [Albert G.] Porter was appointed [United States Treasurer] without consulting them. They admit the app't is capital in all respects, but &c &c &c.

Mr Vice President [William A. Wheeler] does not like Mr Evarts. He thinks E. is not frank to those who speak about appointments. He does not say so, but by an equivocal, non committal way of talking allows them to hope. "When there is no hope tell the man so. He will be disappointed at the time, but it the best way." Mr Wheeler is right. Prompt and square talk is in the long run safest and is just to the parties concerned. I must also bear this in mind.

As soon as the Returning Board prosecutions in La. are ended, and ended rightly, as I am confident they will be, I will hold conferences with judicious members of Congress as to the best way of effecting reforms according to the Cin[cinna]ti platform. Write to D. B. Eaton to send in his report [on civil service reform] and try to push forward the good work!

18th March, 1878.—Mr Conkling in the Senate remarked that the President had 1/6 of the Legislative power of the U. S. Gov't. I suppose he means that the Senate House and President having the whole power, and the President veto and 1/3 of either House being half, the result is [incomplete].

I rise at about 7 A.M.—Write until Breakfast about 8½ A.M. After breakfast prayers—i.e., the reading of a chapter in the bible—each one present reading a verse in turn, and all kneeling repeat the Lords prayer—then usually write and arrange business until 10 A.M. From 10 to 12 in the Cabinet room, the Members of the Congress having the preference of all visitors except Cabinet ministers. Callers "to pay respects" are usually permitted to come in to shake hands whenever the number reaches about a half dozen waiting. 12 to 2 P.M. on Tuesdays and Fridays are Cabinet hours. On other days that time is given to miscellaneous business callers. At 2 P.M. lunch. I commonly invite to that cup of tea and biscuit and butter with cold meat any gentlemen I wish to have more conference with than is practicable in hours given to miscellaneous business. After lunch, the correspondence of the day, well briefed, and each letter in an envelope, is examined. By this time it is 3½ P.M. and I then drive an hour and a half. Returning I glance over the business and correspondence again—take a fifteen or twenty minutes nap, and get ready to dine at 6 P.M.

After dinner callers on important business, or on appointment previously made occupy me until 10½ or 11½ P.M. when I go to bed, and am tired enough to sleep pretty well unless too much worried to throw off the vexations of the day—a thing which, fortunately, I generally can do by a little effort. There is not enough exercise in this way of life. I try to make up by active gymnastics before I dress when I get up, by walking rapidly in the lower hall and the green house after each meal for perhaps five to ten minutes, and a good hand rubbing before going to bed. I eat moderately—drink one cup of coffee at breakfast, one cup of tea at lunch, and no other stimulant. My health is now, and usually, excellent. I have gone to church at least once ever Sunday since I became President. Sunday after lunch, I ride regularly with Secretary Sherman two to three hours. We talk over affairs, and visit the finest drives and scenes near Washington.

NOTES

CHAPTER VI

[1] The reference is to the measure that became known as the Bland–Allison Act. In its original form it provided for an increase in the currency through the free and unlimited coinage of silver. Before passage it was modified to provide for the issuance of a stipulated amount of silver money. Hayes would veto the bill, but it would be immediately repassed.

² Not all the pledges made by both parties in the aftermath of the election of 1876 were observed. In Louisiana the Democrats launched prosecutions against members of the Republican–controlled returning board, the agency which had decided the outcome of disputed votes within the state. One of the members, Anderson, was convicted of altering votes in one of the parishes and sentenced to two years in prison. Hayes was deeply disturbed. Naturally he did not want the circumstances of the election raked up, and he felt that the prosecution violated an understanding to let bygones be bygones. He looked to Democratic Governor Francis T. Nicholls to do something, possibly to pardon Anderson. What happened was that the case was appealed to the Louisiana Supreme Court, which set aside the conviction on a technicality. Hayes would claim that the outcome constituted a vindication of his southern policy, that it proved the better class of whites would act fairly.

³ Bancroft, the historian of the American Revolution and one of the literary figures of the day, made his winter home in Washington.

Chapter VII

MARCH 21, 1878—JULY 27, 1878

21st March, 1878.—The returning board prosecutions are ended by the decision of the Supreme Court of Louisiana. No doubt the Court found legal grounds for its decision. But the favorable fact is that the Court followed the best public opinion of Louisiana in opposition to the wishes of the Bourbons. The Ruffian class, the implacables, and the press were for the severest punishment—determined to persecute the members of the Board to the bitter end. For the first time the better classes have overruled the violent. Pacification begins to tell.

22d March, 1878.—I am invited to witness the Launch of an iron Steam ship at the Chester [Pennsylvania] shipyard of Mr [John] Roach on the Delaware. It will take place two weeks from tomorrow. The hundreds of workmen employed at the yard will be present, and I will be expected to say a few words to them. Why not say something about the need of harmony in their work between enterprise, skill, inventive genius, knowledge labor and capital. The ship is the product of the union of all these. National prosperity in like manner needs friendship and not strife, peace and not war, concord and not discord, Peace and union. The flag which in distant sees is to float over it will give joy to ~~every American~~ the heart of every American who sees it if it is the emblem of ~~Unity~~ both Union and Liberty.

132

25th March 1878.—Yesterday after a thunder shower a cold Nor Wester set in, and at nine O'clock we had a clear ~~night~~ cold wind like midwinter.

Today Senator [Timothy Otis] Howe gives his "excuse" for not being favorable to the administration. He was an eager candidate for Judge of the Supreme Court in the place of David Davis of Illinois. The appointment of Gen [John M.] Harlan of Kentucky soured him.[1]

26th March, 1878.—Gen Schurz had an attack at his office yesterday of heart trouble which prostrated him. He was carried home, and after medical treatment rallied. The attack was alarming. He is a most valuable officer. Senator Howe of Wisc. made his long heralded speech against the administration. It was crammed full of hatred and predjudice. But it showed his malice without introducing any new fact or argument. His grievance is the failure to appoint him judge.

Executive Mansion
Washington

Private

27 Mch 1878

My Dear Sir

I have your letter, and have talked with Sherman about it. We do not differ essentially from your views. At least I do not, and on the leading points I think Sherman concurs. Under the circumstances, I have to hold your resignation without acceptance, not doubting that you will ~~draw~~ withdraw it when full explanations are made.

I trust you will keep it to yourself. If after letters are received you still feel like resigning, it is my earnest wish that you do not do so until we can meet and talk it over.

Sincerely
R B Hayes

Hon. Wm. H. Smith

133

30th March 1878.—Rutherford [Platt Hayes] came from Cornell [University] yesterday morning with a classmate, [Isaac Morse] Underhill, of Norwalk, O., to spend a short vacation. He looks as well as usual. His eyes trouble him if used at night; headaches are also common with him. A rather fine looking good tempered young man.

Mr Dorman B Eaton will probably send in his report during the coming month. The Points of civil service reform which I must call attention to are

1. *To separate office holding from ~~machine~~ political management.* This has in a large degree been accomplished by the order issued in June last. Very generally that the office holders observe the order. Doubtless with some its observance is ostensible or nominal rather than not. But none have resigned. ~~All profess a willingness~~ Public officers generally profess to observe it. The few exceptions to this statement are too insignificant to demand attention. What legislation to define fully ~~more~~ & accurately, ~~correctly,~~ the duties of office holders in connection with elections, may be expedient and necessary it is for Congress to decide. I am not so committed in favor of the measure already referred to, that I shall not be ~~un~~ willing to cooperate heartily with any legislation Congress may enact appropriate to the end in view.

2. To ~~restore the appointing power to its~~ restore ~~to~~ the legitimate and constitutional exercise of the appointing power to the Executive, ~~and Senate~~ Department of the Gov't., ~~with~~ subject to confirmation by the Senate in the case of important offices.   On this point I will quote Senator [George F.] Edmunds

The ~~majority of~~ practice of Congressional appointment is for the time being largely abandoned. ~~By far the largest number of~~ It is generally conceded that Senators and Representatives ~~no longer~~ ought not to seek to dictate appointments and only a small minority in practice now ~~hold the~~ undertake even to influence appointments. But ~~that~~ there is irritation and mis-

134

understanding on the subject. ~~is not to be denied.~~ It is exceedingly desirable that Members of Congress should be relieved from the pressure, demands, of their constituents for places in the public service. This can not be done by Executive action alone. Legislation explicitly defining the duty of Members of Congress on this subject has been attempted heretofore. It is not doubted that the end desired can be attained by appropriate enactments.

3. To provide by legislation appropriate means to secure information as to the fitness of applicants for appointment, and to determine as to the justice and propriety of removals is ~~peculiarly the function of the legis~~ brought to your attention. In the absence of legislation the Executive will seek information wherever it can most readily be found.

4. Let the Cabinet officers have seats in the House of Representatives and in the Senate with the right to speak on questions pertaining to their respective departments. A distinguished member of the House of Representatives made a report on this subject some years ago—in 1865—which presented the subject very ably to the country.

5. Congress should provide for a revival of the Civil Service Commission. My predecessor, President Grant, used the following language as to the beneficial results of the labors of the Board appointed by him. Quote [Quotation not given]

6. In the absence of legislation by Congress to promote the desired reforms, it will not be practicable to give a fair trial to the principles avowed by the general Conventions of the great political parties of the Country prior to the last National election. But it will be my duty to give them practical effect so far as my Constitutional powers will permit and to the extent of my ability. ~~In~~ Such efforts as may be made with a sincere desire to accomplish this, ~~desired ends~~ will it is confidently believed be sustained by the general sentiment of the people.

[Jacob] Collamer, the sound old Senator from Vermont

once said of [George F.] Edmunds "he can see the ~~spot~~ knot hole in the barn door, but he cant see the door."

1st April, 1878.—Last evening I had a very pleasant little dinner party—"quite informal." V. P. & Miss Schurz, the only lady, occupied Lucy's seat. Justice Harlan, Gen Schurz, Dr [George Bailey] Loring, M.C. from Mass., Gen [Ambrose E.] Burnside, Senator from R.I., and Mr. James A. Briggs of Brooklyn, formerly of Ohio. The home folks were Rud's classmate young [Isaac Morse] Underhill, Ruddy, & Fanny. A very friendly, social gathering. Judge Key and Col [Andrew J.] Kellar came in after dinner, and the talk lasted until 10 P.M. Wayne MacVeagh and wife were invited, but "prior engagements."

6th April, 1878.—I go today to witness the launch at the Chester yard of John Roach & Son, of the steamer The City of Para. I will make no speech. But I may give the sentiment

The City of Para. May her voyages be prosperous—and may she long continue to add to the good name and the fortunes of her builders her owners and her sailors.

7th April, 1878.—The launch was in every way successful. I gave the sentiment above with only a word of thanks, and of congratulations to J. R. & Sons.

Lucy returned yesterday morning with Emily Platt, Uncle Wm Cook, Mrs. Carrie Little & dau, Mary, Mrs. Mason, & Miss   Cook, after three weeks absence in charge [of] Birchard.

Saturday, 6 A.M., *13th April*, 1878.—The Republican Congressmen held a Caucus early this week for organization. The feature of the affair was the failure of Senator [Aaron Augustus] Sargent [of California] to procure the passage of a resolution condemning the Civil Service order of the President ~~forbidding~~ which forbids federal office holders from managing the party politics of the Country. His resolutions request the

136

President to rescind this order. ~~He~~ Senator Sargent wishes the doctrine announced that the ninety thousand officials in the Executive branch of the Civil Service shall participate "in meetings, caucuses, conventions, and Committees of a political character." This resolution of Senator Sargent, and the speech of Senator Howe present very fairly the issue between the Senate and the ~~President~~ Republican Party. Sargent and Howe think that Senators should appoint the office holders and that the office holders should manage the politics of the Country. This would be in my judgment a very unfortunate issue for the party to adopt. The doctrine of the Party in 1876 ~~was~~ before the election was that office holders should be appointed by the President and confirmed by the Senate, and that their whole services belonged to the ~~belonged to the~~ Government. The Senators doctrine reverses this. They say we will appoint the officers and our officers shall rule the ~~country~~ party, and our party shall rule the Country. With this Senatorial claim the members of the House of Representatives share very little personal interest. If the patronage of the Government is to be controlled by ~~the~~ Congress, that branch of Congress will absorb it which has the power of confirmation. The Senate will leave to the House only what it does not want. This question of Senatorial patronage is the salient point in the improvement of the Civil Service. It is the interest of the Country that its business ~~should~~ shall be well done and that the area of patronage ~~should~~ shall be limited. But if the office holders are to look after ~~the~~ party politics to make nominations, and to win party victories they will be appointed not for fitness to discharge the legitimate duties of their offices, but for skill in ~~pul~~ wire pulling. No Senator would ~~cut~~ diminish their number. ~~down~~ If ninety thousand are useful, a hundred thousand ~~would~~ will be still more useful. The Howe and Sargent system is that Senators shall make the office holders, and that the office holders shall make the Senators. How many victories can the Republican party gain on such a platform? The Watchword of the people against the office holders would soon be raised, and the party on the wrong side of the question would go under.

I would say the same about the Order as to office-holders. It did at the first elections after its issue disorganize the Party. The accustomed managers were many of them in office. For the most part the office holders obeyed the order. This created disturbance. But the Committees have been ~~re-arranged~~ re-organised. Volunteers have been found to take the places of the regular machine men. The new blood is vigorous. The late elections show it. New Hampshire and Rhode Island ~~show a~~ Republicans fought successful battles with ~~out the~~ new men. The people have always had a certain feeling against the dictation of office holders. "They ought to mind their own business" has often been heard, and still oftener has been thought. Jefferson and the earlier statesmen opposed it. Clay and Webster and other Whig leaders were against it. Howe and Sargent do not represent the best sentiment of the party on this subject. I hear from Milwaukee a protest against Senator Howe's Speech. It is signed by the best Republicans in the principal city of his State. I do not hear of any popular endorsement in his own State of his doctrines. It is said that nine tenths of the Republicans of Milwaukee are opposed to them. I do not defend mistakes in methods. I do not insist on my own particular plans. If better plans are proposed, I shall be ready to support them. But the important ends must not be abandoned. Office holders must attend to the public business, and not become organised political machines. The appointing power may be regulated by law, ~~but it must not~~ to the end that honesty ~~and~~ efficiency and economy may be promoted, but it must not be transferred to the Senate. It must be left where the Constitution placed it.

Office holders who participate actively in politics do not strengthen a ~~good~~ party of principle. People resent their interference. It is felt that office holders are the servant of the public, and ought not to assume to be masters.

It is said that this doctrine degrades the office. Are our present officers degraded? Do you not honor the officer who faithfully attends to his duty? Do the officers feel humiliated? I do not hear of resignations on this account.

Mr Sherman has contracted for $50,000,000. gold, and gold yesterday fell to 100½! It now looks as if we should be at specie payments long before the first of January 1879. We have passed through the suffering, let us have the desired end.[2]

14th April, 1878.—Sherman returned from N.Y. last night. His loan has been very successful. $50,000,000 gold before 1879 at 101½ for his 4½ per cent bonds. The premium on gold almost gone or ¼ of one per cent. If we can practically resume before the elections in the fall it will be a feather in our cap. Now we are hopeful. With reconciliation proceeding well, and resumption secured, as now appears, we are stronger than ever before. Our position on the silver bill enabled the Republicans in the Senate to improve the Bland bill 1 by striking at free coinage, 2 by the device of silver certificates, & 3d by a Commission to treat with other nations.

Sunday, 21st April, 1878.—[Robert C.] Winthrop says something like this Each one of us is engaged in the formation of public opinion. Each of us is in some ~~measure~~ degree responsible for its course and character. "Opportunity, powers, & employment of them." [3]

Sunday, 28th April, 1878.—We returned this morning at 6 A.M. from our four days visit in Philadelphia. It was happy in all of its circumstances. The gentlemen in our reception were Wayne MacVeagh, H. A. Browne, Gen Robt Patterson, James L. Claghorn, Steele [William G. Steel], Col [Archibald L.] Snowden, P.M., Jos[eph] Wharton, Amos R. Little, Brooke, Thos. A. Harrison, Bloomfield H. Moore, J. J. Bagley, Geo. A. Smith, Prest. of Councils Select introduced me at Independence Hall. Near me E. Dunbar Lockwood—

Many things to be remembered. Perhaps most notable was the reception given to Lucy at the Academy of Fine Arts friday evening. About 4000 persons were invited. The attendance was almost universal. The fashionable people, the best people, including church and solid business people. Bishop [Matthew] Simpson & wife,[4] the Friends, and the leaders in charitable enterprises.

The rooms were admirably arranged to accommodate and display the throngs. Paintings, engravings, statuary, and a wilderness of plants and flowers, with music & lights altogether a scene I never expected to see equalled. ~~and~~ Lucy went between 8 & 9 o'clock, and I entered between 8 & 10 or near 10. I this morning asked Lucy how she felt as the central figure of such a fairy scene. "Oh," said she, "humble." "I always feel humble on such occasions. I enjoy them very much, but am humbled by them." This reminds me of my feeling at the great moment of my life, when I heard I was nominated at Cincinnati. I felt a sense of responsibility—a sobered feeling—It was my feeling that with soundness of judgment, with a cheerful and elastic temper, with firmness, with an honest purpose to do right, and with some experience in affairs I could do well in the place. But this is going back. The scene brought to my mind many of the leading events of my life.

In reference to an election by Republicans alone to nominate a postmaster at Binghamton I wrote to Democrats who complained of their exclusion "No regulation has been adopted which prevents any citizen, or any body of citizens from nominating candidates for postmaster. All nominations by Citizens will be considered."

A case in the Quartermaster's Department at Philadelphia shows that I have perhaps unintentionally done a wrong. In the army as to appointments and employments it is said by the Quarter Master Genl *"The President's requests which we must consider as orders."* This did not occur to me when I said "I would be gratified if——could have employment." But hereafter I will uniformly do what I have heretofore intended to do viz give endorsements in conformity with this Mem

"The President does not direct subordinate appointments. In cases of exceptional merit he recommends candidates for appointment if it can be done without injustice to others, and consistently with the good of the service. He would not turn out a worthy officer to replace him with another.

14th May, 1878.—Various "confessions" and statements lately made by [S. B.] McLin & [L. G.] Dennis of Fla., and others of La. as to frauds in the elections have caused the Tilden Democrats, aided by implacable Republicans of the [William E.] Chandler sort to threaten investigations. Yesterday Mr [Clarkson N.] Potter [of New York] offered the resolution to go into it in the House. It is a partisan proceeding for merely partisan ends.[5] If the Republicans manage well their side of the controversy I suspect it will damage its authors. It should be opposed

1. As partial and narrow—If investigation is to be had it should embrace all the questions which have been raised touching the fairness and legality of the elections.

2. It is revolutionary—it looks to overthrowing the solemn adjudication of the Commission as confirmed by Congress. Herein [in this relation] should be given a full history of the origin purpose and understanding as to the Commission—the action of Congress &c &c

3. It will disturb the business of the country.

4. It interrupts the course of pacification between the Sections, and races, and revives sectional strife, and deepens the color line.

5. It is done by Tammany—by the New York rings. It is to continue the rule of N.Y. in the Dem. Party. Trace this power in the nominations of 1864, 1868, 1872 & 1876 in the Dem. Party.

6. It is not in the interest of the South. They want peace, education, improvements, and immigration.

7. It is not in the interest of the Country.

15th May, 1878.—Education is our greatest present National concern. General education is the best preventive of the evils now most dreaded.~~and apprehended~~. In the civilized countries of the world the question is how to distribute most generally and equally the property of the world. As a rule where education is most general the distribution of property is most general. When we see what wealth is doing and what wealth can do we begin to doubt the aphorism, "Knowledge is power." As knowledge spreads wealth spreads. To diffuse knowledge is to diffuse wealth. To give all an equal chance to acquire knowledge is the best and surest way to give all an equal chance to acquire property.

19th May 1878.—The House of Representatives has ordered an investigation of the elections in Fla & La. The resolutions adopted accuse Gov [Edward F.] Noyes and Secy Sherman of crookedness. It will do no more than raise a dust—throw dirt and the like, unless it is intended, as I seriously suspect, to lay a foundation for a revolution. There is a purpose with the real authors to reverse the result of the last election. If they are sustained in the elections there is danger. It is another rebellion!

Look up all letters from Noyes, Matthews, Chandler,   , to see the exact condition of my correspondence. I neither knew nor suspected fraud on our side. The danger was fraud by our adversaries.

I go soon to Hampton [Normal and Industrial Institute] to see the colored school—industrial school under Gen [Samuel C.] Armstrong. I must speak a few words on the education, the training needed by the freed men & women. They need something more than the learning of the school house. Illiteracy must be overcome. But industry, self reliance, self control, economy, thrift, the virtues Dr. [Benjamin] Franklin taught so well, are of still greater importance. The test, one test of the progress of the colored people is, do they own property? Do they own Houses? Do they save and accumulate?

31st May, 1878.—Yesterday at Hon Edw[ard] McPherson's in Gettysburg. A pleasant and satisfactory time. On the way up, Gen [Benjamin F.] Butler told a number of good war stories. The story of his running the battery on the Miss-[issippi] below N[ew] O[rleans]. How a soldier or sailor was blown to pieces by a shell exploding *in* him, which blinded and overthrew Gen B. with his gore and flesh! Also the story of his voucher for a hand organ and monkey purchased to get information which enabled him to sieze Baltimore! Col. [William McKendree?] Robbins of N. C. and Gen [J. Warren] Keifer—both in the whole war on opposite sides made the return trip agreeable with interesting recollections.

The event now on the scene is the investigation as to the election, looking to ousting the Republicans from power by revolutionary proceedings. My views are well shown by Judge Key's letter, Alex[ander H.] Stephens' letter, and an interview somewhat inaccurately reported by G[eorge] A[lfred] Townsend. I never authorise interviews. This one I did not suspect at the time. Talking with Judge [David] Wills on the subject while having a reception [at Gettysburg], Mr T[ownsend] stepped up, and continuing the conversation got up the so called interview out of the items obtained from me.[6]

2d June, 1878.—The election investigation began yesterday with calling as a witness the scamp [J. E.] Anderson. He testified that a letter was given to himself and Webber [D. A. Weber], election officers in the Felicianas,[7] by Sherman to induce them to aid in fraud in regard to the election. He produced a copy as he said of the letter. It is not a letter which sustains the charge even if genuine. He also testified that he called on me soon after I was inaugurated and got from me an

143

endorsement to Secy Evarts to give him a consulship in a warm climate.

The facts are so far as I am concerned He came to me, ~~with~~ one of the throng of office seekers early in my term. He had a strong recommendation from a trustworthy citizen of Steubenville, Ohio, name not now recollected, and testimonials from Senators Matthews and [William P.] Kellogg and Representatives [John Edwards] Leonard, [Charles Bidwell] Darral[l], [Charles Edmund] Nash, [list not complete, all from Louisiana]. Nothing was said which led me to suspect that he had been guilty of any crookedness, or that any promises had been made to him in my name or otherwise. The facts stated were that he had been an active Republican at the risk of his life in Louisiana and that on account of his activity as a Republican he had been driven from his home and business and could not safely return. He appeared intelligent and ~~gen~~ capable ~~and~~. He represented that his wife's health required him to go to a mild climate. Our interview lasted only a few minutes. I therefore gave him the recommendation referred to. Afterwards, and after a small consulship had been found for him, I learned from an anonymous letter signed Bulldozer, and from a note from J. A. Straight facts that made me suspect him. I also learned from Senator Matthews facts that induced the belief that he was trying to levy blackmail. I then directed that nothing should be done for him until his character was investigated. The result was that no office was given to him. My note as to his character is on file in the State Department with other papers. The files show clearly the action by me and the reasons for it.

~~He should be asked if he did not show the President a letter from   of Steubenville, O.~~

As to the alleged ~~action~~ frauds and perjury of Anderson with reference to the election in Feliciana, I never heard of it, until long after his papers were sent to the Secretary of State.

When Anderson was recommended by me for a place in a

144

warm climate there was nothing before me against him, and much in his favor, but after I heard the facts against him I was satisfied we had no place as warm as he deserved, and so he got nothing! Hence his trouble with us now!

Anderson says he told me that the Feliciana business was "a cheat." If so it was on one of the occasions when he was under the influence of liquor, and excited. I gave him no serious attention and got rid of him as soon as possible. I certainly never promised him office, and never intended to give him office after I had been informed of his true character and conduct. He could have been appointed if it had been deemed proper, and he was not appointed on account of the information received about him.

3d June, 1878.—Last evening with Emily P[latt] & Miss [Ellen M.] Kent we had a dinner on the fifteen pound salmon trout caught by Lucy in Lake Saranac, N.Y. Our guests were Sherman, Key, Thompson and Schurz of the Cabinet, and Garfield, [J. Warren] Keifer & [William] McKinley of the House. We talked over many matters. Prof. [Joseph] Henry's unselfish devotion to science. Gen G[arfield] said Prof. H. did show some feeling when [Samuel F. B.] Morse seemed to monopolise the honor of the discovery of the Telegraph. That he was willing to leave him the profit, but his own right to the fame was of value to him! Gen G also spoke of [Louis] Agassiz. "He quit an investigation the moment it became of practical use. Then said he there are enough to carry it forward.["] [8]

Sherman urged the members of Congress to put an item into the appropriation bill giving Prof H's family $500. a year for 23 years unrequited & valuable service in the Light House Board. I trust it will be done.

The testimony of Anderson was talked over. The general opinion was that his story was too thin to do serious harm.

Anderson testifies that June 13, '77 he called   at the White House to see me with Gen Smith (T. C. H.); that Smith saw me, but he did not; that S. came out saying that "the President for political considerations wanted something satisfactory done for him, A[nderson]."

My recollection is that I told S[mith] I believed Anderson was a great scoundrel & that I wouldnt see him, and wanted nothing further to do with him. I certainly did not say I wanted him to have office.

5th June, 1878.—Lucy left home for a visit with V. P. (Mr Wheeler) at Malone in N.Y. and a fishing tour in the Adirondacks, three weeks ago next Friday. She now expects to return home next Saturday. I have been occasionally lonely enough without her. But I have hoped that the trip would strengthen her after the wearing duties of the White House. If this turns out to be so I shall be content. According to present purpose her absence will be from May 17 to June *8th* inclusive.

8th June, 1878.—The weather is very cool for the season. Yesterday I rode out to the [Soldiers'] Home with Webb, Emily [Platt], and Gov [Marshall] Jewell. Good company and a bright bracing air. This morning a cold rain.

Last evening Webb & Emily Platt went on the limited express at 9:20 P.M. to meet Lucy and Fanny in N.Y. L. & F. have been gone three weeks yesterday. Too long an absence. We should always be together. They will reach here tonight on 9:30 train.

I have walked with Scott many mornings lately. He seems to be fond of learning. I have taught him in our walks, items of the Calendar—days of the year, month &c &c and today the year—1878—and the reason for it. He is not a "smart" boy—but sound and promising.

9th June, 1878.—Lucy and Fanny returned last night from their delightful trip to Malone and the Adirondacks—both fattened & browned & invigorated. Great happiness to have them with us once more.

146

11th June, 1878.—We are to start this evening for West Point to witness the graduating exercises.

Had a most delightful sail up the Hudson on the Gov't Q[uarter] M[aster] Boat [Henry Smith] under Capt . A lovely visit at W.P. *12th* & *13th*, and return the P.M. of *13th* down the Hudson in same Boat.

22d June, 1878.—Went with Lucy and [William T.] Crump to Mt Vernon. Slept in Lafayette's room. *23d* went to Pohick Church. Returning, stopped at Mr [Jacob M.?] Troth's a few minutes, and at Mr. [John] Mason's, at Woodlawn. A delightful day. Slept again in Laf[ayette's] room now the New Jersey room. Mrs [Nathaniel Norris] Halsted of Newark N.J. and Mrs   Hudson of Ct. (Stratford), Col [James McHenry] Hollingsworth, and the two McDermotts were friendly hosts. Returned with Maj [Joseph Cabell] Breckinridge on Gov't Boat, [the yacht *Hamilton*], Capt Travis.

The notable political event of the month is the adjournment of Congress on the *19th* (at 7 A.M. *20th*). I went with all the Cabinet to the President's room in the Capitol at 12 M. *19th*. Remained a few hours when the date of adjournment was changed from *19th* 6 P.M. to *19th* 10 P.M. We returned at 8 P.M. Time changed to 1 A.M., again to 3 A.M. then to 5 A.M. and finally to 7 A.M. *20th!* Too many of the enrolment committee of the House were drunk! So of the clerks! The colored member, [Joseph H.] Rainey of S.C. kept sober and alone secured attention to the Sundry Civil Service bill appropriating many millions, perhaps 18,000,000! At last one or two important pages relating to the Hot Springs were omitted, or stolen from the bill. *It should be investigated.*

The family event of the month was the quiet, beautiful wedding of my niece, Emily Platt to Gen Russell Hastings [in the White House, on June *19th*].

1st July, 1878.—We intend to go tomorrow to the Cen-

147

tennial Celebration of the Massacre of Wyoming [Pennsylvania].[9] We shall dine and have a reception at Gov [John F.] Hartranft's tomorrow evening. The next day the 3*d* will be spent in the Valley of Wyoming, and the 4*th* will be spent at Wilkes Barre. I shall probably say a few words at Harrisburg —very few. I may allude to the Centennial anniversaries of the important events of the Revolutionary War. The number of them which occurred in Penna.—and the example afforded by Phila. in 1876.

At Wyoming I may say a word or two about the peculiarity of the event celebrated. The anniversary is not in honor of Warriors or their deeds, or of Statesmen and their achievements. But ~~we now remember~~ in commemoration of the Pioneers—the men and women who encountered disease, and hardship, danger and suffering, to ~~rescue~~ reclaim the wilderness ~~and~~ and turn into civilized homes. We have now on our Western and South Western borders—in Wyoming and Montana, in Idaho and Oregon, in Arizona and Texas large numbers of our Countrymen engaged as pioneer settlers in a struggle with ~~the~~ difficulties and dangers not different from those which the pioneers of the Susquehannah Valley encountered. How can we best aid them? The Indians are the ~~ir~~ most dreaded danger. How to deal with them is a problem which for ~~most~~ nearly three centuries has remained almost unsolved. The founder of Penn'a came nearer to a successful solution of it than any other of the founders of Colonies in the United States. Two leading ideas seem to be ~~required~~ at the foundation of a successful Indian policy. With these always in view the early settlers may have safety.

1. Let all our dealings with the Red man ~~let~~ be characterized by justice and good faith, and let there be the most liberal provision for his physical wants, for education in its widest sense, and for religious instruction and training. To do this will cost money, but like all money well expended it is wise economy.

148

2. If by reason of the intrigues of the Whites or from any cause Indian wars come then let us correct the errors of the past. Always the Numbers and prowess of the Indians have been underrated.

7th July, 1878.–We enjoyed our trip to Wyoming. We dined on the 2*d* at Gov Hartranft's in Harrisburg, and had an agreeable reception in the evening. The clergymen were particularly hearty. On the 3*d* we reached Mr Pettibone's [Colonel Payne Pettebone] in Wyoming, near the Monument, about 9 A.M. or earlier. I spoke in the tent at, off hand, but acceptably. The reports were not well taken [by the press] by reason of confusion. But the reception of the speech by Judge [Asa] Packer, and other intelligent sp people was satisfactory. It ought however to have been written out by me for the press. As reported it looks disjointed. At Wilkesbarre, our stay was most enjoyable. The miners and the wealthy were equally cordial. W[ilkes Barre] is a beautiful Town with a fine site on the Susquehannah. Here our hospitable friends, [William G.] Phelps, Cunningham [possibly Major Charles M. Conyngham], and [George H.] Parrish entertained us.

My next visit is to Ohio. Simply a great Soldiers reunion at Newark. Let me prepare a short speech or two for the press.

Mr [F. W.] Seward at the Gettysburg consecration 19 Nov 1878 said "We shall henceforth be only one Country, having only one hope, one ambition, and one destiny." "*Near graves of the misguided*, with pity for their errors."

Bayard Taylor on Victor Immanuel's death "A single race shall know, One love, one right, one loyalty."

The Home, 10th July, 1878.–Came out to the Soldiers Home tonight. The Cooks–Mag & the twins returned to Chillicothe–

A fine cooling thunder shower. The last few days very hot. 88° in the White House.

12th *July*, 1878.— "Home"—Weather still very warm. Attended yesterday the meeting of the Board of Managers of the Soldiers' Home at the Surgeon General's office in order to make a quorum—seven. Gen [Benjamin F.] Butler presided. He was very polite!

Of [James B.] McPherson, his grand mother after his death said in a letter to Gen Grant ~~after the death of her~~ "I have watched his progress from infancy up. In childhood he was obedient and kind; in manhood interesting, noble and persevering, looking to the wants of others.

Soldiers' Home, 13th *July*, 1878.—A copious rain yesterday afternoon and evening. Cool bright and bracing this morning.

18th *July*, 1878.—The heated term continues—Today the hottest weather. Thermometer in Cabinet room, 85°—in upper Hall, White House, 90°—at window below north front, 94°!!

19th *July*, 1878.—2½ P.M. Cabinet room, 88°. Hall, White House, 93° & window below, 97°—a storm coming. It will cool the air.

We start for Newark tonight viz Webb, William [Crump, White House steward] & Isaiah, [Lancaster, Negro servant] with Gen Devens.

Wednesday, 8 A.M., 24th *July*, 1878.—Soldiers' Home. We left here about 7 [Friday evening, 19 July] after a fine thunder shower, and at the B. & O. RR Depot took the private car ["Maryland"] of Pres't [John W.] Garrett, ~~with~~ Mrs [Harriet Little Platt] Sollace, Miss   Willock of Lancaster, O., Gen [W. T.] Sherman, Gen E. B. Tyler, Gen Devens, Webb & self. A pretty comfortable night. Saturday very hot. The motion of the cars in the Mts mad Mrs S[ollace] & Gen Tyler seasick! Met by crowds at Zanesville & Newark. Got quietly and almost unobserved into Columbus. Found all well at Laura's, and [had] a delightful time. Sunday, a North wind brought relief. 22d [July], Monday, Newark. Weather good and demonstration successful. Stand too weak, *as usual.*

[J. Warren] Keifer's speech good and delivered admirably. I
got off a few words satisfactorily.

Found all well on our return. Absence, four days.

———

Executive Mansion
Washington
24 July 1878

Private

My Dear N[oyes:]

I have your letter of the 21st. You evidently have not heard
of the rule—an ungracious and embarrassing rule—which I
felt it was my duty to adopt against the appointment of relatives to office. No man connected with me by blood or
marriage has received any appointment at my hands. I need
not say that there have been applicants. No doubt a number
have felt severely my refusal to give them places. Generally,
I am glad to be able to say, my course on this subject has
been approved by my own and by my wife's kindred. I
need not argue the propriety of the course. As you say
"Enough is as good as a feast."

You speak of local places which you would like to have.
Such places are usually filled by incumbents of local offices.
Of course, I do not *dictate* or *oppose* such appointments.
I simply let them alone.

This is a hard letter to write. I feel the value of what you
have done. I am persuaded of the warmth and sincerity of
your friendship. More than most men, I suspect, I feel the ties
of kinship and the duties they impose. Your qualifications
and fitness for any duty you would undertake, I know are
ample. But the principle is in the way. Hence this awkward
and, I fear you will think, this cold and unfriendly note.

Sincerely,
R. B. Hayes

H[oratio] S. Noyes
&c &c

———

27th July, 1878.—In conversation with Gen [Lucius] Robinson, [James] Tanner, and a gentleman from Albany, I spoke of the fact that Conklin and Butler were generally regarded as at the bottom of the Potter investigation. Tanner now writes for proof in order to injure Mr Conkling. I reply

26 July 1878

Private

The impression you refer to, so common here, may not be well founded. No doubt it is largely traceable to the World correspondent's disclosures. Whether true or not I see no reason for its dissemination. Certainly I shall have nothing to do with it. My course is not based on personal grounds.

Sincerely

Maj James Tanner
&c &c

———

NOTES

CHAPTER VII

[1] Senator Howe of Wisconsin was one of the Republicans who felt that Hayes in following his reform policy did not take into sufficient account the interests of the Republican party.

[2] Congress had provided during the Grant administration for the resumption of specie payments for greenbacks on January 1, 1879. Secretary Sherman was engaged in building up the gold reserve in the Treasury.

[3] Winthrop was a figure out of the past, a member of a famous Massachusetts family and a Whig leader in the decade of the 1840's. His reluctance to take a strong antislavery stand forced his retirement from politics. He devoted the rest of his long life to scholarship and philanthropy. He was president of the board of trustees of the Peabody Education Fund, to which Hayes was elected in his first year in the White House.

[4] Bishop Simpson was a noted Methodist divine, an orator of powerful persuasion, and something of an influence in the Republican party.

[5] Now began the "Potter investigation" of alleged Republican frauds in the election of 1876. It would drag on for nearly a year and cause Hayes embarrassment, pain, and anger. McLin and Dennis had been election officials in Florida in 1876. They now stated that Florida should have been counted for Tilden and that they had been induced to deliver it to Hayes because of promises of rewards made by Edward F. Noyes, one of Hayes's

Ohio friends. Similar charges concerning Louisiana were leveled at John Sherman. While everything that was promised in 1876–77 will never be known, it seems reasonably certain that the men making these accusations were disappointed office seekers.

6 From statements made by some Democrats, notably Speaker of the House Samuel J. Randall, many Republicans concluded that the purpose of the Potter investigation was to lay a basis for removing Hayes–by court proceedings or impeachment. Postmaster General Key and Stephens, former Confederate Vice President and now Congressman from Georgia, attacked the investigation in public letters. Hayes put forth his views, without exactly meaning to, in the interview with the reporter. Townsend, in the Philadelphia *Times*, May 31, quoted Hayes as saying belligerently he would oppose any attempt to oust him except by the constitutional process of impeachment.

7 James E. Anderson had been a Republican election supervisor in East Feliciana parish in Louisiana. Weber, the supervisor in West Feliciana, was murdered in 1877. Hayes describes the case with essential accuracy, and his designation of Anderson as "scamp" was apt. Anderson, like many other officials in the disputed states, was willing to deal with both sides—and did.

8 Joseph Henry, first secretary and director of the Smithsonian Institution, had died in May. He had aided Morse in the development of the telegraph. Agassiz was the greatest naturalist of his day.

9 In July, 1779, a force of British Loyalists and Indians struck the Wyoming Valley region in one of the grimmest raids of the Revolution.

Chapter VIII

JULY 28, 1878—Nov. 29, 1878

28th July, 1878.—Yesterday afternoon took a sail on Revenue Steamer *Ewing* down the Potomac below Mt. Vernon. Sherman, Key, Mr [J. K.?] Upton, Dr ——— Wilson, Lucy, Sherman's daughter & one other little girl, [E. W.] Clark, Supt of the [Revenue] Service, &c &c. Showery & cool. A pleasant trip.

The event of the week is the South Carolina case. In eight or ten States of the South in the Mountain regions, embracing perhaps sixty counties in all, with possibly a population of a million or more, the tax on Whiskey cant be collected—or if collected it is with a good deal of difficulty. Hitherto there has been a great deal of evasion & some violence and bloodshed. But while public men and the Courts in that region have winked at the violations of law, there have been I think no attempts to array the Governments of the States concerned against the United States. The appearances now indicate that in South Carolina there is danger of this. Gov Hampton is a conservative, and wishes to see the laws enforced without violence. But a State circuit judge in a carefully prepared opinion holds the United States laws unconstitutional.

This is in a case where a homicide was committed by U.S. officers in an attempt to arrest a violator of the Revenue laws. The officers were prosecuted in the State Courts for the homicide. They sought to remove their cases from the State Court into the United States Court. The State Judge, Judge [Joseph B.] Kershaw, held that this could not be done, and refused to allow or order the Sheriff to produce the officers, his prisoners, before the Circuit Court of the United States in obedience to the Writ of Habeas Corpus *cum causa*. This presents a conflict of jurisdiction which may lead to serious results.

30th July, 1878.—The whiskey cases in the South call for wise and firm conduct. No doubt the Government is a good deal crippled in its means of enforcing the laws by the proviso attached to the army appropriation bill which prohibits the use of the army as a posse comitatus to aid U.S. officers in the execution of process. The States may and do employ State military force to support as a posse comitatus the State Civil authorities. If a conflict of jurisdiction occurs between the State and the United States, on any ~~of the~~ question the U.S. is thus placed at a great disadvantage. But in the last resort, I am confident, that the laws give the Executive ample power to enforce obedience to United States process. The machinery is cumbersome and its exercise will tend to give undue importance to petty attempts to resist or evade the laws. But I must use such machinery as the laws give. Without passion or haste the ~~laws~~ enforcement of the laws must go on. If the Sheriffs or other State officers ~~of the~~ resist the laws, and by the aid of State militia do it successfully, that is a case of rebellion, to be dealt with under the laws framed to enable the Executive to subdue combinations or conspiracies too powerful to be suppressed by the ordinary civil officers of the United States. This involves proclamations, the movement of United States land and naval forces, and possibly the calling out of volunteers, and this looks like war. It is like the Whiskey rebellion in the time of Washington. That precedent, if the case demands it, will be followed. Good citizens who wish to avoid such a result must see to it that neither their State governments, nor mobs undertake to prevent United States officers from enforcing the laws. My duty is plain. The laws must be enforced.

2d August, 1878.—Good rains—thunder storms yesterday and the day before. Sultry between showers.

In June my ~~old~~ private Secretary during the *2d* term as Gov. (1870–72), Col [John B.] Neil, came from Salt Lake where he is Ass't P[ost] M[aster], after a consulship. He had with him a gentleman of some apparent importance, Lycurgus Edgerton. It soon appeared that Edgerton wanted to get N[eil] appointed a Consul to some important place in France to advance his, E.'s, interests in selling silver mining stocks in Utah. E. professed to have great influence with Mr Evarts. But he failed to get the office. He failed also to get a place on the Silver Commission which he wanted for himself. Now he threatens to publish damaging things about me if I dont now appoint N[eil] to an office. His exposures are ~~first~~

1. My insincerity and broken promises to Neil in regard to the office sought.

2. That I grossly insulted Mrs Neil by kissing her when she called on me at the White House.

As to the first there is nothing worth remarking on. As to the second. There was no offense. Mrs N[eil]'s father and I were old acquaintances in Cin[cinna]ti before she was born. When she married N., he was my private secy, and both were in the habit of saying they could not have married but for my appointment. A friendly kiss of greeting had been common. I saw no offense taken by her.

But now E[dgerton] proposes to regard this as an insult which can only be *atoned* for by an office! In fact the only offense was the refusal to appoint.

Col N[eil] has nothing to do with this I am confident. Before he left I told him that any vacant office in Utah, it would be proper for him to apply for, and that I would consider the case favorably. But now E[dgerton] kicks this over!

List of [my] Noticeable letters & orders

1. Letter to Wm Hen[ry] Smith declining to quit the army to Stump for Congress, Aug./64.
2. Letter about nomination for Gov., 1865, to Col [H. F.] Devol
3. Farewell order to Old Brigade, 1865.
4. Order in 1862 or early in 1863 at Camp Reynolds.
5. Letter as to Rebel cruelty, 1864, see [William Dean] Howells, [*Life and Character of Rutherford B. Hayes*, page 193].
6. Letter as to Mc Lelland [General George B. McClellan], 1864, see Howells, [page 194].
7. Letter in 1876 to Gen [James A.] Garfield on money question.
8. Letter to Gen [A. T.] Wikoff as to riots & military, 1876.
9. Letters in 1875 [to] Wikoff on the canvass—*selection.*
10. Letter of acceptance, 1876.
11. Letter to Gen [Carl] Schurz during & after Canvass of 1876, selection.
12. Letter to [John] Sherman Nov. 27, [1876] at N[ew] O[rleans].
13. Letter to H. S. Noyes as to appointment of relatives.
14. Letter to [James M.] Dalzell on the candidacy for the Presidency—the "State of Mind" letter.
15. Letters & Diary during pendency of "Count", 1876–7 [letters to William] Dennison, [Samuel] Shellabarger, [William E.] Chandler &c &c.

Speeches

1. Speech opening Canvass of 1866—Extracts.
2. Speech opening Canvass of 1867—Extracts. Also 1868, [*186*]*9*, [18]70, 1, 2, [*187*]*5*.
3. Speech at Sidney, [Ohio], 1867--Extracts.
4. Speech at Soldiers Monument, Youngstown, 1868.
5. Speech at Findlay, 1875, 4*th* July.
6. Speech at Davidson Fountain, Cinti, 6 Oct 1871

7. Speech at Army Reunion of Army of Tennessee, Cinti, ab't 1870.
8. Inaugurals & Gov's Messages, Extracts.
9. Inaugural & Prest's Messages
10. Speeches at Cincinnati & Chattanooga & Louisville, 1877.
11. Speech at Gettysburg, 1878, 4th July.
11. Speeches at St. Paul, Toledo, Dayton, Milwaukee & Pittsburgh, Sept 1878
12. At Saengerbund, Cinti, 186 or 187 when Gov.
13. Oct. 1878. Madison's Home, Winchester & Cumberland.
14. Adoption of 15th Amendment, 13 Apr 1871, Columbus, O.
15. Youngstown, Sept 1879 & Detroit
16. Kenyon College June 1880 & Yale College July 1, [18]80.

_____

Monday, 5th August, 1878.—Lucy left this evening with Birch and Fanny to visit for a week or ten days Judge [Noah H.] Swayne's family at Newport.

Today we had the heaviest storm of rain and hail I have ever seen. With Birch in the Fremont carriage—the grays driven by Albert—we were weather bound in V[ermon]t Avenue near N [Street] over half an hour. No harm done.

Quaker Calendar

"The 4th, 11th, 9th and 6th,
    Have 30 days to each affixed
And every other 31,
    Except the 2d month, alone,
Which has but 28 in fine
    Till leap-year gives it 29."

6th August, 1878.—It is plain that the Civil Service reform has made some progress.

1. No ~~compulsory~~ assessments on office holders are now allowed. If it is charged in any case the officer concerned hastens to deny it. Even the enemies of ~~the~~ reform in the party now give it up. (see [George Congdon] Gorham's letter).

158

2. Office holders have in great degree ceased to interfere in party management. If accused of it, they deny it.

3. Appointments are no longer regarded as belonging to Congressmen.

4. No relatives are appointed to office by the President.

5. No misconduct of any sort—no corruption in office is covered up by the Administration. All officers understand that a betrayal of trust will lead to "speedy, unsparing and thorough prosecution and punishment."

6. Appointments less partisan than any time before since [John Quincy] Adams' time.

7. No partisan service required of any public officer.

Thursday, 8th August, 1878.—[W. K.] Rogers & his wife with Phebe & Andrews [their children] came out to stay a few days with me during the absence of Lucy. It is an agreeable relief. The house was lonely—the table desolate.

I probably go to ~~to~~ St. Paul the first week in September. In the remarks I may be required to make I will ~~deal with~~ present some facts bearing on ~~the~~ our financial condition. ~~of the Country.~~ This is the subject which now attracts the attention, and deserves the careful consideration of the Country. For five years—ever since the panic which began in September, 1873, the whole business of the Country has been greatly depressed. ~~and its industries and labor~~ That depression, wide spread and general, demands and receives, a large share of the attention of thoughtful people. Without entering at all upon the discussion of the political questions which have arisen as to the measures of relief which ought to be adopted I desire to spread before you some facts and figures ~~relating to our financial Condition~~ which seem to me worthy of consideration

1. The condition of the National Debt.
2. The expenditures and taxation.
3. The currency—

159

4. The imports and exports.
5. Transportation.

Sales of public lands.

1. Debt—herein, of bonds & who owns them—rates of interest—time when the debt can be paid—improved credit—
The debt is no longer a foreign debt—it is a debt to our own people.
2. Expenditures & taxation.
[not completed]

Is the condition of the Nation become better or has it grown worse in the last five or twelve years? In respect to Debt, Expenditures, taxation, Currency, Trade with other nations?

9 P.M. In Maine a friend says the friends of the Administration are many of them not disposed to support the Rep ticket because the convention passed no resolutions sustaining the Administration. The truth is they passed no resolution on the subject. They said nothing on the questions of the past—nothing on any subject likely to divide the party. They simply took the right side on the question whether the people shall have honest money. They made this their sole issue. This is like my contest in Ohio in 1875. It is now the real issue before the Country. It is the only very important question. The Republicans of Maine are fighting the battle for a sound currency—for honest money—for a currency of gold and silver and of paper redeemable in gold and silver at the will of the holder. My sympathies are all with them. I hope they will succeed. ~~Let~~ No Republican ought to hesitate in that conflict.

Sol Home, 9th August, 1878.—Nothing brings out the lower traits of human nature like office seeking. Men of good character and impulses are betrayed by it into all sorts of meanness. Disappointment makes them unjust to the last degree.

12th August, 1818.—George H Forster, an able lawyer of N.Y. City, dined with me Friday and talked over the whole situation. The enemies of the Administration have the organization in their hands, and will control the party in the State. But a majority of the good citizens outside of the politicians are sound—so Mr F[orster] says, and in time they will control the organization.

All this is of small importance, if I can keep in the right path, and carry forward the good cause.

30th August 1878.—The weather this month has been cooler than usual—and a great deal more wet. A very great amount of water has fallen.

We start this evening for our home in Ohio—and the trip to Minnesota.

September, 1878.—The address of Nellie Pease is Mr[s.] W[illis] S[edgwick] Merriam, 115 & 117 William St., New York.

October Engagements

In October I go to Baltimore to a Fair, Winchester, & Orange C[ourt] H[ouse]. Ditto, Cumberland? *Peabody [Education Fund] trustee meeting?*

Sunday, 1st September, 1878.—Fremont, O. We left the B & O Depot in [the] director's car (?) viz Lucy, Birch, Webb, Fanny & Scott, with Winnie [Monroe, the nurse], Isaiah [Lancaster] & Wm T. Crump, about 7:30 P.M., Friday 30th, via Newark & Monroeville to Fremont—reaching here about 7:30 P.M. last night. At Depot many friends met us—no speeches—a band accompanied us home. Here Mrs [Helen I.] Savage & her two little boys, Douglass & Clarence & her sister, Mrs [Emma E.] Atwater, & her aunt Mrs   Cook. My cousins (2d) are in possession of our pleasant home & keeping it in beautiful condition. Rutherford is here, making the

161

family circle complete for the first time since the Silver wedding.[1]

Soldiers Home, 26th September, 1878.—Thursday. Yesterday at 10 A.M. we, that is, Lucy, Birchard, Rutherford, Fanny & Scott, with our faithful men, Crump & Isaiah, reached the White House after 26 days absence. A most happy, successful & I hope useful trip. At Pittsburgh, our last stopping place, the reception and welcome was most enthusiastic. Nothing of the sort could have been finer.

I met at Chicago many gentlemen who were very kind to me —Howe [George M.], [Franklin] MacVeagh, [William Taylor] Baker, [Erskine M.?] Phelps, [J. W.] Walker, At the banquet took Mrs Clinton Locke, wife of Rev Dr L[ocke] to the table.

1st October, 1878.—Upon the whole the Western trip was the happiest and most useful trip yet made. It certainly strengthened my administration, and our greetings showed that we were already strong.

I go tonight to New York to attend the meeting of the Board of trustees of the Peabody Education fund.

I go to a fair at Winchester Va, the 16*th*.

On the subject of money we cant be wiser than the Constitution. The money of the constitution is ~~gold and silver~~ coin.

By a law established by the common consent of all mankind the precious metals—gold and silver, have been the standard of value in all Countries and ages, and that law can no more be repealed by ~~the~~ act of Congress than the law of gravitation. It is fundamental and irrepealable. The fathers of our Constitution embodied it in their great work. There it will stand.

* * * By a law resting on the concurring judgment and common consent of mankind in all ages and countries the precious metals have been the measure of value—the money of the world. That law can no more repealed by act of Congress than the law of gravitation. This law will stand. The paper money epidemic will pass away. If the constitution

162

shall be violated, or if ~~the~~ attempts to amend it shall have a temporary triumph, the ephemeral success will be followed by the inevitable calamities which always avenge ~~defer~~ the infringement of fundamental law.

It was my fortune during our great Civil war to become intimately acquainted with the beautiful & historic Valley of the Shenandoah. I came to know it ~~in~~ in a rough school, but under very competent instructors. It is now my happiness to revisit the valley—to renew my acquaintance with its springs, and fertile meadows and fields and ~~beau~~ fine scenery of Mountain and vales with its brave men and fair women under more auspicious circumstances than seemed possible a few years ago. Who could have believed that what is now true and familiar to us all was to occur so soon? The attention of the American people withdrawn from the old Sectional controversies absolutely and entirely and attracted to and engaged about questions of public policy which divide the people of every ~~State~~ section and of every State—and which interest them to the exclusion of the past.

Soldiers Home, near Washington, 5th October 1878.— Yesterday I was fifty six years old. I returned with Lucy, and my old friend John W Herron from New York about day light. The dome as the sun was rising behind it was an object of singular beauty. My first meeting at the Fifth Avenue Hotel ~~was~~ with the Peabody trustees was an agreeable one. Mr Winthrop presided. He is an exceedingly interesting old gentleman. Mr A[lexander] H. H. Stewart [Stuart] of Staunton, Va., impressed me most favorably, as an able, kind and cultured Virginian of the old school. Gen Dick Taylor [of Louisiana] is a witty talker, polite and liberal. Dr [Barnas] Sears, the agent, does the work of the Board, and, I think, does it wisely and well.

Touching my birthday. I was never on the whole happier than I am now. My health and that of my wife also, is very good. Our elevation has not I am sure turned our heads. The

163

abuse of us, and the honest but severe criticism, do not sour us. I try to judge fairly as to what is said, and "to improve" all just criticism. My administration is no doubt stronger than ever before. The appeal to the people on grounds of a non partisan character has been successful. I must in the future be more careful to do only what is wise and right.

I am told by Mr [Joseph H.] Rainey, colored Congressman from So Carolina that in Sumpter and other counties the Whites are resorting to intimidation and violence to prevent the colored people from organising for the elections. The division there is still on the color line. Substantially all the Whites are Democrats, and all the colored people are Republicans. There is no political principle in dispute between them. The whites have the intelligence, the property and the courage which make power. The negroes are for the most part ignorant, poor and timid. My view is that the whites must be divided there before a better state of things will prevail.[2]

How to deal with debts—The value of the public credit and how to sustain it—What constitutes a sound safe and stable currency. No man living or dead has given or can give better advice than James Madison—No man can be wiser. On these subjects no man can be wiser than the Constitution for whose formation & adoption he did so much.

[See] Mr Gladstone in his noted article in the N[orth] A[merican] Review, "Kin beyond the Sea."

Sunday, 6th October, 1878.— My talk at Orange Court House, Va., Wednesday must be very brief, and confined to the character services of Madison. His name is linked inseparably with the Constitution of the United States. He is called its father. No man did more in its formation, and no man did more to procure its adoption by the States. As long as free Constitutional Governments exist his work will be held in grateful remembrance. He was wise on all the questions of his time—More than that his wisdom embodied in our Constitution solves every doubtful question which has arisen since his time—and all the questions of the present epoch.

7th October, 1878.—Received today Photographs taken by Sarony in New York last Wednesday. Lucy's are beautiful—mine good.

10th October, 1878.—Yesterday went with Lucy, Gen Devens, Gen Schurz & Mr [W. K.] Rogers to Montpelier, the residence of [James] Madison. We left the Depot about 6½ A.M. after an early breakfast at the Home and reached Orange C. H., eighty miles, about half past ten A.M. At eleven we started in carriages for Montpelier about five miles distant. On the cars we were joined by Col John S Mosby who had charge of the party,[3] his sister Miss M[osby], Capt Chapman, his brother Mr M. and by Mr   Hill, a senator of M[arylan]d Prince Georges County. At Alexandria, by Lewis Mackenzie, P[ost]M[aster], Mr   Payne & his son the clerk of Court, Miss   at Fairfax by Ex Lt Gov   Thomas ("Judge"), Mr [James V.] Brook[e] senator of Loudon & Fairfax, and others. Before reaching Orange C. H. a Committee of Trustees—Mr   Chapman, Edw[ard]C Marshall, son [of] Ch[ief] J[ustice] M[arshall], Col [John] Willis, a ~~grand~~ nephew of Madison, and others.

A crowd of people met us at Orange—and there was speaking. Our train of carriages on a fair Va road reached the Mansion in an hour. It was a satisfaction to find so admirable a place. The House large, with piazza and tall large pillars like somewhat Arlington—on an elevation with perhaps fifty acres of lawn in front, and a noble view of the Blue Ridge. The great trees were very interesting to me.

A white oak near the grave 21 feet in circumference!

A chestnut on ~~left~~ right flank of lawn 37 feet in circumference.

A Black Walnut right of house fifteen feet—A poplar (tulip) eighteen feet.

The oak and chestnut were low and appletree shaped—the poplars and Walnuts of which there were many tall and beautiful. The place is not well kept up and is for sale cheap. $40,000 certainly would buy it with 1100 acres and probably $30,000. A great lack of enterprise thrift and comfort in that region, but the people were many of them well informed and generally, perhaps universally friendly and well disposed to new comers.

A Mr Brasee, of Baltimore has bought and finely improved an Estate this side of Montpelier eight miles, at Rapidan. His elegant barouche and four with driver were at our service and took us to Montpelier.

On the piazza we were welcomed with hearty handshaking by the present owner, Mr Carson, and by a carefully prepared speech by Col [John] Willis. An interesting and enjoyable day.

17th October, 1878.—Returned this morning from the Winchester Fair—dined lunched elegantly at Judge [A. R.?] Pendletons, who has rebuilt on the Mason place, where house the mansion was carried off to the last brick by the Union soldiers. Mr P[endleton] & Mrs. P. live there in superb style. Their son a young lawyer, is a gentleman by nature, and has with culture and talents. Dined with Gov [Frederick William Mackey] Holliday, & homed at his hospitable old Virginia Home. He is a one armed Confederate soldier of liberal and just sentiments.—Sound on the debt and currency questions. —My list of gentlemen to be remembered is rather longer than usual. The Governor's brother, Dr [Richard J. McKim] Holliday, Capt [William L.] Clark the Mayor, Judge and young Pendleton,

18th October, 1878.—White House. We moved in from the Home this morning in a cold rain storm. Guy [Morrison] Bryan [from Texas] and Miss Tilly Anderson, with little Hally Bryan, are our guests. They will sleep with us tonight in the W[hite] H[ouse] and leave for home tomorrow via St. Louis.

25th October, 1878.—We had an agreeable visit to Cumberland [Maryland] yesterday. The party consisted of Lucy & self, Mr Sherman, Gen & Mrs [E. B.] Tyler, of Balt[im]o[re], Maj. [Thomas P.] Morgan, Mr [Lawrence Augustus] Gobright, & my clerk Mr [George A.] Gustin. We left in the midst of a storm at 7½ P.M. Wed. Col Gilpin (Chas.) & Col [Henry J.] Johnson came down to accompany us up to C[umberland]. At C. yesterday morning the weather was perfect. Mr Lloyd Lowndes Jr as Prest of the [Agricultural] Fair [Association], Gov John Lee Carrol[l], Gov of Md, Mr   Reed, Mayor C.~~Booth,~~ Col   Bruce, [incomplete list], were prominent in our entertainment. I made an off hand talk—desultory, but successful and well received. The Governor was profuse in compliment, and apparently sincere.

This is my last engagement of that sort. Now for my Message and other duties.

26th October, 1878.—I will carefully examine the messages of all of my predecessors—especially of Jefferson, Madison, J. Q. Adams, Van B[uren] & Lincoln, on all the topics of which I shall speak.

I must make a clear firm and accurate statement of the facts as to Southern outrages, and reiterate the sound opinions I have long held on the subject. What good people demand is exact justice, equality before the law, perfect freedom of political speech and action and no denial of rights to any citizen on account of color or race—the same to colored as to whites.

30th October, 1878.—White House. We celebrated last night the 29*th* anniversary of the Cin[cinna]ti Literary Club by a dinner to the members residing or present in Washington. The list is as follows [Ainsworth R.] Spofford, [W. K.] Rogers, T. C. H. Smith, Samuel P. Butler, Gen [Reuben D.] Mussey, R. B. Warden, W[illiam] W. Warden, Jno. E. Hatch of Cinti, Judge C[harles] P. James, Henry Reed, A[aron] R.

Dutton, Cleveland Abbé, Wm. Guilford, Henry C Borden, & self. Also Mrs Hayes, Mrs Rogers, Gen Hastings & Webb C Hayes. Mussey read a good paper. Butler a fine poem. The witty paper of [Benjamin M.] McConkey in 1854 burlesquing the style of R[alph] W[aldo] Emerson, was read by Spofford.

1st November, 1878.—Mr Evarts repeated the remark made about a squeaking voiced Chase opp. to Windson [Windom?] "His voice is admirally adopted to reading fine print."

Mr Ambrose Thompson says our Greenback currency originated with an omnibus driver who called in the absence of change for postage stamps—hence the postal currency.

6th November, 1878.—White House The elections of yesterday ~~are~~ show very gratifying results. The States of New England are solid for sound principles. The crushing defeat of [Benjamin F.] Butler [Democratic candidate for governor of Massachusetts] was one of the best events that had happened since the war. Unscrupulous, able, rich, untiring he was the most dangerous and wicked demagogue we have ever had. When he found he could not rule this administration as he had ~~the last~~ hoped, he declared war on it and me. At the close of his last interview on the Methuen P[ost] O[ffice], he said with significant emphasis "You will regret this"—after a little hesitation, recollecting himself, he said, "because it is wrong!"

Everywhere in the North we are stronger than in any off year since the war, except possibly in 1866 when [Andrew] Johnson was overwhelmed. The South is substantially solid against us. Their vote is light—our side was unorganized—a host of people of both colors took no part. The Whites must divide before we can hope for good results there. The blacks poor, ignorant, and timid cant stand alone against the whites.

In my message I must treat this result as a decision in favor of resumption, undisturbed—in favor of reform, in opposition to all revolutionary schemes which would destroy the stability of our government. It is in one word a verdict against Butlerism.

It is

1. A verdict in favor of a sound constitutional currency—in favor of a currency equal to gold.

1½. A verdict in favor of maintaining unstained the National Credit.

2. A verdict against all revolutionary schemes, threatening the stability of our form of Government.

3. A verdict against Communism, Socialism, and ~~every form of agrarianism~~ repudiation.

4. In a word it is a verdict against Butlerism in all its forms.

5. The only regret is that the better elements of the South ~~which~~ were not so organised as to have a share in the victory. No doubt many good and conservative men have been elected. Probably a large majority ~~may be counted on~~ are in their judgments and consciences opposed to the wild and dangerous doctrines which which the better sentiment of Mass and of the rest of the Conservative States of the North have so decidedly condemned.

We are for

1. A sound constitutional Currency—specie and paper—both equal in value to gold.

2. A maintenance of the ~~national~~ public credit.

3. Equality of rights to all States and for all the citizens of all the States.

4. We are opposed to inflation and repudiation.

5. We are opposed to all revolutionary schemes ~~for~~ hostile to the Stability of the Government.

6. We are opposed to Communism, ~~repudiation~~ Socialism repudiation, & inflation.

7th November, 1878.—Dr Geo. A. Quinby owns & resides at Monroe's home in Loudoun County Va near Aldie P[ost] O[ffice]. It is called Oak Hill and is nine miles from R R at

Leesburg Va. He is formerly from N.Y.—is a good farmer, & prosperous & contented. He invites me to visit him.

[Memorandum] Geo. William Curtis, West New Brighton Staten Island N.Y.

White House 12th November, 1878.—It now looks as if the Nov. elections had settled all questions as to the Presidential title—that *Potterism* is dead. But Butlerism, cheap money schemes still live. The popularity of silver, the unpopularity of Banks, or rather of money lenders as embodied in the National B[an]ks, are strong enough to be corner stones of parties and platforms. They will probably divide the Democratic party, and so strengthen the Republican; but if all the discontent could be embodied in one party, with cheap money and plenty of it as its watchwords, the power of such a party would be ample for mischief, and it might, for a time, rule the country.

In South Carolina and Louisiana, and perhaps in some of the other cotton States grave charges are made that the Constitutional provisions which guarantee equal citizenship have been practically nullified. That by fraud or force or intimidation colored citizens have been disfranchised.

By State legislation, by frauds, by intimidation and by violence of the most atrocious character colored citizens have been deprived of the right of suffrage—a right guaranteed by the Constitution, and to the protection of which ~~good faith~~ the people of those States have been solemnly pledged.

President Monroe in his third annual message, Dec. 1819, congratulates Congress on its meeting in the public buildings so far completed &c &c. The Capitol then first occupied since its rebuilding.

20th November, 1878.—By this morning's paper it is reported that Judge [Walter Quinton] Gresham at Indianapolis was informed by the foreman of the Grand Jury that the President had directed that a certain case, the case of Carey W.

Miller should not be prosecuted by indictment. The Judge replied that the President could not interfere with the duties of the Grand jury—that by their oaths, they were bound to indict if the facts warranted it.

The facts are the M[ember of] C[ongress] from Indianapolis applied for a pardon of Miller. On the ex parte showing a good prima facie case was made for a pardon prior to prosecution. But before finally deciding I preferred to hear what could be alleged on the other side. For this purpose I preferred delay. There was no danger of an escape. The crime had been long known. Therefore the Dist. Atty was directed not to prosecute at the next term, then just about to be held with a view to further inquiry into the facts. It was thought if the young man continued to behave well, and the facts on investigation warranted, that either no prosecution would be ~~made~~ had or a pardon could be properly granted. There was no interference with the Grand jury. The direction was to the District Attorney as to his duties and was in strict conformity with law. ~~and~~ The precedents are also abundant from the days of Washington to Grant inclusive. The President has always been in the habit of giving such instructions. Judge Gresham was hasty. He was *not* well informed as to the facts. When the grand juror—the foreman of the grand jury made his statement he should have inquired of the District Attorney for the facts. The Foreman did not pretend that he had any personal knowledge of the matter. The Judge went off half cocked on heresay, or he blundered grossly if he had the facts.

The direction was to the district attorney as to his action with a view of delaying prosecution until the question of the propriety of a pardon could be investigated. The grand jury were not addressed or approached even, in the matter. The order telegraphed to the District Attorney was in these words * * * "postpone" * * *

24th November, 1878.—Civil Service reforms

1. No dictation of appointments by M. C.'s.

171

2. No money or work for political parties or leaders required.

3. Minor officers to be secure in their tenure as long as their conduct is ~~satisfactory~~ correct official & personal without regard to political opinions.

4. No compulsory assessments.

5. The unsparing prosecution of all who betray their trust.

6. No relations by blood or marriage appointed.

25th November, 1878.—Handed at 9½ A.M. to Mr Sturdevant about three fourths of my message to be confidentially printed, viz, parts

A. Introduction and yellow fever.

B. Treasury.

C. Library.

D. Cruelty to Animals.

E. War.

F. Navy.

G. Attorney General.

H. Agriculture.

I. Postmaster General.

White House, 29th November, 1878.—Thanksgiving dinner yesterday passed off well. Dr [John] Lanahan preached a great sermon at the Foundry [Methodist Church]. God in all human affairs, overruling them for good. At dinner all of the clerks, their wives and little ones. [General Russell] Hastings and Emily, in all at table, 28. A turkey, Narragansett from R. I., gift of Senator [Henry B.] Anthony weight 25 3/4 lbs. Another from Col Linthacum [John Lewis Linthicum], Frederic[k], Md, 23½ lbs. Music after dinner, recitations by little folks. Andrews Rogers in sailor costume, the hero. In the evening Webb, Lucy and I walked out, called on Gen Schurz, Mr Evarts, Judge [John M.] Harlan—all at dinner or *out*—and on McCrary and Garfield who were *in*. Lucy well and in fine spirits—looking her best. Message finished and nearly all printed!

The Senators are coming in daily. The callers thus far are [Justin S.] Morrill & [George F.] Edmunds of Vt, [Theodore F.] Randolph, of N.J., [Simon] Cameron of Penna., [Henry J.] Davis, of W. Va., [John T.] Morgan, Ala., [William Pitt] Kellogg, La., [William B.] Allison & [Samuel J.] Kirkland, Iowa, [Richard] Coke, Texas, [Isaac P.] Christiancy, Mich., [John H.] Mitchell, Oregon, [Alvin] Saunders, Neb., [A. H.] Garland, Ark., [William] Windom, Minn., [Joseph E.] McDonald, Ind., [Charles W.] Jones, Fla., [Thomas W.] Ferry, Mich., [Samuel J. R.] McMillan, Minn., [Thomas F.] Bayard, Del., [Stephen W.] Dorsey, Ark., [Timothy O.] Howe, Wisc., [Henry B.] Anthony, R.I., [David] Davis, Ill., [Richard J.] Oglesby, Ill., [Blanche K.] Bruce, Miss., [John W.] Johns[t]on, Va., [Bainbridge] Wadleigh, N.H., [Henry L.] Dawes, Mass., [Preston B.] Plumb, Kansas, [Samuel B.] Maxey, Texas, [Algernon S.] Paddock, Neb., [J. B.] Eustis, La., [Frank] Hereford, W. Va., [Ambrose E.] Burnside, R.I., [D. H.] Armstrong, Mo., [John J.] Ingalls, Kas., [Newton] Booth, Calif., [George F.] Hoar, Mass., [Stanley] Matthews, O., [Angus] Cameron, Wisc., Gov [Isham G.] Harris, Tenn., [James B.] Beck, Ky., [Matt W.] Ransom, N.C., [Francis] Kernan, N.Y., [Edward H.] Rollins, N.H., [and] [Daniel W.] Voorhees, Ind.

NOTES

CHAPTER VIII

[1] This was the beginning of a long trip to the West that would prevent any diary writing for almost a month. Hayes and his party traveled as far as Fargo, North Dakota. The ostensible purpose of the tour was to deliver an address at the Minnesota state fair at St. Paul. But actually Hayes wanted to bring a message to people at all points—that the country was on a sound economic basis and that resumption of specie payments would bring greater prosperity. At St. Paul and in speeches in other cities he defended the financial policies of his administration and upheld the principle of what he called "honest money."

2 This is an unusually frank analysis of the Southern problem—and of the failure of his policy to accomplish its objectives. He had hoped to create a conservative white Republican support that would recognize the rights of the Negroes. Reluctantly he was beginning to acknowledge that it might not work out as he had expected.

3 Mosby was the famous Confederate guerrilla who in 1864 had operated in the same general area where Hayes had served.

Chapter IX

DEC. 4, 1878–MARCH 18, 1879

4th December, 1878.—My Message was sent ~~in~~ to the two Houses of Congress on the 2*d* soon after 12 M. It seems to be generally well received. Such stalwarts and irreconcilables as the New York Times are severe in their strictures upon it. No doubt the Bourbon press, which represents the extreme sectionalism of the South will be equally bitter. This was ~~to be~~ expected. It will doubtless continue to the end of my administration.

I am likely, I fear, to lose Gen Devens from the Attorney Generals office by his acceptance of the N[ew] Engl[and] Cir[cuit] judgeship.[1] It is difficult to fill his place satisfactorily. If our stalwarts would permit it, I should ask A. H. H. Stuart of Va. to take his place. The probability is that the attacks on such a course by the bitter brethren would damage the good cause of pacification, more than his appointment could benefit it.

* * * I had a slight chill followed by fever today, but have not been sick enough to drop any work or duty.

8th December, 1878.—Now for the Civil Service in case the N.Y. appointments are confirmed. The first step in any adequate and permanent reform is the divorce of the Legislative from the nominating power. With this, *reform* can and will successfully proceed. Without it reform is ~~difficult~~ impossible. When the N.Y. nominations are confirmed, in case that is the result I can go ahead with public efforts to reform the Service. A special message must be prepared to go in with Mr D. B. Eaton's report. I will make the principal point—the first point—as above indicated. Argue it fully. The people must be educated to expect and require their M.C.'s to abstain from appointments. They must not expect them to obtain places. Congressmen must not claim to have a share of the appointments, either principal or minor places.

9th December, 1878.—Weight on White House scales in ordinary clothing, hat off—190 lbs.—Bad cold continues. Chill & fever gone.—

11th December, 1878.—7½ A.M. x x Cold not so bad—chills &c gone.

14th December, 1878.—7½ A.M. Weather good—health good.

16th December, 1878.—Yesterday, Sunday, a gloomy rainy day. In the evening the V.P., Gen Sherman, Dr & Mrs [John Maynard] Woodworth, Judge Matthews, the Atty Genl. & Maj [William] McKinley, called. Mrs W[oodworth] at the piano in the Red room. "Grandfathers clock" and other plantation melodies made a cheerful evening. Gen [Sherman] discussed the death of [Princess] Alice, the war of the English agst the Afghans—the routes to India and Australia. Noble steamers, well equipped, no accidents—and our visit to N.Y. the 30th to attend the Bryant memorial exercises of the N.Y. Historical Society.

The political event of the last week, is the opposition of Conkling to the N.Y. appointments. This is a test case. The Senators generally *prefer* to confirm [E. A.] Merritt and [C. K.] Graham.[2] But many, perhaps a majority, will not oppose Conkling on the question. Senatorial courtesy, the Senatorial prerogative, and the fear of C's vengeance in future control them. He is like Butler, more powerful because he is vindictive and not restrained by conscience. The most noticeable weakness of Congressmen, is their timidity. They fear the use to be made of their 'record'. They are afraid of making enemies. They do not vote according to their convictions from fear of consequences.

17th December, 1878.—Bright and beautiful.—How to get the requisite information to appoint Postmasters without practically giving it to the Members of Congress is one of the questions. Last night I took up the papers in the Lebanon, O., case. There were eight competitors. Three women—two widows of officers. Three or four of the men were were well qualified and well supported by the people. I appointed a crippled private soldier. He was getting a smaller pension than the ladies received—poor, honest, moral and religious, with the requisite business qualifications.

21st December, 1878.—The first snow of the winter this morning. One or two inches whitens the ground and it is still snowing.

Dined with the Cabinet and Gen Sherman and Mr Justice [Samuel F.] Miller last evening. Mr J[ustice] Miller did the most of the talking—in a fine natural way and in the most charitable and friendly spirit. Of [Nathan] Clifford he told anecdotes—favorable ones—and spoke in the highest terms of his conduct both matter and manner, as president of the Electoral Commission. "Marshall could not have done better." [3]

23d December, 1878.—Last night Evarts & Sherman went to N.Y. to attend the New England dinner. Congress has taken a recess until Jany 7, /79—Mrs [Linus C.] Austin of Cleveland, has been with us since Tuesday, 10th. Rutherford came from Cornell Saturday morning. Birch will be here the last of this week. Frank Hickok & bride, Mr [John N.] Jewett of Chicago & Mrs. J[ewett], Charlie Anderson & bride. Enough to make the House merry New Years day.

24th December, 1878.—1. Col Herron of Pittsburgh—Pension agent. Marshall, P. O.— 2. Fire Comm[issioner]s—Schurz.

— 3. Mr Mills wants a battery of guns for Houston Co[unty], also Galveston Co. 4. Reply to Bryant Memorial [committee]. 5. Chicago, U.S. Court rooms—Get better rooms some how? How is it? 6. To Gen Hawley—Hyde of Tenn. should be appt'd. 6. Hyden to be a copyist? See Gen Payne! 7. Spofford about Presidents' portraits.

25th December, 1878.—A happy day for Fanny and Scott. Lucy not quite well. Mrs [Linus C.] Austin and Lizzy and Lena Scott visiting us. Ruddy at home. More presents than ever before. But a long day! We are prosperous—our main ideas more acceptable than ever—Resumption seems assured—The Southern policy safely vindicated.—We both long to be at home, and free and at peace! Two years more of responsibility, care, and labor!

27th December, 1878.—There is a world of useful information on public affairs in J. Q. A[dam]s' Diary.

In 1835, Apr, May, &c., Mr A[dams] was much interested in the bill to restrict Presidential patronage, advocated by Clay, Webster & Calhoun. He offered it, and supported the House agst the pretensions of the Senate. The whole subject was thoroughly investigated by him for future use in the debate he looked for in 1835-6.

He says "A public life ought to be a perpetual sacrifice of resentments."

"In the turbid stream of political life, a conscientious man must endeavor to do justice to all, and to return good for evil, but he must always expect evil in return."

See J. Q. A's Rept on the Smithson bequest—He speaks admiringly of Halleck in 1836, Jany—.

26th [28th] December, 1878.—Twenty six years ago [on December 30, 1852] we married. A happier event for me—for both of us—than either of us then ventured to expect. All of our children are now here. Birch from Toledo, Rutherford from Cornell, and Webb and the dear little ones. We also have Mrs Austin, Lizzie and Lena Scott, and two daughters of my friend [John W.] Herron from Cincinnati—Jennie, now Mrs Charles Anderson, with her husband, and Nellie [later to become the wife of William Howard Taft]. A fine company who make the house ~~vocal~~ alive with laughter, fun, and music.

[*Genealogical memoranda*]

I. Matthew Beckwith of New London, Hartford, Branford, & Lyme, Ct., from 1639 to 1680 m (Eliz?)

II. Matthew a son of pre[ceding], Lyme, by 1[st] w[ife] Eliz, had

III. Elizabeth, [daughter] of pre[ceding], b 4 Feb 1679 m[arried] *prob[ably] to James* Birchard, my ancestor, 17 Mch 1679 & had s[ons] & d[aughter]s.

I. Joseph Jacobs prob[ably] came from Engl[and] to Windham Co., Ct—Mansfield or Windham ("near the line"), had w[ife] Sarah.

II. Dr Joseph Jacobs Jr. m[arried] 8 Nov. 1728, Marah (Martha?) Storrs, d[aughter] of Samuel Storrs, one of the proprietors of the Town of Mansfield, d[ied] 15 Sept. 1790, in 87*th* yr. ~~8 Nov 1728.~~

III. Sarah Jacobs dau. of pre[ceding] b[orn] 13 Dec 1735 m[arried] Elias Birchard (my gr[eat] grandfather), 25 Jan 1758.

I. Samuel Storrs, Barnstable, fr[om] Sutton, Nottinghamshire, Engl[and], m[arried] 6 Dec 1666, Mary dau. of Thos Huckins; he rem[oved] to Mansf[ield] & d[ied] 30 Apr 1769.

II. Samuel, a son of pre[ceding], b. 17 May 1677, m[arried] Martha, had s[ons] & d[aughter]s, & d[ied] 9 Aug 1727.

III.   Martha? b[orn] Feb 1704 m[arried] Dr Joseph Jacobs Jr., 8 Nov 1728.

IV.   Sarah, dau[ghter of] pre[ceding] m[arried] Elias Birchard, 1758, see above.

———

I.   Thomas Huckins,* Barnstable, had liv[ed in] Boston & was standard bearer of [an] art[illery] co[mpany], 1637-9, m[arried] 1642, Mary Wells.

II.   Mary Huckins ~~dau of pre.~~ dau. of pre[ceding], bapt. 29 Mch 1646, m[arried] 6 Dec 1666 Samuel Storrs (see ane . . .)

*Thomas Huckins was the sixth on the roll of the A. & H. Art Co. of Boston & was Ensign of the Co. in 1639. See Hist. of A & H Art. Co. He emigr[ated] to Barnstable & ~~died at sea after~~ m[arried] Mary Wells in 1642 Left chil[dren]. See [James] Savage, [*A Genealogical Dictionary of the First Settlers of New England* . . . Boston, Little, Brown and company, 1860. Four volumes. Volume I, pp 151-2; Volume 2, p. 487].

I.   Thomas Newberry of Dorchester, 1632-5, m[arried] Jane & had

II.   Rebecca Newberry, m[arried] Rev John Russell & removed with him to Hadley.

III.   Samuel Russell, son of pre[ceding] m[arried] Abigail Whiting.

———

[The] V. [Fifth] Vol[ume of] Holinshed's *Chronicles* [*of England, Scotland, and Ireland*], p 243, about year 980 A.D., contains the account of the valor of the first noted man of the Hayes family. "An husbandman with two of his sons, busie about his work, ~~with two of his sons~~ named Haie, a man strong and stiffe in making and shape of bodie, but in-

180

duced with a valiant courage." * * * "caught in plow-beame in his hand." * * * "The King gave him armes three scutchons gules in a field of silver, a plow-beame added thereunto, which he used instead of a battel axe when he fought so valiantlie in defense of his own countrie."

———

Belle Nicholson [Isabella Eugenia Nicholson] knows the history of the Webb family farther back than any one I have met.

About 1791 Isaac Webb married Lucy Ware at or near Winchester Virginia.—He was Lucy's Grandfather. *His* father was also named Isaac and resided in Richmond County, Va., North Farnham parish. He died when his son (Lucy's gr[and]-f[ather]) was six months old. His wife was Fanny Barber; *prob[ably]* the daughter of Capt Wm. Barber, one of the vestry of North Farnham parish. See [William] Meade, Hist. of Ch in Va. [*Old Churches, Ministers, and Families of Virginia* (Philadelphia, 1861), two volumes].

Isaac Webb, the gr[and]f[ather] was Captain.

Absence from W[ashington]

1878

1.	N. Y.	4
2.	Phila., Apr 24–27	4
3.	Hampton School May	2
3½.	Gettysburg, 30 May	1
4.	West Point, June 12 & 13	2
5.	Wyoming, July 2,3,4 & 5	4
6.	Newark, O., July	4
7.	Ohio & Minnesota trip, Aug 30–Sep 25	27
8.	Madison's Home, Oct. 9.	1
9.	Winchester Va., Oct. 16	1
10.	Cumberland Md. Oct 24	1

51 [days]

1st January, 1879.—We returned last night from New York. Mr [George William] Curtis' address at the Academy of Music on [William Cullen] Bryant was excellent and admirably delivered. He was plainly dressed in a black frock coat, buttoned—read from Mss, lifting the sheets and throwing them over to the left pile which grew as the other on the right dimished. With a good strong voice, ~~suffi~~ he delivered, rather than read his address for one hour and fifty seven minutes without a break, or moments hesitation, in superb style.

The applause was frequent, moderate usually, the most enthusiastic when he repeated with fervor the sentence quoted from my inaugural. A Reception afterwards at Mr Frederic De Pyster's. Returned ~~via~~ as we went in Tom Scott's car with Evarts, Senator [Francis] Kernan, Gen Sherman, Gen Devens, Dr [George Bailey] Loring, and Miss E[varts], Miss K[ernan], Miss L[oring] & Mrs S[herman] with Birchard and Sherman E[varts].

Weather for our reception and the day held favorable—not bright—cloudy—cool, but frozen dry and hard.

Before eleven A.M. snow fell pretty rapidly making a dismal day. But the floral decorations, the smilax and foliage plants, the music and gas made the rooms cheerful—the crowd was gay—the garb and ornamental costumes of the Diplomatic Corps, of the Naval and Military gentlemen, lent brilliancy to the scene. The crowd of people was not so large as last year —more colored people—more Congressmen, and more of the young—perhaps also more of the old people of the District. Our visitors enjoyed it vastly.

2d January, 1879.—A severe storm from the west put the mercury down rapidly this afternoon. Three of our guests left this evening notwithstanding. Mrs [Linus] Austin for Cleveland (her home) and Mr & Mrs [John N.] Jewett for

Richmond, Va. Lucy has a difficulty in her throat, and is in bed taking medicine tonight.

3d January, 1879.—Coldest day. 1° below zero in front of the house north side, 3° below by thermometer in waiting room at 9½ A.M.!! The sun shining beautifully, and only an ordinary wind blowing! Is not this unprecedented in Washington?

Lucy is better, but still abed with her throat.

4th January, 1879.—Still very cold—slightly milder than yesterday. Resumption [of specie payments] has gone off well so far. More gold brought in for notes, than notes for gold! A great event if it sticks, as I believe it will.

I am meditating a California trip with Gen Sherman. One car for me and my party—one for him and his friends. I have invited to go with me the Vice President, John W Herron & wife of Cinti & Mr Wm D[ean] Howells & wife of Cambridge. Lucy and Webb with our orderly William T. Crump will also go, and possibly Rutherford or Birchard. Possibly the Secretary of War & wife will also be my guests. Say ~~in all~~ for my car 10 or 11 persons.

10th January, 1879.—I am blamed for the pardon of [Ezra Hervey] Heywood convicted in Boston of sending obscene matter through the mails. A man guilty of circulating writing or publishing obscene books—books intended or calculated to corrupt the young would find no favor with me. He ~~crimes~~ should be punished ~~without~~ surely. ~~But~~ In the case referred to the pardon was granted on ~~grounds~~ principles perfectly well established in reason and by safe precedents

1. Imprisonment imperilled his health as shown by the certificate of respectable medical authority.

2. There was no intention to violate the law, and

3. In my judgment the law was not in fact violated—the pamphlet was not ~~in any~~ obscene matter.

Indeed, I think the real objection to Heywood's act ~~was not, and~~ is not that he discussed a question in an objectionable

183

manner, but that he was on the wrong side of the question. That he maintains the wrong side of the question as to marriage I entertain as little doubt as those who assail me. But it is no crime by the laws of the United States to advocate the abolition of marriage. and to be [?] Pamphlets or books on the wrong side of that question may be obscene publications, ~~but~~ so also may writings on the right side of the question. ~~In~~ In this case the writings ~~may have been~~ were objectionable but were not obscene, lascivious, lewd, or corrupting in the criminal sense.

22d January, 1879.—In presenting the argument against the Senators' right to dictate appointments a quotation from Madison's Speech in the first Congress [would be apt]. See [*Congressional*] *Globe*, Mar 19, 1869, p 163

2d February, 1879.—The contest in the Senate over the confirmation of my New York nominations for the Customs offices is close and as yet undecided. If confirmed against the votes and efforts of *both* of the N.Y. Senators, the decision will be of great value. It will go far to settle

1st the right of Senators to dictate appointments

2d It will decide in favor of keeping the offices out of politics.

In that case I will lay down the law to my New York offices according to the ~~strictest~~ doctrines of the strictest sect of Civil Service reformers. Two or three officers holding confidential relations with the chief officers may be left to their personal preference, but the great mass of appointments must be impersonal, and on principles that will stand the test. I shall say to Gen [E. A.] Merritt disregard all influence, all solicitation, all pressure—even if it come from me, or his immediate chief, the Secy of the Treasury. In this way the question can be fairly tested, and the value of the Civil Service rules have an impartial trial in this, the most important office in the Country.

I put the issue on solid grounds in a short Message which I

sent to the Senate on Friday 31st [January]. In the preliminary skirmishing we have had slightly the advantage, and we seem to be gaining. Judge Matthews leads ~~the~~ on our side. Postponement has seemed to be our policy. Matthews beat Conkling 28 to 26 last Monday on postponement, and 35 to 26 last friday on the same question. The decisive vote will be taken tomorrow, Monday.

4th February, 1879.—We are successful. The New York nominations, [E. A.] Merritt and [Silas W.] Burt, were confirmed against Arthur and Cornell, after five or six hours debate by a vote of 33 to 24. Thirteen (13) Republicans voted to confirm. There were two or three others who were of the same mind, but were controlled by promises. One or two would have voted with us if their votes had been needed. I will now write to Gen Merritt my views and wishes as to the conduct of his office. Something like this

My Dear General:

I congratulate you ~~most heartily~~ on your confirmation. It is a ~~great~~ great gratification to ~~me~~ your friends, very honorable to you, and will prove I believe of ~~great~~ signal service to the Country. My desire is that the office be conducted on strictly business principles, and ~~with~~ according to the rules for the Civil Service which were adopted, or recommended by the Civil Service Commission in the administration of Gen Grant. I want you to ~~feel~~ be in making appointments and removals perfectly independent of mere influence from any quarter. Neither my recommendation, nor Mr Shermans, nor that of any Member of Congress, or other influential person, must be specially regarded. ~~in this matter~~. Let appointments and removals be made on business principles, and according to rules. There must, I assume, be a few confidential places filled by those you personally know and trust, ~~personal friends,~~ but restrict the area of patronage to the narrowest limits. Let no man be put out merely because he is a friend to Mr [Chester A.] Arthur, and no man put

185

in merely because he is our friend. The good of the service should be the sole end in view. The best means yet presented seems to me to be the rules recommended by the Civil Service Commission, and ~~adopted~~ approved by ~~the last~~ President Grant. I shall issue no new orders on the subject at present. I am glad you approve of the Message and I wish you to see that all that is expressed ~~and~~ or implied in it is faithfully carried out.

Again congratulating you, and assuring you of my entire confidence I remain

Sincerely

R B Hayes

6th Feb 1879

My Dear Sir

I beg you to receive my sincere congratulations on your confirmation. My desire is that the result may prove advantageous to the country. I have written Gen Merritt that I wish the office conducted on business principles, and under sound civil service rules. You were on the commission under Gen Grant. I therefore request you to have a conference with Gen Merritt and Gen [C. K.] Graham and agree upon a ~~brace~~ body of rules for the government of your offices, based on the rules ~~refuted~~ reported by the commission with such alterations as you deem advisable.

Sincerely

R. B. Hayes.

To Hon. Silas W. Burt

6th Feb. 1879

My Dear General

My hearty congratulations on the result of Monday's work in the Senate. We must see that our pledges are faithfully kept. Let the offices be conducted on business principles, and under fixed rules, and the public will be content. Please confer with Gen Merritt and Mr Burt, and agree upon a course of conduct.

Sincerely

R. B. Hayes

Gen. C. A [K.] Graham.

14th February, 1879.—There can be no complete and permanent reform of the Civil Service until public opinion emancipates Congressmen from all control and influence over Government patronage. Legislation is required to establish the reform. No proper legislation is to be expected ~~until until~~ as long as Members of Congress are engaged in procuring offices for their Constituents. It is not for me to lay down rules for the personal conduct of Members of Congress on this subject. I shall certainly give due weight to information ~~reported by~~ received from Congressmen whether it is volunteered or given on my ~~solicita~~ request. The end the public are interested in is the independence of Congressmen ~~from~~ of all responsibility for appointments, and this depends ~~on the~~ largely on the people themselves. Let government ~~patronage offices~~ appointments be wholly separated from Congressional influence and control, except as provided in the Constitution and all needed reforms of the Service will speedily and surely follow. Impressed with the vital importance of good administration in all departments of Government I must do the best I can unaided by public opinion, and opposed in and out of Congress by a large part of the most powerful men in my party. I had written a letter to Gen Merrit which taken with my Message embodies the leading principles on which I desire the officers appointed by me to administer their offices. I will have them printed together, and send them to important offices, as occasion seems to demand.

20th February, 1879.—Both houses have passed a bill intended to prevent the Chinese from coming to this Country in large numbers. I am satisfied the present Chinese labor invasion—(it is not in any proper sense immigration—women and children do not come) is pernicious and should be discouraged. Our experience in dealing with the weaker races—the negroes and indians for example is not encouraging. We shall oppress the Chinamen, and their presence will make hoodlums ~~and~~ or vagabonds of their oppressors. I therefore would consider with favor measures to discourage the Chinese from coming to our shores. But I suspect that this bill is inconsistent with our treaty obligations. I must carefully examine it. If it violates the national faith I must decline to approve it.[4]

The [E. H.] Heywood case, convicted of sending obscene matter in the Mails

Private

Feby 21, 1879

My dear sir:

With no time for letter writing, I say a few words touching the subject of your note to Mrs. H[ayes].

Public men are so used to abuse and misrepresentation that a level headed man cares nothing for it. But it does touch me to find that *you*, knowing me as *you do*, can for a moment be disturbed even by such an article as the enclosed. False *certainly*, and malicious probably the article is. *One* man was pardoned after serving six or eight months on the decided recommendation of the Pardoning officers of the Bureau of Justice, on grounds perfectly settled and unassailable, and which are considered sufficient by every Christian man to whom I have named them, including the best and most trusted men of the M.E. Church, clerical and lay. The man is a very dangerous man, openly opposing religion and marriage. *I do not discuss his pardon publicly, because I believe it my duty to suffer misrepresentation rather than give him the increased influence for mischief which my advertisement would surely do.*

I have had almost eight years experience in the use of the pardoning power. I act upon rules as to leading cases which are perfectly sound in the judgment of all well informed people. In this case I was right. But to say so as I might, with the reasons for it, would do injury. Let it pass in silence, as one of the mistakes, if you please, of the President.

[R. B. Hayes]

Rev. Dr. R. M. Hatfield
 Evanston, Ill.

23d February, 1879.—The Chinese bill now likely to pass both houses—has passed both but is waiting action of the House on Senate amendments—attracts much attention. As I see it, our treaty with China forbids me to give it my approval. The treaty was of our seeking. It was proposed by our Minister to China, Mr [Anson] Burlingame. He became the Ambassador of China to this Country, and in Washington negotiated it with Mr [William H.] Seward. It was first ratified by our Senate and sent to China for ratification there. It was applauded by all parts of this Country. The Pacific Coast joined in this. It is now claimed that it has proved unsatisfactory and pernicious, and the bill in question seeks to prevent the mischiefs complained of by a measure which violates its most important provisions. We have accepted the advantages which the treaty gives us. Our traders, missionaries and travellers are domiciled in C[hina]. Important interests have grown up under the treaty, and rest upon faith in its observance.

One of the parties to a treaty cannot rightfully by legislation ~~for~~ violate it.

~~The~~ When a question of national faith is involved, we should deal with all nations on ~~with the weakest~~ the same principles—footing. We should deal with China precisely as we would expect—and wish other nations to deal with us under similar circumstances.

The whole subject was thoroughly understood when this treaty was made. For twenty years the Chinamen had been coming. Complaints were made. Laws passed to prevent it. We chose to enter into the treaty. If we assuming it to have been a mistaken policy. It was our policy. We urged it on China. Our minister conducted it.

In the maintenance of the National faith it is in my judgment a plain duty to ~~decline to allow~~ withhold my approval from this bill. We should deal with the China in this matter precisely as we expect and wish other nations to deal with us.

All the protection which the treaty gives to Chinese subjects, who have come to America in the faith of that treaty would be withdrawn. In like manner our citizens who as missionaries and in Commercial pursuits ~~would who~~ are domiciled in China would be left without treaty protection.

Under these articles the Chi have the rights of the most favored nation in this Country.

We stand for the sacred observance of treaties.

We abrogate without notice, without negotiation, the vital articles of a treaty of our own seeking, and it may be truthfully said of our own making. No precedent for such action except in cases which justify war.

Grant that the results are unsatisfactory and pernicious.

We make no complaint to China before taking action.

No change in facts has occurred since the treaty was made ten years ago. No new and sudden emergency has arisen. The same causes of complaint.—The same facts were there before our eyes.

Our Countrymen on the Pacific Coast with great unanimity, and with the utmost earnestness desire a change in our relations with China. They are entitled ~~to our~~ to have, and they should have our sympathy in this matter. If we could put ourselves in their places it is absolutely certain that we should think and feel as they do. With this opinion We should at once devise ~~enter afor~~ appropriate measures to give them assurance of relief. This can be done long before there is any material increase of their present difficulties without any violation of the national faith, and without any real or substantial departure from our traditional policy on the subject of immigration.

26th February, 1879.—Last evening we had a new sort of gathering for the White House. An official entertainment to the Diplomatic Corps. Guests invited, and refreshments. The difficult point was to draw the line among officials and the exclusion of all unofficial persons. It was solved as follows: We invited all members now in Washington of this and the next

Congress, all Cabinet and U.S. judicial officers in the City, the heads of bureaus, Army officers of the rank of Colonel and upwards, Naval officers of the rank of Captain and above, the Secy of the Smithsonian, head of Agriculture, printing [bureau], elected officers of House and Senate, all ex-representatives to Foreign powers, Ex-Speaker Winthrop,   .
The only private citizen invited was Mr [William Wilson] Corcoran.

Mr [George] Bancroft spoke warmly about it—said it was the finest affair ever had in the White House— Many others talked in a similar strain. It was no doubt a successful and enjoyable affair. Lucy and I received and shook hands with the stream of people about two hours as they were coming in, and after a few minutes promenading, I with Mrs [William] McKinley, Lucy with Mr Geo Bancroft (the venerable historian) we again took our places in the East room fronting the main entrance and a little back of the central chandelier, and again shook hands for an hour with the departing guests. We did not enter the dining rooms until after ~~the~~ eleven when the affair was happily over.

28th February, 1879.—Our party to the Diplomatic Corps was all that could be desired. One mistake was made. We did not include among "officials" the reporters—the gentlemen of the press. Strictly they are not officials. But their connection with Congress is so intimate and important that they might properly be included with the officers of Congress. Nothing sinister was intended. It was not considered. But it has ~~Hence~~ great irritation, and ~~with many~~ accounts of the affair corresponding with the feelings of the writers have been sent out. The exclusion of wine from the list of refreshments has turned out exceedingly well. There is a good deal of dissipation here. At the receptions of the British Minister, and at that of the Mexican Minister disgraceful things were done by young men made reckless by too much wine. Hence the necessity for our cause is obvious and is commended in unexpected quarters.

Many of the Foreign gentlemen speak of it with approval. We shall stick to it.

The Veto of the anti Chinese bill is generally approved East of the Rocky Mts, and bitterly denounced West of the Mts. I was burned in effigy in one Town! No doubt a population without women—without wives and mothers—that cant assimulate with us—that underbids our laborers—~~will be~~ must be hateful. It should be made certain by proper methods that such an invasion can not permanently override our people. It cannot safely be admitted into the bosom of our American Society.

9th March, 1879.—The 45*th* Congress adjourned without making provision for the support of the Army, and for the ~~payment of the~~ payment of the civil list. I therefore immediately called a special session of the 46*th* Congress to meet the 18*th*—two weeks after the adjournment of the 45*th* Congress.[5]

The appropriation bills were defeated by a disagreement between the House and Senate. The House insisted on the right to force its views on several questions of general legislation upon the Senate ~~under~~ by the threat of defeating appropriations if the Senate did not yield. The Senate adhered to its own views—hence no appropriations for the purposes named. Now the question will come to me. The Senate and House in the 46*th* Congress being both Democratic will insist on the right to repeal the Election laws, and in case of my refusal will put the repeal on the appropriation bills. They will stop the wheels—block the wheels, of government if I do not yield my convictions in favor of the election laws. It will be a severe, perhaps a long contest. I do not fear it—I do not even dread it. The people will not allow this Revolutionary course to triumph.

See [Allen G.] Thurman in [*Congressional*] *Record*, Mch 8 [3], p 13. Quote in reply to this Jackson's claim to *represent* the Nation.

18th March 1879.—The House organized today by electing Mr [Samuel J.] Randall Speaker. Tomorrow I will send in my Short Message to Congress in Special Session. An important struggle then begins. The Democrats will attempt by coercion of the President to secure a repeal of legislation which I deem wise and important. This is to place the executive "under the coercive dictation" of a bare majority of the two Houses of Congress. This is a mode of evading the Constitutional provision as to the Presidents participation in legislation. It is "a measure of coercion", a revolutionary measure.

I must resist it to the last extremity. I say first: I object to the repeal of important legislation designed to protect the elections—to secure the purity, the honesty, the sanctity of the ballot box.

But what is of far more importance I object to the bill because it is an unconstitutional and revolutionary attempt to deprive the Executive of one of his most important prerogatives. To coerce him to approve a measure which he ap in fact does not approve.

The measure is "attached to an appropriation bill as a means of coercion."

No precedent shall be established with my consent to a measure which is tantamount to coercion of the Executive. I stand for "the equal" and Constitutional "independence of the Executive."

The independence of the different departments of the government are essential to the progress and the existence of good government.

Loving the order, the peace, the perpetuity of our institutions, I must go on to the end of my term.

If in these laws there are provisions which interfere with free and fair elections, let those provisions be so amended as to secure such elections. All attempts to improve them have my sympathy, and all wisely directed efforts to that end shall have my support.

I will not be driven to consider the repeal of these laws under unlawful duress and menace attached to appropriation bills. Mch 8 [3] p—.

If separate bills are presented for the repeal of laws authorising soldiers to be sent to the polls at elections to keep the peace—and to repeal all laws prescribing test oaths See [James B.] Beck [of Kentucky in *Congressional Record*] 8 [3] Mch [page] 10, I would consider them and approve them.

But to attach ed these measures to appropriation bills for the purpose of coercing the action of the Executive presents a very different question.

As to some of the measures which it is sought to repeal, I would regard it a duty to approve separate bills framed in the usual way for that purpose. And as to all of them, I would consider with favor independent measures modifying amending and improving them without impairing their efficiency. But presented in a way and for the purpose of coercion I cannot even consider their merits.

NOTES

CHAPTER IX

1 Devens eventually decided to remain in the cabinet.

2 Since the autumn of 1877, Hayes had been carrying on his fight to establish executive control of appointments. The particular battle was with Senator Conkling over positions in the New York Custom House. Conkling was able in 1877 to prevent confirmation of Hayes's appointees. But after Congress adjourned, the President suspended Arthur and Cornell, Conkling's men, and made interim appointments of his own. Now Hayes was offering the names of Merritt and Graham for two of the top posts. A third nominee was S. W. Burt.

3 Justice Clifford, although a Democrat, served as president of the Electoral Commission. Despite the opinion of him quoted here, he considered the work of the Commission to be partisan, viewed Hayes as a usurper, and refused to enter the White House during his presidency.

4 Chinese immigration to the United States was permitted under the Burlingame Treaty of 1868 with China. When the treaty was negotiated, the Chinese were welcomed as needed laborers. But in the intervening years a strong feeling had developed against their presence, especially on the

Pacific coast. The legislation before Congress would in its final form limit the number of Chinese coming in one ship to fifteen and abrogate two clauses of the treaty—one recognizing the right of men to change their home and allegiance and another providing for the protection by each government of the citizens of the other living under its jurisdiction. At stake in the matter, as Hayes grasped, were some serious questions. Could one party to a treaty unilaterally repudiate a part of it? And could the Senate by legislation alter the nature of a treaty?

5 The Democratic House had attached to the army appropriation bill a "rider" repealing the law authorizing the use of troops to maintain order in elections. The Democrats had also affixed riders to the appropriation bills to the executive and judicial branches. These amendments were not acceptable to the Republican Senate; hence the special session.

Chapter X

MARCH 21, 1879—MAY 28, 1879

21st March, 1879.—Yesterday was Webb's birthday. He is twenty three years old. Without the scholarship I wish he had, he is yet a boy to be content with. He is honest, cheerful, very sensible, and full of social and friendly qualities, with good habits and principles. My war horse "Old Whitey" died yesterday at Fremont. Two dispatches were received telling the fact. Little Fanny in the presence of strangers spoke lightly of it, but she had a good cry over it alone.

We had Gen Garfield and Mr [Frank] Hiscock of the House with Dr [William?] Waddle [Waddell] and Miss Devens at dinner last evening. The talk was very interesting— chiefly on the political situation.

The threatened dead lock on the appropriation bills is maintained, but the manner in which Democrats will present it is not yet known to the Republicans. ~~if it~~ Perhaps it is not yet decided how to do it. Many of our Senators are in favor of vetoing all bills repealing either the discretionary test oath, the right to preserve peace at polls, and the election laws. My inclination is to approve the first two measures if presented to me separately, and ~~to~~ I shall certainly veto any repeal of the election laws which does not substitute equally efficient measures in their place.

But it is conjectured that these measures will be presented

to me as riders to different appropriation bills. Suppose this is done how shall I treat the appropriation bills which contain the repeals which I would approve if they were separate bills? Is not this a sound view. The repeal, for example of the discretionary test oath, is attached to an appropriation bill as a measure of coercion. I will not consider the merits of the bill so presented. The appropriation bill is essential to the continuance of the Government. It ~~will appear~~ is perfectly well known that the Executive approves it. It is the duty of Congress to pass it. The rider is attached to it to get rid of the Constitutional exercise of the veto power to defeat that measure in case the Pres't does not approve it. This is the first attempt in our history to break down the functions of the Executive by ~~the threat of~~ coercion. I cannot approve it.

22d *March*, 1879.—The Democratic members of the two Houses of Congress have held caucuses, and appointed Committees to decide the course they will take as to the measures which caused the dead lock between the H[ouse] and S[enate] at the ~~last~~ end of the last session. It now seems probable that they will put all of their repealing measures into one bill. A bill which will repeal the jurors' oaths, the law authorising sodiers to keep the peace at the polls, and the ~~act~~ law which provides for the appointment of deputy marshalls to protect the polls. If presented to me I should probably feel it to be my duty to veto such a bill.

The law as to the appointment of marshalls ~~at the~~ to protect the ~~elections~~ supervisors and prevent violence and fraud may require extensive modifications. But that there should be such officers—officers as impartial as possible, is almost a necessity. Do not the States provide some such machinery for State elections? Is mere supervision enough? Do not the States provide for keeping the peace at the polls at State elections? Should not the Nation do it at National elections? Whatever force by means of civil officers the States provide should be provided by the Nation.

Mem. Get the laws of a few of the leading States—the new and the old.

Experience has shown that the protection and conduct of National elections can not safely be left to the States.

I cannot consent to the repeal of the election laws enacted by Congress, unless others equally effective are substituted.

Believing that the National authority is ample ~~for the protection, and secu~~ to protect and secure free and fair Congressional elections ~~at Congression~~ I must insist upon retaining the existing laws until ~~other and~~ more efficient and better are enacted.

If national military force is not allowed to keep the peace at the polls civil authority should be provided for that purpose.

The enactment into law of this bill will turn over to the mere local authorities, the most important National elections. The constitution ~~did~~ does not contemplate this. It provides Art I, Section 4, "The Times, Places and Manner of holding Elections for Senators & Representatives, shall be prescribed in each State by the Legislature thereof; but the Congress may at any time by Law make or alter such Regulations, except as to the places of choosing Senators. * * *

The principle of the bill is a denial of the right and duty of the Nation to legislate for the security of Congressional elections.

The State may have its military at the polls and its police, but the Nation is to be powerless. Or rather, The bill admits the right the duty and the necessity for National Supervision, but denies the power to make it effective.

23d March, 1879.—The Democrats in Congress show signs of receding from their revolutionary programme. They now talk of trying to remove the objectionable features in the election laws. But the claim still seems to be all but universal that the National government has no right to use force either military or civil to protect the freedom of the elections. The

States alone are to be allowed such powers. *They* may have both military and police forces, but the Nation is to be confined to mere supervision, observation, and the like. This will not do. The authority of the National Government must be maintained.

The proposed compromise measure does not protect the polls from military interference. There may be soldiers, police, and the posse comitatus at the polls. But they must be under State authority. The National Government alone is forbidden to exhibit force to keep the peace, and protect electors. This is not the ~~true~~ principle of the Constitution. This whole power is expressly vested in the United States.

The facts in which the law had its origin are well known. In the opinion of many well informed citizens the election ten years ago in the first State in population and political power was carried by frauds. The true result of the State ~~and~~ Presidential and Congressional elections were ~~changed~~ revised. ~~The result of the~~ An investigation confirmed the belief of the public and this law was enacted.

Recent elections in several States have shown that State regulations are not to be relied on to secure free and fair elections.

It is believed that if the Congressional elections at which members of the present ~~Congress~~ House of Representatives were chosen had been free and fair, and their results correctly reported and acted upon that there would have been a majority of the present House opposed to the bill I am now considering.

With the experience of the last twenty years before us we are forced to the conclusion that the ample powers which the Constitution confers to regulate Congressional elections should be exerted in furtherance of laws as equal and impartial in their operation as can be devised. If the present laws need changes in order to render them more effective and at the same time more impartial ~~and~~ less expensive, and less liable to abuse, I shall cheerfully unite with Congress in securing such modifications of the existing Statutes. But to repeal ~~these laws~~ without substituting better—especially if it be done on the principle that the National authority is to be subordinate to the State is in my judgment wholly inadmissable.

~~With~~ If there had been free and fair elections in the States during the last few years there would now be Republican majorities in both ~~branches~~ Houses of Congress—in the Senate and in the House.

The question presented by this bill is not whether we shall have the present law or a better one but between this law and no National law at all for the protection of the elections.

If the present laws are not so ~~in~~ efficient ~~& expensive~~ as may be desired—if notwithstanding these laws great outrages have been committed against the freedom and fairness of elections it is our duty to provide wiser Statutes.

It is not to be denied that in the last elections great wrongs were done—the laws ~~protec~~ conferring suffrage on Citizens were not regarded in some parts of the Country. These provisions should be enforced. Let us have an effort to do it.

Is it not the plain duty of the National Government to make such regulations respecting the election of Members of the House of Representatives as will secure free and fair elections? In case the States fail to do it?

The debate on the adoption of these laws.

The debate on the Tariff bill in 185–.

Suppose the President should say I will sign no bill on any subject of general legislation until the appropriation bills are passed?

I do not call in question the motives of those with whom I am unable to agree, but believing the tendency of this bill is to deprive the President of the Share in legislation which is conferred   embodied   upon him by the Constitution I can not approve it. The attempt to pass a measure ~~under~~ a measure that the Government ~~will~~ shall be stopped if the President declines to yield his convictions of duty has never yet succeeded —has never before been made.

To ~~yield~~ consent to it is to make a radical change in the character of the Government. The House of Representatives ~~becomes~~ in case this principle is established becomes the Government. With the sole power to originate the measures upon which the existence of Government depends, and with the doctrine established that the House may legitimately refuse to act unless the other branches of the Government obey its commands, the House of R ~~become~~ will become a despotism with unlimited power.

If in all of the States ~~at~~ the last Congressional elections had been ~~With~~ free and fair elections— ~~with proper laws efficiently enforced~~ this bill would it is believed never have been passed by Congress.

For my ~~position~~ views on fair elections see Message on Registry laws in Ohio, and the last regular message.

It is the right and duty, and the necessity exists, that the President should exhaust ~~every~~ his constitutional authority to secure to every American citizen possessing the qualifications of an elector the right to cast at each congressional election one unintimidated ballot and to have it honestly counted. The existing legislation enacted ~~for this~~ with this end in view—for this purpose—is not so effective as it should be—it may be liable to abuses, but it should not be repealed without providing in its stead ~~some~~ a measure more wisely framed to accomplish the desired object.

Authority exists in most of the States to use the military at the polls. (?) If the red shirts can be present at the polls in S[outh] C[arolina] why can not the blue coats be called in also? [1]

Authority exists in the States also to marshall civil affairs at the polls to keep the peace, to make arrests and the like—may not the Nation do the same?

The views of this subject contained in the last annual message may be here repeated.

To protect the right of citizens, and to secure ~~for~~ peaceful and fair elections, the States generally have provided laws authorizing at State Elections the military to keep the peace, and to protect the voters—there are also laws authorizing civil officers, sheriffs, police and the like to maintain the freedom of the State elections. In the absence of regulations by the National authority the States would still have soldiers at the polls, and civil officers authorized to make arrests.

But the Constitution confers supreme authority on the National Gov't as to the regulation of the National Congressional elections.

25th March, 1879.—The Constitution makes the National laws ~~of Congress~~ supreme in the regulation of Congressional elections. But if the laws now on the Statute books regulating the elections are repealed, without the enactment of others in their place the State governments ~~alone~~ will have full control of them. ~~at these elections.~~ State Executive officers may have state troops at the polls—state sheriffs and police may be there to exercise all the authority conferred by these laws on National officials.

The complaint is that there are to be soldiers and officers of the law at the Polls. This is not changed by this bill. It merely puts State soldiers and officials in place of National soldiers and officials as safeguards for National elections. The experience of the past is against this change.

Washington, 26th March, 1879.—I begin a new book in the midst of serious and perplexing events. A dead lock on appropriation bills. The Debates so far have ~~given~~ been very ~~little~~ meagre. Mr [George F.] Hoar in the Senate today made a prepared speech against the Democratic revolution. Conkling yesterday spoke on the election of new officers in the Senate. The Dems turned out all of the old election officers. C managed to drag in by the heels his hatred of me. Poor man he will never forgive me for having beaten him in the Cinti Convention. He has been a traitor to his party three times. His treachery stopped short of results only because he lacked the back bone required to make it notorious and effective. Once in 1876 in the election—in 1877 in the Electoral Count—and in 1878 in the Potter Committee's attack on the Presidential title. I showed my disregard of his attack yesterday by sending to the Senate today the name of one of his friends, President A[ndrew] D. White [of Cornell University], a capital man, for the Berlin Mission.

27th March, 1879.—The question still lacks adequate statement. If the two houses of Congress make the approval of any measure of general legislation a condition without which they will refuse to make the requisite appropriations to carry on the Gov't should the President yield to that coercion?

[George Ticknor] Curtis [in *History of the Origin, Formation, and Adoption of the Constitution of the United States* ... (New York, 1858)] 2*d* Vol., p 257 "The [Constitution ... gives] authority of [to] Congress at 'any time' to *'make* or alter such regulations' ... when exercised *must be paramount*, whether a State regulation exists at the time or not."

The authority of the general Government to regulate by law *at any time* the ~~election~~ Congressional elections ~~at "any time"~~ is paramount.

Whatever is to be done in regard to elections, here is ample power to do it. Whatever the States may do as to their elections the United States may do as to Congressional Elections—and that, as Curtis says, *"whether a State regulation exists at the time or not."*

Believing that the National government under ~~this section~~ the Constitution has power to enact and enforce laws regulating Congressional elections so as to secure fair and peaceful elections, and convinced that the necessity for such legislation exists I cannot approve any measure for the repeal of ~~existing~~

the present laws on that subject ~~legislation~~ which does not provide wise and efficient safeguards in pursuance of the ~~4th~~ fourth Section of the first Article of the Constitution for the elections which are under the National control.

By the constitution Congress has ample power to *"make"* *"regulations"* prescribing "the times, places, and manner of holding elections for Senators and representatives" in Congress.

Congress is thus invested with all the powers now exercised by the States in relations to these elections, and can prescribe election districts, provide for election officers, the mode of announcing, authenticating, and declaring the result, and prescribe offences for officers, voters, and others—in all respects affecting or connected with such elections. The Constitution "authorizes Congress to do supremely whatever the State legislatures may do provisionally on any part of the subject.

Note.—Mr [Daniel] Webster, in regard to the right of suffrage, lays down "two great principles of the American system: 1. The right of suffrage shall be guarded, protected, and secured against force and against fraud. 2. Its exercise shall be prescribed by previous law; &c. 6, Webster's Works [Boston, 1857], p 224.

The laws which it is proposed to repeal are safe guards of honest elections—of fair & peaceable elections.

27th March, 1879.—I am convinced that it is my duty to exhaust every executive authority committed to me by the Constitution and the laws to secure to every citizen having the requisite qualifications the right to cast one unintimidated ballot and to have it honestly counted.

These laws ~~were~~ framed as safeguards of honest elections, adopted by more than two thirds majority in both houses of Congress, approved by the President, carried into effect during the last eight years in many States, ~~acted~~ upon without serious question of their validity by any Court of the U.S. called into action on the suggestion (application) of both political parties in different States, with a very general conviction among the people that National laws are necessary to secure from violence and fraud the National elections. I cannot consent to their absolute ~~and~~ repeal. If ~~laws~~ National legislation (laws) can be framed which will better secure ~~greater~~ impartiality, less expense ~~and~~ or ~~more~~ greater efficiency I will cheerfully cooperate (concur) with Congress in such legislation. But if it is sought to repeal this or any other legislation ~~under the~~ and to obtain the approval of the President by the threat that ~~the Gov't will be~~ Congress will grant no supplies to carry on the Government unless such approval is had, I am compelled by my convictions of duty to use every constitutional authority (means) at my command to prevent ~~such~~ the repeal upon such terms.

Every measure should stand or fall on its own merits. This should be the fundamental principle in legislation.

The ~~correct~~ true principle is correctly stated above.

28th March, 1879.—The appropriation bill for the Army was introduced into the House yesterday in accordance with the Caucus plan and considerable progress was made towards its passage. There is tacked to it the repeal of the right to employ the army to keep the peace at elections. I do not regard the measure thus tacked to the Army appropriation bill as of vital importance. The army as a matter of fact can not and will not be used for that purpose. But the measure is objectionable. ~~as~~ It applies to all elections National as well as State, and ~~seems to appl~~ denies therefore the right of the Nation to keep the peace at the National elections which by the Constitution are ~~within~~ under the National control, and at the same time prevents leaves the power to the States to use State troops ~~to~~ at the National elections. There should be no such discrimination against the National authority. If the presence of the military at elections should be forbidden, the prohibition should apply equally to all ~~troops~~ soldiers, to those of the States as well as to those of the Nation. A general ~~prohibition~~

and equal measure framed to accomplish the purpose of pre-vention any ~~military~~ soldiers wether State or National from interfering in the elections would meet my approval.

The Army can be supported without these appropriations several months, and in case of great necessity they might be postponed until the next regular session of Congress.

Let every measure stand or fall on its own merits.

This repeal prevents persons in the Civil Service of the U.S.—the civil as well as the military officers of the U.S. from keeping the peace at the polls. It is not the military force of the U.S. alone, but it is the civil power also which is to be excluded from the elections.

The President's right is to exercise his discretion and judg-ment upon all bills presented to him, without constraint or duress laid upon him by a coordinate branch of the Gov't.

29th March, 1879.—This is a controversy wh[ich] cannot and ought not to be compromised. The Revolutionists claim that a bare majority in the House of Representatives shall control all legislation, by tacking the measures they can't pass through the Senate, or over the President's objections, to the appropriation bills which are required to carry on the Govern-ment. They claim the right to do this under the Constitution and say it is according to the practice and precedents in England. In the presence of this claim it is idle to talk of compromises as to the particular measures which are used as riders on the appropriation bills. These measures may be wise or unwise. It is enough to say in regard to them, that used as they are to establish a doctrine which overthrows the Con-stitutional distribution of power between the different depart-ments of the Government, and consolidates in the House of Representatives the whole law ~~of~~ making power of the Gov't ~~of legislation,~~ and with it ~~will attempt sooner or later~~ the judicial and executive authority as well, we will not discuss or consider them ~~even~~ when they are so presented. Let the ap-propriation bills be passed in the usual and orderly course of legislation. Let there be no attempt to coerce either the Senate or the Executive. And then at the proper time in the proper way we will be prepared by repeal or amendment to get rid of whatever is objectionable in the existing legislation. I am not a believer in the continuance of the test oaths—I do not ~~care~~ wish to see ~~either~~ soldiers either under the State or the National authority at the polls—I would have all of the regulations as to the safeguards of the elections impartial fair and economical. But none of these questions ought to be even considered ~~when~~ under the revolutionary threat that unless the President yields up his discretion and judgment concerning them, ~~and to present~~ the revolutionists ~~favor~~ will destroy ~~ing~~ the Government.

Unquestionably the true rule or legislation is that each measure should stand or fall on its own merits. This wise and salutary rule has however been departed from so often, and the practice has been so long established by the action of all parties that I may not now insist upon its non observance as a ground for withholding my approval to bills submitted to me. There are also ~~perhaps~~ it is believed ~~more than~~ several cases in which the House has practically carried its point against the Senate or the Executive ~~by the~~ by tacking the measure to the (under pain of losing) appropriation bills. But no ~~other~~ example has been found in our legislative history in which this has been attempted on the ground that the until the opening of this controversy at the ~~beginning~~ close of the last Congress.

To tack political legislation (measures) ~~on~~ to appropriation bills and to threaten ~~with~~ that no appropriations will be made unless the political measures are approved is not in my judgment constitutional conduct.

30th March, 1879.—To incorporate political measures in appropriation bills ~~to me~~ and think to make the approval of such legislation by the President ~~a~~ the condition on which appropriation bills for the support of the Government can alone be passed ~~this~~ is ~~surely~~ revolutionary and unconstitutional.

To attach conditions to an appropriation bill is revolutionary and unconstitutional. I cannot consent to consider even—to discuss conditions attached to an appropriation bill for the purpose—the purpose not disguised, but openly avowed and asserted to be as a proper and constitutional exercise of the power ~~of the House of Representatives~~ of a mere majority in the two houses of Congress to compel the President to give up his right to exercise his discretion and judgment upon all bills presented to him. It is the principle of coercion embodied in this bill which can under no circumstances receive my approval. It is an attempt to compel the President to approve a measure of general legislation under the penalty of, if he ~~fails~~ withholds his approval, of stopping the operations of Government by ~~stopping~~ denying the supplies necessary to carry them (it) on.

The object of this struggle is the removal of National authority in any efficient form from the polls, even at National elections. State authority with force at its back, both military and civil, is to be permitted to remain but all National authority whether military or civil is denied.

No case has been presented in the debates on the question in which a bare majority of the two houses of Congress has claimed the right, or undertaken, to coerce the President by tacking political legislation to appropriation bills.

31st March, 1879.—We had at family dinner yesterday, Sunday, my kinsman Linus Austin of Cleveland, Senator and Mrs [Henry L.] Dawes, ~~and wife,~~ Mr & Mrs [Samuel] Shellabarger, Mr [Frank] Hiscock, Gen [Anson G.] McCook, Gen [J. Warren] Keifer, and the young people, Miss McDowell of Chicago, [Aurelius Milford] Tracy, classmate of R[utherford's] at Cornell, and W[ebb] & R[utherford.] An unusually chatty and lively dinner. Gen K[eifer] explained the word GerryMANDER—all knew the ~~connection~~

history of the first part of the word in its connection but Gen K. explained that the animal the misshapen district resembled was the Sala*mander*—"Oh no said one it is a Gerry-Mander. Mr Dawes explained how caucus came from caulkers with whom Sam'l Adams and [John] Hancock arranged beforehand to control the public meetings in Faneuil Hall and the old South Church. I told how the Ohio "Tin pan" was a translation (*sic?*) of the latin name of the Saloon called the tantine. A *Res-taur*-ant is called because it is a *bully* of a *thing*.

The talk was mainly on political topics. Garfield's speech [Anson G.] McCook thought the finest speech he ever heard. All praised it. Mr Evarts and the young ladies, came in during the evening—also Senator [George F.] Hoar and Gen Devens. — Mr Evarts regards the controversy as growing out of the wish of party leaders to make issues for the next Presidential election. That the Dems began it—and that the Republicans are now in it. That the Administration should keep out of it. He doesn't seem to see that it is merely a new form of the old conflict between ultra state rights, and the National doctrines. The S[tate] R[ights] men are for putting all power in local authorities. We believe the National authority should be exerted to protect elections ~~in~~ which ~~the~~ are National, so far [as] the Const[itution] sanctions. We have none too many safeguards for the elections. Mr Hoar agreed with me that in the present situation I may properly veto any appropriation bill which contains political legislation tacked to it for the purpose of compelling me to approve it under the threat that otherwise the Gov't shall be stopped for want of supplies, no matter what may be the merits of such legislation. In doing it the history of this Extra Session may be given to show the purpose of the House in attaching ~~the~~ a political measure to the appropriation bill.

They mean to obtain and establish a precedent (which will lead to) for the consolidation of all of the powers of the

Government in the hands of a bare majority of the H, of R.

The present controversy is in no sense partisan and it is not a question of race or color. The old question States Rights always seems closely related to Sectional and race conflicts, but this is chiefly as a reminiscence. No present interest of a Sectional character is involved. The laws concerned are mainly employed in the densely peopled regions of the North.

The law proposed to be repealed was passed by the concurrent action of both political parties, and became a law by the approval of Pres't Lincoln.

2d April, 1879.—Wherever United States laws are violated there should be United States authority ~~forces~~ civil or military to enforce them.

The practice of annexing general legislation to appropriation has become a serious abuse. Every measure should stand on its own bottom. The two houses of Congress and the Executive should insist upon a return to the old method of legislation on this subject. If ~~I do not wish in advance~~ there were no other objection to this measure than the fact that it ~~couples with~~ embodies in an appropriation bill essential to the support of the Gov't legislation which is not pertinent to the general purpose of the bill would be a sufficient objection, the bill having passed by a bare majority vote, to justify the President in withholding his approval of the bill.

When did the practice of tacking general legislation to appropriation bills begin? What debates upon it have been had?

There has been and there will be no such use of the military of the U.S. to keep the peace at elections, as justifies a discrimination against the military of the Nation. If there is to be such prohibition it should include also the military of the States. What the States may do as to State elections, the United States should not be forbidden to do as to National elections.

3d April, 1879.—There is no urgent demand for this measure on account of military interference in elections. No complaint of such interference has been heard from any ~~part of the States that such interference occured~~. quarter at the recent elections, or at any election ~~since~~ under the present administration. There is no pretence even that the military power of the United States has been exhibited at or near any place of election. The army is fully ~~impo~~ employed, ~~and is not sufficient for~~ guarding the frontiers and the territories. There is no practical necessity for ~~the measure~~ prohibiting ~~of~~ the military forces of the United States from keeping the peace at the polls and no petitions, memorials or complaints have been received from the people. If the necessity existed for ~~denying~~ preventing military interference with elections this measure is not broad enough. The National elections should be protected from ~~State~~ all military interference. The State military force should be excluded ~~also~~ as well as the National forces. The power of the United States to regulate and control the Congressional [elections] is ample and supreme. If military interference is feared in the future, there should be no discrimination against the United States at these elections. Let the States forces be prohibited. ~~But the practi~~

But the practical importance of this measure is not in its provisions against military at the polls. It forbids all United States ~~authority~~ power from being present at the polls to keep the peace. The prohibition extends to the civil authority as well [as] to the military. The terms of this bill are "No military or naval officer ~~of the~~ or other person engaged in the ~~military~~ civil, military or naval service of the U.S., shall order, bring &c &c

In short this bill denies to the United States the power to protect its own election by either military or civil authority. This power is granted to the U.S. (conferred upon the United States) in express terms by Sec[tion] 4 of Art[icle] 1, and may be exercised at any time. The power granted is ample and supreme. It is as follows,

> [The Times, Places and Manner of holding Elections for Senators and Representatives, shall be prescribed in each State by the Legislature thereof; but the Congress may at any time by Law make or alter such Regulations, except as to the Places of choosing Senators.]

Under this clause of the Constitution the act which the bill before me seeks to repeal was passed fourteen years ago. All political parties in Congress united in its support. It ~~passed the~~ was approved by President Lincoln, and under it, it is believed, no man's right to vote has been interfered with. Certain it is that no complaint of such interference has been heard during ~~my~~ this administration.

The whole case stated.

My objections to the bill are as follows,

1. The measure of repeal is uncalled for, and wrong.
2. The method of annexing it to an appropriation bill is wrong.

Under the first head, the following are the points

1. No demand for it—no practical ~~harm~~ necessity for it.
2. The National military and not the State forbidden.
3. The U.S. Civil as well as the military authority withdrawn.

Under the Second

1. All tacking of political legislation on appropriation bills is objectionable.
2. This case is one of an attempt to coerce the President, and herein of the history of this attempt at the last session.— its consequences—and my purpose.

Enlarge on the denial to the Genl Govt of the power to

enforce its own laws of unquestioned Constitutionality—the denial of power to protect its own elections.

If military power at the polls is not desirable the State military power should be forbidden.

———

It has been said that the President possesses no part of the legislative power of the Government. This is not the doctrine of the fathers. Gen [Andrew] Jackson says [*The Statesmen's Manual: The Addresses and Messages of the Presidents of the United States* ... compiled by Edwin Williams (New York, 1846–1849)], 2d Vol 844

"The legislative power, *subject to the qualified negative of the President*, is vested in the Congress of the United States."

5th April, 1879.—This is a late Spring—cold windy and, this morning, snow! Webb started with Fanny last evening for Fremont. He expected to begin gardening at home, and to plant trees and shrubs.

The bill has two parts— It makes appropriations and *it amends the election laws.*—the laws relating to the elections.

When was the first restriction placed on the power of the U.S. to keep the peace at the polls, and elsewhere? Has it not been a power always used? Prior to the Act of Feb 1865 The U.S. forces might be placed under civil or military authority whenever the officers in command of them might in their discretion order.

Suppose the Gov of N Y calls on the President under the 4*th* Art of the Const and the circumstances require action at the polls on election day, does this bill forbid it? See Art 4, Sec 4.

6th April, 1879.—The cold gale is at an end—a calm bright morning.—Still cold for the season.

The House is to *originate* Revenue bills—but this method claims for the House the right to originate all legislation.

Where matter ~~not pertinent~~ is tacked to an appropriation

213

bill ~~which~~ which is not pertinent to it, it ought not to become a law unless two thirds of both Houses consent to it.

Sec 6. of the Bill makes criminal the acts of Marshalls which are authorised by the genl election laws and yet does not repeal those laws? Keeping the peace is a duty of the Marshall under the gen[eral] election law?

What is the reenactment of the Act of 1865 in the Revised Statutes? When? Did the reenactment imply approval by Congress? 1873 or 1874.

Act of June 18, 1878 prohibits use of Army as a posse comitatus—

5529 Rev[ised] Stat[utes] prohibits army from interferring
2003 prohibits interference
2024 [also]

These three sections cover the whole subject.

The only interference with elections that has been complained of was under instructions of Atty Gens under Sec 2024.

Bill 4867, Posse Comitatus, House [of Representatives], yeas, 154; nays, 58. Senate, no division.—

Quote [Abram H.] Hewitt p. 4686 Vol 7, [*Congressional*] *Record*, [House Proceedings, June 15], 1878: [Francis] Kernan, p. 4240, Vol 7, [*Congressional*] *Record*, [Senate Proceedings, June 7,] 1878.

The executive power to approve or return without approval, according to the conscience and Judgment of the President is a *trust*.—It cant be given away without a violation of official oath. It is my duty to guard ~~the~~ as a trust the powers conferred on the office which has devolved upon me.

No power denied to the army by this ~~law~~ bill now belongs to the army. If there was doubt on this question the act of June 18, 1878 removed it. The last elections for Members of Congress, and all ~~other~~ of the recent elections in all of the States have been held without so far as I am informed a single ~~any~~ complaint even of Military interference.

The following is Act of 1878 so far ~~the~~ as it is applicable to the present purpose. [not completed]

See Garfield's speech in Apr 5 [March 29, 1879?] [*Congressional*] *Record*.

7th April, 1879.—The question as to United States regulations of Congressional elections is in no sense a sectional question or a question of the Civil War. The legislation grew out of a belief that the vote of the largest State in the Union had been defrauded of its true result at [the] Pres[idential], State, and Congr[essional] election in 1868. The violations are found in all parts of the country. Let the legislation be fair, impartial, and with ample guarantys against oppression and corruption. I shall cheerfully cooperate in such legislation.

8th April, 1879.—In 1792, May 2d, Marshalls were given the same powers *to execute* the laws of the U.S. that Sheriffs have in the States.

The Confederate Constitution contained this provision, Sec. [Paragraph] 20, [Section 9], Art 1,

"Every law, or resolution having the force of law, shall relate to but one subject, and that shall be expressed in the title."

Since the passage of the Act of June 18, 1878 no soldier ~~has~~ of the U.S. under orders has been seen at the the place of any election in any State.

Let it be understood that to tack to an appropriation bill any legislation plainly foreign to ~~the~~ its general purpose will imperil the adoption of the law.

The United States troops can not now be lawfully used to interfere with any elections under the pretext that they are keeping the peace at the polls. This prohibition by the foregoing Statutes, framed for the purpose of preventing it, and which are amply effective to that end. See ante p

The objectionable features of present laws should be removed. The laws should be impartial, non-partisan, fair and effectual to ~~as~~ safeguards of the purity of elections. But the safeguards are necessary. The Nation has the constitutional power to enact them. I can not consent to the repeal of existing laws except in connection with the adoption of measures to take their place which are free from the objectionable features of the present laws, and at least equally effective as safeguards of honest elections.

13th April, 1879.—My opportunity to examine the ~~testimony~~ evidence in the case of Gen [Fitz John] Porter is too limited to express a decided opinion as to the finding of the Board, but the character of the Board, and of the investigation and finding are such that I deem it my duty to send their report and the evidence to Congress as presenting a case which deserves their attention.[2]

17th April, 1879.—Riding out with Lucy this P.M. I saw the first peach trees in blossom. A very late spring.

26th April, 1879.—The Army appropriation bill passed the Senate yesterday about 4 P.M. and when we returned from our ride before 6 P.M. Mr. [John] Hanna, M[ember] of C[ongress from Indiana], met me with the enrolled bill ready for my approval. We had the Ch Justice [Morrison R. Waite], Mr [Samuel M.] Young of Toledo, Mr [Robert] Cummings Mr [George W.] Davis of the same place, with [their] wives to dinner—also Mr John H [M.] Boalt, to a family dinner which passed off well.

I put the last paragraphs to my veto message last night. It is now printed. I have read it to Schurz and Devens—They approve. Col Thompson approved the substance of it as I stated it to him. Webb is a treasure ~~also~~ in such a case. [W.K.] Rogers assisted and now at 4 P.M. I am ready to send in my veto. It will not go in until day after tomorrow, Monday.

27th April, 1879.—The civil appropriation bill passed the House yesterday. It will no doubt pass the Senate. The House adjourned–until Tuesday. My Veto of the Army Appro bill can not go in until that time. I must now prepare to veto the

Civil bill. The message may allude to the veto of the Army bill for the general grounds as objection and state briefly

1. The authortiy of the National Govt to regulate (an ample word) the Congressional elections

2. The necessity for such regulation as shown in N.Y. and the South.

3. Refer to the abusc of tacking incongruous legislation to appro. bills.

4. Which is wholly inadmissable if it is done to coerce another branch of the Gov't.

If the election laws are imperfect or objectionable let others more perfect and less objectionable be substituted. Amendment and not repeal is the true remedy.

28th April, 1879.—I read my veto message last evening to Judge Carter [David K. Cartter]. He said "it is all gold—pure gold." "It will be your great act" and the like. Schurz and Devens approved of it decidedly after hearing it all read. I told the points of it fully to Col Thompson and he approved. Sherman, Key, and ~~Devens~~ McCrary fully endorsed my general views before the paper was written. Mr Evarts on hearing my account of it Saturday evening fully approved. I may not call a Cabinet meeting to hear it. There is betting and selling of pools here and in New York on the question whether I will sign or vcto. Friendly Republicans all feel confident that I will sign. [veto?] Hostile Rep[ublican]s profess to be in doubt, and I *hope* I will *sign*. Their number is now small—only the implacables—the patronage brokers.

30th April, 1879.—I sent my veto message to the House yesterday. It was received, but by reason of the death of Rush Clark, a popular member from Iowa, it was not read. If I had known of his death in time I would not have sent the message to thc House yesterday. It was given out to the press as soon as it was delivered to the House. It seems to be well received.

Now for the other bill—the Civil bill. I may deal with it

217

very briefly—merely refer to the former Message, and in a few propositions state my objections to it. I will insist on the constitutionality of the election laws, and on their necessity. They have been in force (*how long?*). Committees of the house (*how many?*) have examined—made investigations as to their operation. The only report I have seen is very laudatory.

The two committees, one from each party agree that the election of 1868 was a monstrous fraud— Mr [William] Lawrence Committee estimates the fraud at 25,000 in New York City alone. Mr [Samuel S.] Cox in his report estimates [it] at more than twenty per cent of the total or not less than ~~30,000~~ 35,424, or 22.72 per cent nearly 23 per cent of the total vote was fradulent.

1st May, 1879.—The message was read in the House and the further consideration of the subject was deferred. In the Senate nothing on *the* topic of the day was done. Caucuses were held but with what debate or result I· do not yet know.

The last utterance of the coercion doctrine was on the 17*th* [of April]. Mr [Thomas Montague] Gunter of Arkansas said

"I assert that we only exercise the high prerogative conferred on us by the Constitution of the country when we attach such legislation as we deem vital to the interests and liberties of the people to the appropriation bills and say without the one you cannot have the other. Like the Indian chieftan [who led his people in their migration until he found a country beautiful beyond comparisons and striking his spear into the ground said,] 'A-la-bam-a', 'here we rest.' " Record 27 Ap p 25 [*Congressional Record*, Volume 9, Appendix, page 34].

It seems not improbable that the Democrats will decide to pass a separate bill forbidding the presence of troops at elections. This is fine and simple. I may sign. They yield two points—the right to *use civil force* at elections —and the claim I make in favor of *separate* bills for general legislation. If a Senator or representative I might vote against such a measure as uncalled for, and needless, believing as I do that the soldiers of the U.S. should not be used at the polls.

3d May, 1879.—Webb and Scott have gone to Fremont. It is very gratifying that all of the children are so fond of their home. Mrs [John W.] Herron and her Willy will come this morning. We are now waiting breakfast for them—[They come] on Pan Handle RR from Cinti.

Mr [Thomas J.] Henderson states squarely the principle of the present position of the House—but I hear Lucy's welcoming salute to the good dear friends. "Why are there not more of the young folks?"

Sunday, 11th May, 1879.—Webb and Scott returned from Fremont after a pleasant visit, this morning about 8 A.M.

The Democrats have not been conservative nor or as I think politically wise. They have passed an affirmative new measure which repeals for the day of election many valuable laws. They call them war measures, and seem to think that as the War is ended these laws should now be mustered out. We are ready to muster out the soldiers, but we dont muster out the flag nor the powers of the law and of the Constitution which enabled us to gain the victory. We dont muster in again the evils that caused the War. Besides it is for the victors to say what shall remain—not for the vanquished.

15th May, 1879.—My veto has been well received.[3] I am congratulated by Senators and Representatives, and by people of all sorts. I am glad to have had an opportunity to do something for the true principles of the Constitution. My first veto maintained the prerogatives of the Executive, and the separate and independent authority of each branch of it [the Government] against the grasping ambition of the House of Representatives. The second maintained the right of the Executive branch to exercise power enough to enforce the laws, and now I am likely on the Civil—the Legislative, Judicial and

Executive appropriation bill with its rider repealing the election laws, to have an opportunity to do something for purity and fairness in elections.

Mr [Francis] Kernan [of New York] in his speech yesterday (see it) admitted the fairness—the conspicuous fairness of the Elections in 1874,5,6 & 7.

17th May, 1879.—We grow corpulent as age creeps on us. Lucy weighed yesterday 170 pounds. I weigh 193, and little Scott aged 8 years following his parents weigh 82.

In treating the question of as to the necessity for the election laws show the State of opinion about the probability of fraud at elections. Quote [Thomas F.] Bayard's despair of good government in great Cities—[Horace] Greeley's letter to Tilden, &c &c.

18th May, 1879.—Mr [William Wallace] Eaton of C[onnecticu]t described our Gov't as "a representative republic of sovreign States!!"

It is claimed that the election of Congressmen is a matter wh[ich] concerns the States alone.—that these elections should be controlled by the States, and not be regulated by the United States.

21st May, 1879.—Lucy and little Fanny left last evening with Mrs [John W.] Herron and Willie for Ohio via B & O RR. We have had a delightful visit from Mrs. H. Good, sincere, dear, friends!

24th May, 1879.—A novel spectacle in this city for some days past. The same thing doubtless in all of the large cities. The Post Masters, Collectors and sub-treasurers have had authority to sell small four per cent bonds—not more than $100 to the same person, so art as widely to distribute them among small investors—among the people of small means. These bonds are now at a premium of two to four per cent. Speculators employ parties to buy for them. $2 is made every time $100. is bought. The poor themselves also rush to get them. The consequence is great crowds of negroes, women boys &c &c gather daily at the Treasury in long procession—each in turn to get his $100 worth of bonds. This morning as early as 7 A.M. the whole open space at the north end of the Treasury was filled with the "cue" of investors. Some go to sell their places in the cue or procession, and do so at from ten to twenty cents or more according to proximity to the selling desk.

25th May, 1879.—The veto message of the Civil appropriation with its attachment of clauses repealing the elections is printed for final revision and correction. My habit is, if time permits, to write my documents, to print and then, having them before me in satisfactory shape, to make the final additions and corrections. I have not in such work been careful as to style, except to have my papers state principles in a way to satisfy men of ability and culture that the statement is sound, and to so phrase and put my propositions that the plain people can readily understand them.

I rode out yesterday with Wm Henry Smith Wm Penn Nixon of Chicago. Both talked pleasantly of the improved condition of public sentiment towards the Administration. Nixon is connected with the Inter Ocean which has been hostile.

The exodus of Colored people from the South still attracts some attention. Its effect is altogether favorable. The tendency will be to force the better class of Southern people to suppress the violence of the ruffian class, and to protect colored people in their rights. Let the emigrants be scattered throughout the North West—let them be encouraged to get homes and settled employment.

Lucy and Fanny are still in Ohio. It is lonesome without them.

The annexation to the U.S. of the adjacent parts of the continent both n[orth] and s[outh] seems to be, according to the phrase of 1844, our "manifest destiny." I am not in favor of artificial stimulants to this tendency. But I think I see plainly that it is now for the interests of both Canada and the United States that properly and in order, and with due regard to the feelings of G[reat] B[ritain] the two countries should come under one Gov't. If it were known that we would probably pay the whole or part, of the Canadian debts, or would assume to pay them, would it not stimulate the feeling in favor of annexation in Canada?

28th May, 1879.—Lucy and Fanny returned last night after a short trip to Ohio. Birchard came with them. Also Howard [B.] Smith and his bride, Lizzie McKell. Lucy went out to Chillicothe to attend their wedding. It is very gratifying to see the heartiness and warmth of friendship for Lucy. Her large warm heart, and lively sympathy for or with all around her with a fair share of beauty and talents have made her wonderfully popular. Old Joseph, the veteran at the [Soldiers'] Home who takes care of our house there, told Dr and Mrs [Ebenezer H.] Bushnell who are visiting us that "the old soldiers love and worship her. She is so *human*—not cold, or lofty with them." At the Christian Y.M.A. [Young Men's Christian Association] reception Monday evening, a young man from Indianapolis told an incident. "A sweet lovely little girl of eight returning from Church with her good grandfather—not a Church member—said to him "Grand Pa ~~I wish~~ why dont you belong to the Church—I wish you would be a Christian," and the Grandfather greatly moved, thought of it until he did join the Church—a decision due under Providence to that little girl. That grandchild is now the wife of the President of the United States," and the house came down!

NOTES

CHAPTER X

[1] The red shirts were the rifle clubs that by threatening to intimidate Republican voters, or by actually doing so, had helped the Democrats win South Carolina in 1876.

[2] The case of General Porter went back to the Civil War. Accused of disobeying orders at the battle of Second Bull Run, he was subjected to a court-martial, found guilty, and cashiered from the army. Almost immediately he began what would be a long struggle to have the verdict reversed. The case was complicated by politics. Porter had been known during the war as a Democratic general, and now most of his supporters were Democrats. Not unnaturally, most Republicans tended to think he was guilty. Hayes himself, who had been within ten miles of Bull Run during the battle, had previously believed Porter was derelict. The President agreed, however, to appoint a board of army officers to look into the matter. This agency reported that Porter was inocent. But Hayes, for some reason, chose not to act. He merely transmitted the report to Congress with no recommendation. Perhaps he hesitated because Garfield, a member of the original court-martial, objected to changing the verdict. Porter did not secure full vindication until 1886 and the administration of Grover Cleveland.

[3] The Democrats modified the army bill in some of its provisions, hoping the new version would be acceptable to Hayes. But he vetoed it also.

Chapter XI

JUNE 2, 1879—OCT. 5, 1879

2d June, 1879.—It is now reported that the joint Dem caucus committee has agreed on a plan of operations with regard to the dead lock. It is in effect a back down. But it does relieve the party to some extent from its awkward predicament. It may in some of its features be quite as objectionable as former measures. This will depend on details which I must carefully examine.

Birchard left for Toledo last night. Rev. Dr. Bushnell and wife go to Annapolis today. Our young kinspeople, the bride and groom, Howard Smith and Eliza McKell are still with us.

The new plans of the Democrats are too foggy in the rumors of them that I do not see clearly the way out. If they propose to defeat old laws, laws long ago placed on the Statute books, or constitutional provisions, they can do it in two ways. 1. Simply appropriate for other objects but not for them. 2. They can prohibit the enforcement of these laws, or the use of money appropriated, or the incurring of obligations in their enforcement.

I probably could not veto a bill merely because it fails to make all the appropriations which are required. I should [not] oppose a bill wh[ich] contains nothing but what is right. If it is not enough, and the omission is important, I may call a special session to supply the deficiency. But if their new bills deprive by prohibition the Executive of authority which belongs to him by Existing laws or Constitutional provisions it will require a veto.

Copy.

Executive Mansion
Washington

Private

2 June 1879

My Dear Sir,

I need not attempt to tell you how much I regret the conclusion you have reached as to remaining in England as our Representative. The feeling I have on the subject is increased by the considerations which you name and which compel me to acquiesce in your views. During your whole stay in that important and most conspicuous service, I have rested with perfect confidence in your judgment and tact and character. I have known that in every thing which pertains to public duty, and personal conduct in private affairs, you would in all things be an honor to the country and to my Administration. Your appointment I felt to be a privilege when I made it and I shall always count it as one of the most fortunate facts in my conduct of the office I hold. If you adhere to your purpose to return in August, and I beg you to change it if you feel that you properly can, I shall nevertheless still feel under very great obligation to you, for remaining in England so long as you have.

This is written hurriedly, but you will not I trust doubt that it is the expression of my most deliberate and sincere feeling and sentiment in regard to your service.

Sincerely
R B Hayes

Hon John Welsh
   Legation of the U.S.
   London.

4th June, 1879.—5 A.M. Forty five years ago this morning I started in the Stage on my first journey from my home at Delaware, Ohio. Mother, Uncle B[irchard] and Sister Fanny were with me. We started at or about 4 A.M. I was permitted to ride on the outside with the driver. Going to visit kinsfolk in New England—to Vermont and Massachusetts—to see Mountains! the Lake! Steamboats, canals, cities! All of my dear kindred—mother, uncle, sister, long since dead. How I loved them, and I do love them still!

————

The Democrats instead of squarely backing out of their awkward position, or manfully sticking to it, seem disposed to creep out of it in a way to enable them to say that they have gained something by their contest. They cant repeal the laws they object to. They therefore propose to cripple the Govt in its efforts to enforce them.—to make it impossible to enforce them. The laws remain unrepealed. The Dem. plan is to prevent their enforcement.

This plan also embodies the principle that the House may coerce the Executive. It refuses appropriations for the most necessary duties of the Gov't unless the Ex[ecutive] signs a bill which contains provisions which it is known he does not approve. In the regular official and Constitutional methods his views of duty have been communicated to the House. As to the great body of purposes for wh[ich] appropriations have been proposed by the House, there is absolute and complete concurrence. As to one subject not ~~a question~~ strictly germane to to an appro[priation] bill, but general legislation—there is a difference of opinion. The House insists that no appro shall be made unless the Ex yields his convictions on this subject of gen'l legislation. Having failed to secure the direct repeal of the election laws—it is now proposed to prevent their enforcement.

6th June, 1879.—Lucy and I have had a few minutes to talk

226

on this laborious, anxious, slavish life. It has many attractions and enjoyments but she agrees so heartily with me as I say "well I am heartily tired of this life of bondage, responsibility and toil." "I wish it was at an end! I rejoice that it is to last only a little more than a year and a half longer."

We are both physically very healthy—unusually capable of bearing the fatigues incident to the place. We can travel longer, night and day without losing our spirits than almost any persons we ever meet. Our tempers are cheerful. We are social, and popular. But it is one of our greatest comforts that the pledge not to take a second term relieves us from considering it. That was a lucky thing. It is a reform—or rather a precedent for a reform which will be valuable.

7th June, 1879.—The nomination of Gen [Thomas] Ewing in Ohio for Governor may prove disastrous to the Republicans. He is an able man—a good popular debater, and of excellent private character. He is the ablest and most consistent of the Greenback leaders. His aim will be to secure the votes of both the Democrats and the National or Greenback parties. Combined they out-number the Republicans, perhaps 30 000 votes. What should be the Republican plan? The energetic presentation of the best issues. What are the issues, and which of them are, for the Republicans, the best?

1. The conduct of the Ohio Legislature and the administration of State affairs.

2. The conduct of the Democratic party in Congress.

3. The financial questions.

In a spirited contest state issues and State affairs lose their importance as the canvass progre-proceeds. But in this case they are very greatly in our favor, and should not be lost sight of. The long session, the gerrymander, the abuses in the State institutions, and the taxes and expenditures all furnish topics of more or less significance.

But of far more importance is the Democratic proceedings in Congress. The revival of the nullification and secession

227

doctrines of [John C.] Calhoun will be influencial and salient points for attack. The extra session, the attempt to crowd and cripple the Executive and the Genl Gov't, the dismissal from office of Union soldiers and the like.

I suspect, however, that more important than all is the position and record of Gen Ewing in favor of irredeemable paper money and against coin and his opposition to resumption *and* to honest money. His speeches should be carefully examined, both those made in Congress and on the stump. His opposition to [Allen G.] Thurman in 1876— The outgivings of Democratic hard money papers and men should be utilised. This is a real living issue. Gen E[wing] is squarely, and I suspect honestly, on the wrong side. Let it be pushed from the beginning to the end of the canvass, and, the best results possible will in my judgment be obtained. *A collection should be begun at once of all resolutions in conventions or in Congress —all bills presented—all Speeches made by Ewing &c &c.*

11*th June*, 1879.—Soon after the inauguration in 1877 Lucy received a fine large copy, 2 vol[ume]s, of the Doré Bible from an unknown friend. We now have learned from Mrs Secretary [Richard W.] Thompson that the giver is *James N Jones of Boston*. Writing to Mrs T[hompson] about it he says

"In regard to the Doré Bible I merely had a curiosity to know whether it had been received. I would much prefer that Mrs Hayes should be kept in ignorance from whence it came. Shortly after the inauguration I spent an evening in her Company, and I was so much pleased with her gentleness of character that I determined to send her something, and I knew of nothing more fitting than the best of all books. It was not sent for any sinister design or purpose. I have an utter loathing for those who act for a prospective advantage. So I adopted the anonymous way I did in sending it to her. Of course I should feel gratified in having an autograph letter from the wife of our good President, but I must forego that pleasure—however I leave that matter entirely in your hands to do as you think best."

The judicial bill is the only one I have any doubt about. It leaves the election laws without the means for their enforcement. If that was all, there would be no ground for a veto. Perhaps it goes further. I must look into it. It prohibits any officer or any department from ~~contracting~~ incurring any obligation or ~~incur~~ contracting any liability. This is intended to nullify the law leaving it unrepealed. Does it have that effect. May I direct the Marshalls to appoint deputies, notwithstanding this provision? May the Courts appoint supervisors —may these officers act? If not it amounts to a repeal of the law.

No duty devolving on Congress is plainer than the duty to provide the necessary means by suitable appropriations for the enforcement of the laws. Title 26 is in force. It provides that—it makes it the duty of certain officers to make appointments of deputy marshalls and supervisors. The duties of these officers remain. By this bill it is provided that they shall not be performed. Their performance involves the liability of the United States to pay ~~for~~ such officers. All officers & each Dept. are forbidden to do this. It is tantamount to a repeal of the law for this year.

The execution of the law is required during the next fiscal year in but a few districts and is of comparatively small importance. But it is wrong in principle.

Several of the questions presented by this bill have been examined in prior communications, and my views in regard to them have been fully presented to the House of Representatives. These questions are

1. As to tacking legislation on appropriation bills, with a view to forcing the Executive to ~~com~~ approve the legislation in order to obtain the appropriations.

2. As to the constitutionality and necessity for the election laws embraced in Section 26 of the Rev[ised] Stat[utc]s.

13th June, 1879.—Rutherford will probably reach home this morning from Cornell. He has finished his junior year. Webb is still at Fremont. Scott and Fanny are very happy taking their first lessons at the swimming school. *Lucy very well*. Birch returned to Toledo after the Lizzie McKell Smith wedding.

14th June, 1879.—Rutherford returned yesterday. Rather thin, but in good health. He is slightly lamed by an injury to his foot four or five years ago by "Young Ned" in rearing and jumping, coming down on his foot. His taste and capacity as a scholar are for the Natural Sciences. Quick in this direction, he is slow in others.

Will the Attorney Genl give me his opinion about the appointment of a Collector in Bangor, [Maine] after Congress adjourns? The vacancy occurred during the last regular session by expiration of term.

I want to get from Mr [Edward] Clark, the architect of the Capitol, [Andrew Jackson] Downing's plan for laying out *as one park* all of the public ground from the Capitol to the Potomac. This has been a favorite hobby of mine. Last night I learned from Mr [John A.] Kasson that it is not an original thought of mine—or rather that Downing long ago urged the same thing. At the meeting of the [Washington] Monument Commission today I will talk to Mr Clark about it.

20th June, 1879.—The Congressional contest with the Executive is near its end for the present.[1] The Legislative bill is in such a shape that I can sign it without a question. The bill is awkwardly framed, but there is no objection to the appropriations which it contains; it can be executed, and the fact that proper appropriations are omitted is not a ground for a veto. The army bill is supported by the great majority of the Republicans in Congress, by the Republican press, and by the Administration. It contains a clause which prevents the Army from being used as a police force at the polls. The rule as to the use of the military at elections was stated by me as follows in the ~~second~~ veto message on the Army bill. The doctrine there laid down has been received as sound by the Republicans of the Country—and I think also by Democrats generally who are not blinded by the partisan excitement of the time. It is the business of "the ~~civil~~ police" the civil authorities, to make arrests of the disorderly and of repeaters and of others guilty of violating the ~~laws~~ election laws at the polls. They will thus keep the peace at the elections. ~~In these d~~ The Marshalls are authorized to appoint deputies enough with ample authority to do this under ordinary circumstances. If these civil authorities are unable to do this the military will aid them in all cases.—not at all as a police, but as part of the military power of the Country. They may be used whenever it is necessary to enforce the laws. That is to say whenever the opposition to their enforcement is too powerful for the ordinary police or other civil officers to overcome the military may be employed to suppress such opposition. This was the law when Congress met. It is the law now. It has not been changed. Before the assembling of the Extra session my views were correctly published in the [*National*] Republican of this city. The action taken since by me is in strict conformity with that publication.

So much for the past. But the important thing is the present situation. The issues now presented to the Country cover all the points of the controversy. The Democrats refuse needed appropriations unless the Election laws are repealed or nullified in the same measure. This raises the

1. question of their right to dictate to the President what measures he will approve. It deprives him of his veto power.

2. It raises the States rights question, by denying to the nation powers with respect to the National elections which the States are left free to exercise.

3. The right & Expediency of *any* National election laws. —we have offered them amended and improved laws.

231

4. It admits the right and duty of National supervision by leaving untouched the Supervisors.

Wednesday, 25th June, 1879.—My fourth veto message at the present session was sent to the House Monday.[2] It seems to be well received by party friends and has certainly thrown our adversaries into the greatest confusion. In a vote yesterday in the House our side on the question of adjournment without appropriations had a majority of 22! Seventeen Democrats and all of the Greenbackers united with our friends!

Judge [Allen G.] Thurman has backed out of his ~~great~~ "vast question" doctrine, and is one of the most urgent advocates of ~~mak~~ appropriations without any riders! It is not yet decided, after several caucuses, what to do. But the probability seems to be that the Democrats will pass a judicial Expenses [bill] without the objectionable section—the second section, and also without any provision for Marshalls or their deputies. Another bill for the Marshalls, with the objectionable rider attached will also be sent to me.

Weight today after eating heartily my noon lunch is 190 pounds.

27th June, 1879.—Yesterday attended Commencement exercises of the Catholic College—Georgetown [University]— in the large unfinished Hall of their fine new building. The young men's performances were creditable. Many prizes were distributed to members of the lower classes. Weather very warm—room airy and cool.

The Democrats have introduced their bills in the form anticipated. The judicial Expenses bill was passed through the House. Its riders are the repeal of the test oath law, and the provision for non partisan juries. This bill I shall approve. The Marshalls bill with its objectionable rider will probably pass today and may reach me tomorrow. I think it is not necessary to repeat in a veto message the arguments heretofore used.[3] A simple recapitulation of the objections will suffice. I will probably show the importance of the Marshalls and the deputy marshalls of the United States, which they propose to leave unprovided for if I refuse to approve their objectionable partisan legislation.

———

1st July 1879.—I today handed S.M. Shoemaker the following note for wh[ich] he will send me in a day or two $7000. from Adams Express Co.

Fremont, Ohio
7 July 1879

On demand the Birchard Library of Fremont Ohio promises to pay to the Adams Express Company or order Seven thousand dollars with interest at six per cent payable semi annually.

Birchard Library
By R B Hayes
President

Endorsed
R B Hayes.

The above is from memory—probably is literally correct—is certainly substantially so.

———

I have heard arguments by [Robert G.] Ingersoll and [Thaddeus B.] Wakeman in favor of pardoning D. M. Bennett, convicted of sending obscene matter through the mails—viz a pamphlet of a polemical character in favor of free love. While I am satisfied that Bennett ought not to have been convicted, I am not satisfied that I ought to undertake to correct the mistakes of the Courts—constantly persisted in by the exercise of the pardoning power. There is great heat on both sides of the question. The religious world are against the pardon, the unbelievers are for it.

3d July, 1879.—I am now experiencing one of the *"ups"* of political life. Congress adjourned on the *1st* after a session

233

of almost 75 days mainly taken up with a contest ~~with~~ against me. Five vetoes, a number of special messages and oral consultations with friends and opponents have been my part of it. At no time—not even after the nomination at Cincinnati, has the stream of commendation run so full. The great newspapers, and the little, have been equally profuse of flattery. Of course it will not last. But I think I have the confidence of the Country. When the [New York] Tribune can say "The President has the Courtesy of a Chesterfield and the firmness of a Jackson,"(!) I must be prepared for the reactionary counterblast.

My convictions have been adhered to equally against party friends and foes. Party friends have insisted that I ought to extend the veto to the 1. repeal of the test oaths, 2 to the jury clauses which provide for men of opposite parties as officers to prepare the lists from wh[ich] juries are to be drawn and 3. to the clauses against the use of the army "as a police" at the polls. But I steadily resisted, and in the end have I think vindicated the power of the National Government over Congressional elections, and the separate authority of the Executive department of the Gov't.

Inasmuch as I stood firmly and successfully against the dictation of my own party leaders in the Senate I have a feeling that the applause given to the firmness exhibited agst the pretensions of the adversary as to the powers of a bare majority of Congress, is not altogether unreasonable.

We go today on the Tallapoosa to spend the 4*th* at Fortress Monroe.

Soldiers Home, 7*th July*, 1879.—We came out to the Home for the Summer on our return from the "ocean voyage" Saturday evening 5*th* July.

On the 3*d* at 3 P.M. we ~~went~~ started down the Potomac on the U.S. vessel (S[team] B[oat]) Tallapoosa Capt [David G.] McRitchie. Our party consisted of Sec of the Treasury, War Navy and Atty Genl and Mrs [Richard W.] Thompson

234

and 2 dau[ghter]s & 2 sons, Mrs [George W.] McCrary and
and Gregory—my boys Webb & Rud. We reached
fortress Monroe early on the 4th—Salute fired—Escorted by
Gen [George W.] Getty and troops to the Fort. At his house
until firing of bombs and large guns at a target—interesting.—
In the afternoon we steamed out of the Chesapeake passing
near Cape Henry, into the ocean for two or three hours. Returning we visited the great unfinished fort on the Rip Raps.
A huge mass of good masonry—with blocks of granite almost
enough perhaps to complete it.

Fireworks at the fort at night—also at the Hampton Home
and fr on vessels in the Roads.

Left F[ortress] Monroe about 10 P.M.

[On the] 5th, A.M. about 7 o'clock reached the vicinity
of Washington's birthplace sixty miles below W[ashington]
in Westmoreland Co[unty] at Pope's creek. Water shallow
anchored a mile out. Sent a boat ashore to spy out the land.
After breakfast, boat not in sight, the four Secretaries, Capt
McR[itchie] and Webb in a cutter attempted to land. Too
shallow. The sailors carried us ashore. With Webb pushed
out, from left of Pope's Creek. Found a Mr Muse ploughing.
Engaged him to show us the birth place one mile off by a cir-
cuitous route, by reason of slo marshes, to the pile of brick
where the Chimney stood. A beautiful clump of big trees also
showed where the Home of the Washingtons stood. It is
perhaps sixty yards from Popes Creek and in a direct line
half a mile from the Potomac. It has fine views of the River.
The land is covered with sea shells, not barren— This is one
of the first visits to the Home of Washington—certainly the
first by President and Cabinet. A monument is to be erected
at the spot simply to mark it. It will be often visited hereafter.

Wrote today to Gov Ramsay [Alexander Ramsey] of
Minnesota inviting him to take the place of Secretary of War
on the retirement of Mr McCrary who is to be judge of the
Iowa Circuit U.S. Court.

The Home, 8th July, 1879.—This has been an unusually cool and dry summer—No rain at the Home for a long time—not I am told since June 10*th*. Last night there was a slight shower.

I walked this morning about 2½ miles passing out of the N.E. gate near the Cemetery, and returning through the E[ast] gate into the Tulip avenue and west of the Hospital by the power House to the Scott statue.

10*th July*, 1879.—Yesterday the Surgeon of the Home, Dr [David Lowe] Huntington left word that there was at the hospital an old soldier named Sergt Gaines who fought under [Major George] Croghan at the defence of Ft Stephenson [during the War of 1812].

This morning taking my six o'clock walk I called at the Hospital and inquired for Sergt Gaines. I was told that he was the old gentleman wearing a straw hat sitting on the porch. I approached him—he arose with a pleasant smile and greeted me with genuine politeness as I told him that I was President Hayes. He was rather below medium height, with a good kindly face, and an intelligent looking man. In reply to questions he said:

I enlisted at Knoxville, Tenn., in 1812 at the age of fourteen. I was eighty last Christmas—was born in Frederick Md.—went to Lexington Ky to an Uncle named Daviess—from there to an Uncle at Knoxville. He died, and I soon after enlisted in Capt[Francis W.] Armstrong's Company, Col Addison's [William P. Anderson's] Reg[imen]t—the 24*th* Infantry. My name is William Gaines. We marched to the Ohio River—spent the winter—crossed the Ohio and marched to Franklinton [Columbus, Ohio] the last town before reaching the Black Swamp. Then to Ft Findlay and to Ft [Meigs]. At the time of the battle under Croghan [at Fort Stephenson, Lower Sandusky], we had been stationed at Ft Seneca ten miles above Lower Sandusky. Croghan was weak, and five men from each Company were sent down to reenforce him. Five were from my Company. We reached the Fort just as the

236

enemy, the British, were landing below. The fort was on the edge of a hill—on the hill side our defence was pickets, and logs placed ready to roll down on the enemy if they attacked on that side. On the West side were two block houses—one at the S.W. corner and one at the N.W. corner, and a deep ditch reaching between them. The firing began within twenty minutes after we reached the fort. Only one man was killed on our side—a young fellow from my Company. He said he meant to kill one British soldier. He lay down on the top of the block house to shoot. A cannon ball took off his head. He was from Tennessee. His name was Samuel Thurman. The 19th and 17th Inf. had men in the Fort. I saw a number of officers there that I knew. We soon after crossed the Lake in open boats, landed at Malden and overtook [the British General Henry] Proctor and defeated him at the Thames.

Touching the [D. M.] Bennett case. I must stick to my rule to mind my own business—to see that the laws are executed—not to trench on the province of the Legislature, or of the judiciary. The pardoning power must not be used to nullify or repeal Statutes, nor to overrule the judgments of the Courts. Palpable mistakes, hasty decisions, newly discovered facts may all furnish occasions for pardons.

The true rule as to obscene matter is does it tend to excite the passions or to inflame the sensual appetite, or desires of the Young? Does the ~~publication~~ book or pamphlet belong to that class of ~~lite~~ publications which are sold secretly to the Young?

The fact that it is atheistic, or infidel, or immoral in doctrine, does not make it obscene.

11th July, 1879.—The most important and interesting ~~case~~ question before me is the Case of Bennett's application for pardon. I am turning it over carefully, trying to see all of its bearings. The pamphlett is a wrong headed affair—a free love argument—an argument against the institution of Marriage.

Its doctrines are opposed to all my principles and notions. But it is a controversial or polemical document [such] that its publication and sale are open and public in the State of Massachusetts where it originated, and in the State of New York where the prosecution and conviction of Bennett were had. It may therefore be assumed that no law of these States has been violated by its publication and circulation. ~~It has been prosecuted~~ Only two prosecutions for its circulation have been had. (It is sold by the thousand. The notoriety given to it by these prosecutions has given to it a wide circulation).

It has ~~been prosecuted as obscene~~ been alleged to be obscene in two cases under the Statute of the United States against the circulation of obscene matter through the mails.

12th July, 1879.—Yesterday about 9 A.M. Gen [John Grant] Mitchell, Laura, Lilly, Fanny, Jennie and John [Mitchell], with the veteran nurse of the family arrived. The older ones go to Gen [Joseph H.] Potter's for the present. We dined with Gen P[otter].

7½ to 12 last night, heavy showers—a good rain but not yet enough.

Sunday, 13th July, 1879.—We used in the early days of anti slavery movements hold conventions in Ohio on the 13th of July because it was the date of the ordinance of 1787—"The Jeffersonian anti slavery ordinance," as [Salmon P.] Chase was fond of calling it.

I heard a strong sensible and practical sermon by Dr [John] Lanahan on self examination this morning. I have not yet missed attending morning service, since I came to W[ashington] in March, 1877.

At church thought of this course of observation in my talks to people this fall. Avoid mere electioneering topics. Call attention to what I said a year ago to the effect that we were on the threshhold of better times—that the true course—the wise course was to let well enough alone—that resumption would come if there was no more tinkering, and that until it came there could be no solid prosperity—and that with it good times were certain. Now the Resumption fires are starting up in all directions.—the good times are coming—coming and have come. And what now is wisdom—what is good conduct. What will keep the times good? What will enable us to feel that resumption has come to stay? Again I say let well enough alone. The policy which brought resumption and better times, will make resumption and prosperity permanent.

The one thought I would like to lodge in all minds is keep out of debt—if in debt now is the time to get out of it in the only safe way, by honestly paying them. The honest payment of debts is the safest way to get rid of them.

But let every man, every corporation, and especially let every village town and city—every County and State get out of debt and keep out of debt. It is the debtor that is ruined by hard times.

14th July, 1879.—Took no morning walk—

An intelligent writer in a recent review (periodical) says ~~it~~ "Panics it has been observed recur about every twenty years in this Country, and about every ten years in England." Burke says about the causes of popular distress,

18th July, 1879.—A cool north wind has driven off the hot waves of the 16*th* which was our hottest day—Thermometer 101°, and under awnings on the Avenue, 110°!

Laura [Mitchell] and the darlings [are] still with us. Webb is at Mouse Island [in Lake Erie] with Birch and friends.

The talk of a small addition to the house [Spiegel Grove], with a larger portico leads me to catalogue things needed

1. A large cistern with a portion wall—some distance from house.
2. An elevator for trunks &c &c
3. Color.
4. French roof—or cottage roof.
5. Drainage and sewerage.
6. Sliding & arched doors.

239

7. Water—gass—& heating apparatus.
8. Water closets—.

19th July, 1879.—I have, ~~some~~ after very careful consideration, reached the conclusion that I ought not to pardon [D. M.]
Bennett. To do so would be, to nullify the law as expounded
by the judicial department. This would be an improper use
of the pardoning power. An abuse of it. No doubt in cases
near the line between what is right and ~~wrong~~ what is forbidden—it is a mistake to prosecute.

In this case Heywood [Bennett] wrote a book, [*Cupid's
Yokes: or, The Binding Forces of Conjugal Life* . . . Princeton,
Mass.] in opposition to marriage, and in favor of free-love
practices.— He put into it many passages not required for the
argument—in language and sentiment indecent, which enable
the seller to advertise it as "spicy," as "rich, rare and racy,"
and which add greatly to the demand for it. In short, obscenity
to make money, may be truthfully alleged of it.

While I maintain inflexibly the authority of the Executive
department against all attempts to cripple it by other departments, I must not magnify it at the expense of the just prerogatives of either the judicial or legislative departments.

20th July, 1879.—East or N.E. wind—cool weather since the
extremely hot day—the 16*th*.

24th July, 1879.—Sherman made an effective speech at Portland, [Maine] yesterday. He is now a candidate for the Rep
Pres[idential] nomination. I would make two criticisms [of
his speech:] 1. It gives ~~too much~~ encouragement to sectionalism 2. It is not sound on the financial question.

On the latter question he expresses the opinion that legal
tender notes ought to be, or may very well be a part of the
paper currency of the Country. Now in my opinion 1. these
notes are not in time of peace, a Constitutional Currency and
2. they are are a dangerous currency—depending as they do
wholly on Congressional discretion as to their amount—their
issue—and all of their functions.

26th July, 1879.—The long drouth has had a slight check—just enough of a drizzling rain to lay the dust, *24th*, *25th* and early this morning.

[James] Parton in an article ["The Traditional and Real Washington"] in the Magazine of American History [Volume 3, number 8, August 1879, page 487] says Washington was in favor of a single Presidential term of seven (7) years—

"The term of seven years is probably as long as any man can advantageously hold the Presidency. The strain upon the faculties of a good man is too severe to be longer borne, and a young country must needs grow faster than an elderly mind. . . ."

This is true. The strain is hard to bear—it grows harder as time passes.

Sunday, 27th July, 1879.—A cool beautiful fresh morning. Yesterday we had copious showers—the first in a great while. Last night the children had charades. Fanny Hayes and Fanny Mitchell as boys!

28th July, 1879.—Gen Mitchell came this A.M.

Soldiers' Home, 1st August, 1879.—The death of Judge [Isaac Clinton] Collins is surprising and a great calamity to his family and my friends, John [W.] and Harriet [Collins] Herron. He seemed assured for of a long life. A young man with me in [Cincinnati] at the bar and in the Literary Club, his death breaks a circle of the most intimate and dearest friends. He was amiability itself. With a fair and good mind, his excellent disposition, and rather elegant literary culture were his noticeable characteristics.

3d August, 1879.—If we would prolong the period of good times—postpone the return of Hard times and soften their severity, Keep out of debt. When hard times come and begin to pinch that man suffers least whose debts are least—and the same is true of City County State and Nation.

A grave man of dignity, but of moderate ability was appointed to office to the surprise of every body. Tallyrand said "To have never said anything, and to have never done anything is no doubt a prodigious power! But it ought not to be abused!"

8th August, 1879.—The Democratic platform of Maryland is sound on the currency. It is in substance

The Currency of the country should be firmly established on the basis of coin which is exchangeable at its face value in all the markets of the world.

10th August, 1879.—Cold for the season after several very warm days.

Geo W. Jones an intimate friend since College days has been with me two or three days. He talked of the Cinti visit and old times.

Look up Lincoln's Messages and Speeches for his opinion as to the results of the War—the questions settled by the War.

The less public officers have to do with the management of party politics the better it ~~is~~ will be for the public service, and for their party.

Capital and enterprise cannot afford to oppress labor, or to allow labor to suffer from injustice and oppression. The Exodus will teach this truth to the landowner and the Merchant in the South.

We want a currency ~~which~~ that will pass at its face value in all the markets of the Commercial world. Whoever supports measures which will degrade our currency below this high standard is the enemy of our prosperity.

The ~~tenth annual~~ *7th* Cincinnati Industrial Exposition ~~of the business of Cinti~~ opens at a most fortunate period in the Com[mercia]l ~~of~~ history of our Country. ~~The~~ The revival of ~~reviving~~ prosperity ~~wh~~ is surely & rapidly extending to every branch of useful industry. With values fixed and measured by a currency which is worth its face value in the markets of the world; with business no longer perplexed by an uncertain and fluctuating standard; with a well grounded confidence in

242

the future ~~pervading the minds of~~ shared alike by men of capital, of enterprise and of business capacity; with crops of wheat and cotton and corn abundant, and bearing fair prices; with health again returning to the fever stricken South, the merchants, manufacturers and workmen of Cincinnati may well be confident and hopeful as they invite their countrymen from far and near ~~to their growing and beautiful attractive City to this attractive central City.~~—to the attractions & the instructions of this beautiful Central City of the American Continent.

14th August, 1879.—The weather still continues cool. ~~and~~ The Conkling scandal is the newspaper sensation of the time. This exposure of ~~his~~ C's rottenness will do good in one direction. It will weaken his political power, which is bad and only bad.[4]

15th August, 1879.—We had a good little shower last evening which has laid the dust, and which gives us a fresh cool morning.

No doubt I am somewhat affected by the Washington malaria. Symptoms, slight headache at night—bad dreams, a tendency of blood to the head—flushed face at times &c &c &c not serious, but I shall be glad to get away next month.

Soldiers' Home, *17th August*, 1879.—Very heavy rains the last two days—Six inches fell the *15th*—5 inches in one shower of two or three hours! Rain last night also.

This morning I wrote Hon. J. S. Newberry that I would, if still thought best, accept invitation to State Fair, Detroit, *18th* & *19th* Sept.—to Gov [Shelby M.] Cullom of Illinois that ditto ditto for *29th* and *30th* Sept. at Springfield. In order to be at Indianapolis on *1st* & *2d* Oct.

19th August, 1879.—Clear and cold of the great rains.

Webb left ~~for~~ on a long trip with Secretary Schurz to the Western territories last evening.

"He that mindeth his own business is better than he that taketh a City."

21st *August*, 1879.—Lucy had a severe headache yesterday but is better this morning. I have dull headaches at night which leave me when I rise. Judge [David M.] Key says he has the same and attributes it to the Washington Malaria. The weather is beautiful. The rain thus far in Aug. is ten (10) inches! This has no precedent in recent years.

Birchard came yesterday morning. He looks strong and healthy—rather a fine intellectual looking young man. He in good spirits.

Gen Schurz and Sherman in Ohio—Col Thompson ~~returned~~ left last night for Va. Gen Devens returned yesterday.

———

Executive Mansion
Washington

Private

21 Aug. 1879

My Dear Sir:

I hardly know how to thank you for your kind offer of the interesting collection of Japanese articles, nor what to say about it.

I do not wish to accept presents of great value. Tokens of friendly feeling, as books, canes &c &c I receive as a matter of course. In case of applicants for office I make it a rule not to accept any presents, and where presents are accepted before applications are made, ~~the~~ I do not appoint the givers. My preference in this matter is either to return the articles or to pay for them, if the cost is not beyond what I am willing to invest in such curiosities.

I have written in great haste.

Sincerely
R B Hayes

Dr R. T. Hayes
  Los Angelos
  Calif.

———

Soldiers' Home, 2d September, 1879.—Our darling's [Fanny's] birthday—We have tried to make it a happy one, and certainly it is her best. She is twelve years old. She had a ~~crowd~~ bevy of her young friends to lunch and dine with her. Will & Phebe Rogers—Alice Joe and   Potter, McCrary,   LeDuc, Russell Kilbourne, Andrews Rogers, Fanny Fay,   . Her presents are, Lady of the Lake, Encyclopedia of Poetry, Whittier's Poems, a casket, Paper Knife, Jewelry, [list not completed].

Have been writing Speeches for Youngstown, for Detroit &c &c.

5th September, 1879.—Monday morning we go via B & O RR to Cincinnati. Our party will consist of Lucy, Birchard, Fanny, Scott, Isaiah [Lancaster] & Winnie [Monroe]. Gen Sherman and his aids Col. [John E.] Tourtellotte and [Col. John Mosby] Bacon, will accompany us. Our plan is to stop over our train at Chillicothe to see Uncle [Matthew] Scott Cook and other relatives of Lucy there. We remain three days at Cinti. Thence to Fremont. I am to go to Youngstown the 17*th* and to Detroit the 18*th*.[5]

8th September, 1879.—6½ A.M.—Soldiers Home, Washington. We go this morning. The thunder storm last night cooled the air and laid the dust. The morning is beautiful. All ~~feel~~ are well and in good spirits.

21st September, 1879.—Sunday, Fremont, [Ohio].—After about two weeks of rather severe travel with receptions, speech making, and handshakings we are at our restful home in Fremont.

Our tour has in all respects been prosperous and agreeable. We go to Kansas tomorrow.

5th October, 1879.—Sunday. Fremont.

Our western trip has been most enjoyable. At Chicago, the evening of the 22*d,* our welcome was enthusiastic and hearty —and so on the 23*d* throughout the day in Illinois down to and including Quincy. We were late at Hannibal, Mo. It had rained—the night was dark and threatening, and a few young-sters were persistent in calling "Hayes" "Hayes" "President Hayes" &c &c. I finally stepped out and talked a few minutes —was treated with respect, but the papers got it that the crowd was insolent and violent! Nothing of it in fact.

24th, we breakfasted at Col [A. D.] Jaynes' beautiful home in Sedalia, and had a fine reception by the citizens of this growing Town.

Thence into Kansas at Ft Scott, and to Parsons in the eve-ning. Great interest and friendliness in Kansas everywhere with large and enthusiastic crowds of laboring intelligent Americans.

Gov [John Pierce] St. John and wife with us throughout. The Neosho Fair was in the newer part of Southern Kan[sa]s, but numerously attended, and very interesting. 25th.

26th, A.M., we were at Ft Dodge. Capt [James Heyward] Bradford and ladies. The Arkansas nearly dry. At Larned, a Fair and great spirit.

Evening with noise, fire works, and welcoming shouts, at Topeka, at the agreeable home of Judge and Mrs [N. C.] M[a]cFarland.

27th, Receptions at Topeka. [and] Lawrence. (A most interesting visit to the University—a noble view from its tower —a beautiful reception in the large hall of the University.

At night, a most uproarous welcome at Leavenworth—especially by the colored people.

28th, Sunday. Spent delightfully at Gen [John] Pope's. Visited the wonderful views of the grand country around Ft Leavenworth.

Church in the excellent Military prison, A.M., and at the Episcopal army chaplain's services in the evening.

29th, warm welcomes at Atchison, and St. Joseph, Mo. and all along the route to Hannibal.

Evening a beautiful reception at the Congregational Church —a handsome church—with capital music. Nothing better than

Hannibal with its supper, in the basement. Col [William Henry] Hatch, M[ember of] C[ongress] particularly happy in his remarks.

30th, Entered Springfield, Ill. at daylight—with Gov & Mrs [Shelby M.] Cullom and dau[ghter]s.

All most agreeable—see papers.

The tomb of Lincoln, and its Monument &c &c with the associations are most impressive. His old home is neglected— It may as well be taken down as left so.

1st Oct, reached Grand Hotel, Indianapolis. This was *the* reception of our tour in all respects. They rate

1 Indianapolis
2 Cincinnati
3 Detroit
4 Springfield, Youngstown, Topeka, Neosho, Hannibal, &c &c.

3d Oct, reached Fremont—visited County Fair—Home— rest—content.

The *4th*, my birthday. Fifty seven years old. Let me try to live during my remaining years a useful life. To make others happy and to make men and women better to the extent of my powers—this must be my aim.

At noon, today, Sunday, Fremont, 5 Oct. 1879, the mercury is at 80° +! Rev Thos [H.] Wilson preached his first sermon in our M.E. Ch[urch]. Short, and full of impressive feeling. (At one P.M., 82°+) (3 P.M., 84°+!)

NOTES

CHAPTER XI

[1] Hayes here records his opinion that the battle with Congress is nearing an end with victory in sight. The Democrats had enacted the army bill with, as Hayes notes, no really restrictive rider. They also removed the riders from the legislative and executive bills. But they retained restrictions in the judicial bill—forbidding payments to marshals who were used to enforce federal

election laws and repealing a law setting up an oath to bar former Confederates from federal jury service.

2 This is the veto of the judicial bill.

3 Congress had bowed by passing a measure providing for expenses of the judiciary. Although the bill repealed the test-oath for jurors and made no mention of payments for marshals, Hayes accepted it. But a separate measure restricting the employment of marshals encountered another veto.

4 The scandal referred to involved Conkling and Kate Chase Sprague, wife of Rhode Island's former governor and Senator William Sprague. Conkling and Kate were rumored to be lovers, and at this time Conkling visited her at her summer home at Narragansett Pier. There Sprague appeared and threatened the Senator with a shotgun. The encounter was a press sensation.

5 This was the beginning of a tour that would take Hayes to Michigan, Illinois, Missouri, and as far west as Kansas. In his speeches he praised nationalism, condemned the denial of rights to Negroes in the South, and defended the gold standard. All in all, he was more frankly political than was customary on such trips.

Chapter XII

OCT. 6, 1879—APRIL 28, 1880

Fremont, 6th October, 1879.—8 A.M. 68°—. 2 P.M., 84°—.
Wm Henry Smith and his wife left our house for their home
at Chicago (Lake View) at 10:30 P.M. last night.

We talked over many matters. Our place we shall call
Birchard Grove, after its former owner, Uncle Sardis Birchard.
His name Spiegel Grove—fanciful and eccentric does not stick.
We never used it.[1]

7th October, 1879.—Last night at a meeting of Trustees of
Birchard Library, I offered, in order to put the institution on
a solid basis, to assume the indebtedness, about $14,000. and to
take for it, the Birchard & Boalt tract in Toledo—that is to
say the Library interest in it nominally $15,000. This puts on
me a burden of $7000. the debt to the Express Company. But
my desire to see Uncle's monument (the Library) in good
condition, compels me to this course.

Birchard Grove, 10th October, 1879.—The hot weather continues without abatement. 84°+ in the shade every day for a
week, and more.

The tall elm N.E. of the porch lost its leaves a fortnight or
more ago, and is now leaving out again!

We had a charming visit to Mrs Judge [Ebenezer] Lane the
8th & 9th at Sandusky. I saw many old friends. Judges [Cooper
K.] Watson and [Ebenezer Brown] Sadler, Mr Oran Follett,

Mr   Haywood, [Rollin B.] Hubbard, [John M.] Boalt,
the Marshes, [Chris. C.] Keech, [the] Macks, [Jacob A.]
Camp, the Moss(es), ~~Barney~~ Barber, [incomplete].

11th October, 1879.—Yesterday Mr G[alusha] A. Grow
of Penna and I[saac] F. Mack of Sandusky held a meeting
here. We invited them to dine with us. Mr [John Crocker]
Sherwin M[ember of] C[ongress] of Aurora, Ill., Mr
Cheesebrough of Detroit, Gen   Leake of Chicago, Dist.
Atty, were here with citizens of Fremont viz [Dr. James W.]
Wilson, [Anson H.] Miller, Gen [Ralph P.] and S[tephen]
Buckland,   Mower, [Issac M.] Keeler, [Homer]
Everett, [George J.] Krebs—an agreeable dinner party.

Birchard Grove, 14th October, 1879.—Election day.
Weather still warm, 65° at 8 A.M. Smoky and Indian Summer
like.

Rutherford came from Cornell to cast his first vote for
[Charles] Foster and the Rep[ublican] ticket. Three voters
~~among~~ in the family besides myself. The election is important.
If F[oster] has a good majority and we have the Legislature so
as to secure Judge [Allen G.] Thurman's seat in the Senate,[2]
it will improve the temper of all sides towards the Administration, and strengthen us for good works. Ohio also needs a
change. The Dem party has good and able public men, but
they are powerless in the presence of the bad and reckless
elements of their party. This is perhaps too strong a statement.
But it is true that if not powerless they are at least unable to
control the general course of their party. ~~in the wrong direction.~~ On the other hand the reckless public men of the Rep
Party are compelled to take their direction from the better
elements of their party.

I am glad my ~~voters~~ boys voted. To vote is like the payment
of a debt—a duty never to be neglected, if its performance is
possible.

Birchard Grove, 15th October, 1879.—The election, as at
present appears, has gone strongly with us. Foster's majority,

I judge, will reach fifteen thousand. This is a valuable victory. Two questions were debated mainly. The Currency and the Supremacy of the Genl Gov't. Inflation and Statesrights are badly beaten. It is a verdict in favor of a sound an honest currency—a currency of gold and silver of paper convertible into ~~gold~~ coin at the will of the holder a currency which will defraud no man,—a currency worth its face in the markets of the world. It is a judgment in favor of the perpetuity of the Union, the Supremacy of the National Government and the enforcement of the laws. It ~~says to the legislature~~ is the voice of Ohio that Congress should make all appropriations needful and proper to enable the Executive department of the Govt to ~~enforce~~ execute all laws ~~held~~ not declared to be unconstitutional by the Supreme Court, and that the Executive ~~will~~ Dept of the Govt will be sustained in ~~its~~ the faithful ~~execution~~ enforcement of all such laws.

Washington, White House, 21st October, 1879.—Returned this morning, after a Six weeks absence in Seven States viz Ky., O., Mich., Ind., Il., Mo. & Kansas.

17th had a fine reception at Columbus. 18th, had a fine reception at Delaware. 20th, B & O via Newark, Cambridge, Barnsville, to Washington 8 A.M., 21st.

25th & 6th October, 1879.—25 with Gen [Albert J.] Myer, Capt.   Howgate, Lucy, Webb & Mr Herman A Brown of N.Y. down the Potomac in Yacht.

Executive Mansion
Washington
27 Oct 1879

My Dear General,
    Mrs Hayes and myself will be glad to receive you and Mrs Grant, with any members of your family who may be with you, as our guests on the occasion of the unveiling of the Statue in honor of Gen [George Henry] Thomas. It occurs on the 19th & 20th of next month, and long enough after the

251

Chicago Reunion to enable you to be present, if other engagements do not prevent.

Preparations are making to give you a hearty reception
here. Your welcome back will be a warm and friendly one.
We shall be glad to have you remain with us as long as it
may be convenient for you to do so.

With best wishes,
Sincerely
R. B. Hayes

Gen U. S. Grant
&c &c
(Galena, Illinois)

White House, 5th November, 1879.—The Republican victory yesterday was complete everywhere in the North except
in New York. In New York we carry the Legislature. This
means the election of a Republican Senator in the place of
Mr [Francis] Kernan. We also elect the Governor by reason
of the bolting of the Tammany Democrats who refused to
support the nominee of Mr Tilden, Gov [Lucius] Robinson
and voted generally for [John] Kelly. The remainder of the
Republican State ticket is, I fear, beaten. Our full force was
not at the polls. Many Republicans opposed to machine politics
were disgusted by the Conkling control of the Convention,
and the nomination of Mr [Alonzo B.] Cornell.[3] I did all I
could to save the cause, by urging friends to lay aside their
opposition. But there was too much Conkling in the ticket.
Hence its weakness and probable defeat.

With a popular nomination for Governor and no ~~dissent~~
dissatisfaction in the party we should have elected our whole
ticket. New York would have been no exception to the general
course of Republican success this year. All of the Northern
States have done better for the Republicans this year than they
did last year except New York. In New York alone have the
Republicans failed to do as well as last year. Last year our
plurality was about 40,000. This year I fear we are beaten on the

popular vote. There is but one cause for this viz too much of Roscoe Conkling and his machine politics.

The defeat of Gov Robinson is the defeat of Tilden and foreshadows his overthrow next year either in the Democratic National Convention or at the Polls.

14th November, 1879.—I directed framed full length photos of myself to be sent by express to Mrs Minerva Justice Everett [of Fremont, Ohio] and Kenyon College. They were taken by Landy, Cincinnati, 12 Sept. 1879.

26th November, 1879.—I sent to the printer last evening the last revise of the Message. Its topics are finance, Mormonism, ~~civil~~ a paragraph about the South, and Civil Service reform. There was small difference of opinion in the Cabinet about the questions discussed in the Message. Col Thompson and Mr Evarts looking at the political effect say we should do nothing to change the issues now before the Country. I recommend stopping silver coinage and retiring the Greenbacks. Both Mr E[varts] and Mr T[hompson] fear the effect of this. It seems to me sound policy however to do both. ~~things~~ The sooner we take the true position, the easier it will be to convince the people of its wisdom.

Lucy and Fanny went to Phila. to spend Thanksgiving with Bishop Simpson.

28th November, 1879.—I spent Thanksgiving day,—yesterday—at Bishop Simpson's 1807 Mt Vernon St in Philadelphia. With Isaiah Lancaster, my servant, I left here on the 5:30 P.M. train on the Baltimore and Potomac RR. We travelled in the common car. Heretofore since I became President I have had a special car when travelling. Being without a "party" I preferred to go without fuss. I had a ticket to Baltimore. But paid forty cents—apparently for Isaiah, but I didn't understand it. A family ticket which I had, included I suppose servants. I was as polite as the conductor, and made no remark. Fare was paid from Baltimore to Phila. for both of us—I think 3:00 each. On my return I paid $15.00 for fare on B. & O. and for sleeping births—two sections, leaving Phila. at 11:30 P.M. Soon after lying down the Conductor told me he had orders to return my fare. I took it without counting. This morning at 7 P.M. before leaving the car the conductor told he had ~~made~~ orders to return me the fare paid on the *26th* and gave me 3:00. This was for fare I suppose leaving me to pay for *my* own sleeping birth. All of this pleasantly done, but I suspect I make less trouble if I ask for a special car.

On the way up a Mr Sutton of the Eastern Shore—clerk in the great whole sale store of Jacob   & Co., Phila., took a seat by my side. I got much interesting information about his business and the trade generally.

At Bishop Simpson's met the family and Lucy and Fanny. A happy home—a cheerful pious family—a family of good works and most loveable character. The Bishop and his son Barney met me at Broad St Depot at midnight, or near it. Mrs Simpson is a warm hearted and motherly lady who is full of good works. A home for aged women, and now for Orphans are her pet hobbies. The Fair is in the interest of the Orphans. Mrs   Bowie, a married daughter, wife of a Methodist Episcopal preacher in Harrisburg, was visiting her parents. Two sweet dau's, a blonde and a brunette, young ladies, completes the family. The Bishop's eloquence and success are due to a tender sincere nature, great modesty, good culture, and a sound common sense. These high qualities added to unshaken faith in Christianity, and in its vast importance make him a man of great power in the pulpit and in private life. He possesses also unusual love and capacity for hard work.

Thanksgiving day we rode N.E. six or eight miles to attend the opening of an improved church in Frankfort. The Bishop preached a hopeful sermon. A collection to pay for the church improvement, was tolerably successful.

Returned and dined with the Bishop's family, also Pres-[iden]t [William H.] Allen of Girard College—and a few others. After dinner callers—[Wayne] MacVeagh and others.

Then a drill of a military company of Orphan boys in front of the House. In the evening at the crowded Fair in the great hall—hand shakings and great enthusiasm. At 11:30 P.M. left Phila. for W[ashington]— (home!). Lucy and Fanny remained for ~~da~~ a day or two longer. A rapid, busy, delightful trip.

Private

7th Dec., 1879

My dear Sir:

I agree with you. I know of no good reason why Mr B[laine] and I should not be on the best of terms with each other. In the first year of my administration he said and did things which I thought needlessly hostile—for example, his speech at Woodstock on Mexican affairs. I have understood that he was offended by an appointment which I made in Maine. He was opposed to it. I thought it was my duty to make it. There was certainly not the least *intentional* disrespect to him in the act itself or in the manner of doing it. I sincerely regretted that he felt as he did about it.

The Cin[cinna]ti platform, my letter of acceptance, and my convictions, led me to oppose the Senatorial usage by which the appointing power of the President was usurped by Senators. This was the cause, for a time, of much irritation. I regarded the controversy as a difference of ~~opinion~~ principles, and I never allowed it to disturb my relations with any Senator if I could avoid it.—In the affair referred to I have suspected that some misapprehension caused the feeling that was exhibited. I have throughout regarded Mr. B as a gentleman with whom I would like to be on good terms. I do not wish to be understood as intimating that explanations are needed on either side to bring us more cordially together. I do not feel that the past stands in the way of good relations.—

Thanking you for your friendly suggestions, I remain

Sincerely

R. B. Hayes

Hon. Wm Walter Phelps.

14th December, 1879.—Col Josiah W Ware has been visiting us for several days. He was born 19 Aug 1802 Frederick Co[unty], Va., near where he lives, near Berryville, Va.

He says ["] I knew your wife's grand mother after whom she was named Lucy Ware Webb intimately and corresponded with her. When she was about 60 or 70 years old her hair was cut short and was white as snow. She was a perfect specimen of hospitality. She was very fine looking—had as fine a face as you ever saw—full of kindness and benevolence. She was rather fleshy, not too much so, about the height of Lucy Hayes. I also knew ~~Lucy~~ Cousin Lucy's grandfather Isaac Webb. He was a very small man—of an active figure. I first saw them at their house near Lexington Ky—about 12 miles, I think, east of L[exington] about 1825.

["]James Ware, the great Grandfather ~~Ware of~~ of Mrs Hayes lived in Clark County Va. The family came from Gloucester County Va where there is a Ware church and Ware river. Some of the family moved to Georgia & one of them was a U.S. Senator from Ga. The Great gr[and]mother of Mrs Hayes, wife of James Ware, was Catherine Todd.— I think it Catherine—not positive.— The Todds were from Caroline County, Va.

["]Charles Webb married one of the Miss Wares—*Isaac Webb another*, and Dr Scott married another.

["]Lucy's father, Dr James Webb was a very handsome man. He had black hair & dark eyes, and was tall and straight.["]

18th December, 1879.—The Committee of the Republican party for the Nation met here yesterday. This is the first official movement towards the Presidential election. The Committee in a general way were harmonious. They were apparently about equally divided in their preferences for next President between Grant and Blaine, with a decided balance of power for Sherman. If New York could with a fair degree of unity, present a man like say the Vice President [William A.

Wheeler] or Gov [Hamilton] Fish he would probably be nominated. The general popular favorite is Grant. But many thoughtful men dislike a departure from ~~the~~ Washington's precedent—dislike the third term, and many more fear a return to the unfortunate methods and men of Gen Grant's former administration.

Executive Mansion
Washington
13 Dec 1879

My Dear Sir,

Your note of the 12th inst. tendering your resignation of the office of Secretary of War with a view to the acceptance of the position of Judge of the Circuit Court of the United States for the Eighth Circuit is received, and the resignation accepted.

The expression of personal regard with which the tender of your resignation is accompanied are very heartily reciprocated and the termination of our intimate official relations is attended with the very gratifying reflection that your eminent capacity for usefulness in the public service will be transferred to the responsible duties of the important and permanent judicial position to which you will hereafter devote your attention.

With the best wishes for your success and happiness

Sincerely
R. B. Hayes

Hon Geo. W. McCrary.

———

19th December, 1879.—My friend Thos Donaldson [of Philadelphia, Pa.] brought me a Navajo blanket, made by Indians in New Mexico, and is a present from Gen Henry M Atkinson of Santa Fe, the U.S. Marshall. It is a very fine one—water proof of read [red] and white colors—dark red.

25th December, 1879.— This Christmas day is given up to the little folks—Fanny and Scott. They are very fond of each other, and noticeably thoughtful of one another's wishes. This is shown always when an opportunity occurs. They received many gifts. I got a knife from the Clerks, slippers from Mr Stevenson of Brooklyn & a silk gown from Lucy.—Mr Stevenson (John W.), cor[ner] N[ew] Y[ork] Avenue & Pacific St., Brooklyn, sent Lucy a Japanese silk gown.

1880

13th January, 1880.—Two things that may be important have been considered.

Last Friday, the 9th, I directed the Secretary of the Navy to order two of our national vessells to ~~occupy the~~ sail to the ports in the Chiriqui grant—one on the Gulf of Mexico and one on the Pacific Coast between Panama & the proposed Nicaragua canal. The purpose is to establish naval stations in these important harbors. It is claimed that an American citizen Mr Ambrose [W.] Thompson, has procured a very important grant of the lands surrounding these habors, and of the right of way connecting them. Mr Thompson conveyed to the United States by an arrangement with President Lincoln an interest in his grant. If it shall be deemed best by Congress to take possession of this interest, the presence of our ships, and the establishing of our coaling stations will give us a foothold which will be of vast service in controlling the passage from Ocean to Ocean either at Panama or at Nicaragua Lake.[4]

The other affair is the appointment of a Governor for the Territory of Utah. This under ordinary circumstances would be a common Administrative act. But an appointment in the place of the present very reputable governor means a change of policy towards the Mormons. Now the territory is virtually under the theocratic government of the Mormon Church. The Union of Church and State is complete. The result is the usual one the usurpation or absorption of all temporal authority and

power by the Church. Polygamy and every other evil sanc-
tioned by the Church is safe. To destroy the temporal power
of the Mormon Church is the end in view. This requires agitation. The people of the United States must be made to ap-
preciate ~~the~~ to understand the situation. Laws must be enacted
which will take from the Mormon Church its temporal.power.
Mormonism as a sectarian idea is nothing, but as a system of
government it is our duty to deal with it as an enemy to our
institutions, and its supporters and leaders as criminals.

18th January, 1880.—The winter of 1879–80 thus far has
been one of the mildest of winters, except in the far north-
west. Six fair days this month. A lovely New Years day and
then a week of gloomy weather. Heavy fogs in the morning.

24th January, 1880.—Bright & warm.

Judge S Newton Pettis has sent Mrs Hayes from Meadville,
Pa., *a vicina [vicuna] robe*. It seems to be of Lama hair.

Saturday, 31st January, 1880.—We get every week gifts of
small value from all parts of the country. I must bring up today
my arrears of acknowledgments. A basket of large handsome
red seedling apples from Minnesota—a watch case and tidy
from Vermont, a lawn rake from Dayton, Ohio.—a biography
of Eminent Abstainers from England—Indian trinkets from
Alaska—a robe from Pennsylvania—Photographs of Indian
pupils at Carlisle—Autographs of Patrick Henry, and letters of
Webster, Clay & Calhoun from the Eastern Shore of Virginia
&c &c all recent accumulations.

1st February, 1880.—Dr [Jedediah H.] Baxter vaccinated
the houschold on the 23d January viz Lucy, Webb, Fanny,
Scott and myself—also our guests, Nannie and Lizzie Jones,
Miss Jennie Halstead, Nettie Ferguson, &c &c. The ladies "in
the French manner —what is the French manner? Why the
way they do in France! But how do they vaccinate in France?
Why, dont you know?" &c &c. That is to say, the under-
pinning. All took well, and the ladies have all been limping
ever since!

Last night *after dinner* we were weighed. R B H, 197; Lucy, 177; Webb, 150; Rud, 140; Fanny, 81; Scott [not given]

When I came into the White House ~~eight~~ nine (9) presidential portraits were wanting to complete the list. I have added Grant, Jackson, John Adams, Madison, Monroe, Tyler and Harrison. I must get Buchanan and Johnson, and then each of my successors ~~by w~~ will have to add the portrait of his predecessor.

5th February, 1880.—A cousin of my wife having a son in law at West Point as an instructor wanted me to detail her son also to duty at the same desirable place. To this I replied

5 Feby 1880

My Dear Mrs—

You are perfectly correct in thinking—I agree with you that nepotism and favoritism prevail in the army. You might find examples of it in Washington as well as at West Point. ~~But~~ I do not expect in my short term of service to get rid of ~~it~~ this abuse. But I intend that my example shall shall be a protest against it— At any rate I do not permit myself to add to the weight of the precedents in favor of the abuse. Two young men who have their records yet to make, belonging to the same family in soft places at West Point would ~~hardly~~ neither be useful to them nor ~~for~~ creditable to the service. If they and their friends give it a little thought I am confident that they will so consider it. In this matter ~~you will~~ I hope you will not regard me as other than your and their friend.

Sincerely
R B Hayes

———

7th February, 1880.—Mr John M Morton son of O[liver] P. Morton, nominated by me for Collector of Internal Revenue at San Francisco was rejected by the Senate by a large majority. The California Senators opposed him, and under the doctrine called Senatorial courtesy they succeeded in rallying agst him a majority of both parties. Mr Morton is in all respects worthy. But there is an evident purpose to re-establish the doctrine that the Senators from a State are entitled to control the Federal offices of their State. This has been greatly shaken during my administration. In many conspicuous cases it has been broken down, or at least disregarded. The strength of the usage in the Senate is shown by the fact that many Senators, Political friends of Senator Morton—many of them ~~political~~ intimate personal friends of the great leader, who had promised Mrs Morton to sustain her son's nomination, deserted at the pinch and voted against him, or dodged. Among those named to me who did this are Conkling, [Hannibal] Hamlin, [William B.] Allison, [list not completed].

The object evidently is to re-establish the usage, so that the next President will not venture to question it. Now the question is what can I do to counteract this. I can emphasise my dissent by leaving Mr Higbee [William Higby] the present incumbent, in office until the Senate adjourns and then appoint Morton in his place. Under this appointment, Morton can hold his office until the end of my term, March 4, 1881. This is worth thinking of.

The most important subject now under consideration is as to the Canal across the Isthmus connecting the waters of the Atlantic and the Pacific. The French Engineer, [Ferdinand M. de] Lesseps, the chief man in building the Suez canal is actively at work organising or trying to organise a Company to enter upon the work. The time has come when the American doctrine on the subject ought to be explicitly stated. In my judgment the United States regard ~~this~~ the commercial communication whether by railroad or canal between the two oceans across the ~~narrow part~~ Isthmus at any of the points which have been suggested as essential to their prosperity and safety. The right of free passage at all times, in peace or war, for the purpose of commerce or for defence the United States deem essential to their safety and prosperity. They wish it to be understood by all concerned that the United States will not consent that any European power shall control the Railroad or Canal across the Isthmus of Central America. ~~With due regard~~ With due regard to the rights and wishes of our sister republics in the ~~territories~~ Isthmus, the United States will insist ~~upon American~~ that this passage way shall always remain under American control. Whoever invests capital in the contemplated work ~~will~~ should do it with a distinct ~~notice~~ understanding that the United States expects and intends to control the ~~use of the~~ canal in conformity with its own interests.

The highway between that part of the U.S. which is on the Atlantic and the Gulf of Mexico and that part of our Country which is on the Pacific must not be allowed to pass under the control of any European Nation. The control must be exclusively either in the Country through which it passes, or in the United States, or under the joint control of ~~the ten~~ the American Republics. The United States should control this great highway between that part of our Country &c &c &c &c

This great highway must not be controlled by Europe. It must be held and controlled ~~by the~~ by America—by the American Republics.

Sunday, 8th February, 1880.—A bright beautiful day. The last reception of Lucy and myself for this season was last night. It was the largest and gayest throng of the year. Many could not get in, and left without reaching the door. Others got in and left without entering the Blue room—going out through windows because they could not get out at the door. A very good natured and well behaved crowd.

Scott Russell is nine years old today. Weight, 84½ [lbs]; height, 4′ 6⅜″.

The interest of the U.S. in the communication—the interoceanic canal or Railroad does not rest on the Monroe doctrine alone. That great highway connects on the part of our Country which is on the Atlantic with that which is on the

Pacific. It is of vital importance to our prosperity and our safety. It is a part of our general system of defensive works. It is essential for National defense. It will not be permitted to pass into the control of any hostile nation. We shall deal justly with all other nations in regard to its use. We shall deal liberally with the sister American Republics which are interested in the work and in the territory through which it passes. But it may as well be understood that the United States will not permit ~~any European control or powers~~ it to be held or controlled by any European Nation.

11th February, 1880.—Our diplomatic reception last evening was very successful. The Senators and Representatives quite generally attended.

The event of yesterday however was my presentation to the Cabinet of my views on the Inter-oceanic Canal. As my opinions were matured distinct and decisive I first gave my opinion and then asked for theirs. I said in substance that I thought that existing circumstances furnished an occasion for an explicit declaration of the views and purposes of the United States with respect to a ship canal across the Southern part of North America. That our principles should be at an early day announced. That in my view our position did not rest alone upon the Monroe doctrine. That paramount interests were involved. That the Control of the Canal ~~would~~ was essential to our prosperity and safety. That the ocean highway from that part of our Country on the Atlantic to that part of our Country on the Pacific must always be under our Control ~~or wh~~ that if it passed into European control our security, our peace, our commercial and general prosperity, and our commanding and natural position among the Nations would be endangered. That our interest in the subject was greater than that of all European nations put together. It was therefore my purpose as soon as it could properly be done to take occasion by special message to Congress to communicate these views to them. In this way all concerned—all who proposed to take part in the construction of the Canal would be informed of the principles of the United States on the subject.

I then expressed the hope that the members of the Cabinet would concur with me in my views thus expressed, and called on them for their opinions. I was glad to find no opposition in to the general scope and purpose of what I had said.

Mr Evarts at some length explained what he was doing in regard to the question. That he was collecting the treaties, the correspondence, and all that existed on the subject showing the history of the matter. He did not decidedly speak of the necessity for prompt action, but seemed to regard *early* action as desirable.

Mr Sherman in a single sentence decidedly concurred with me.

Gov. Ramsey also gave spoke favorably express, and added considerations showing the importance of American control over the canal.

Mr Thompson with a smile said "You know these have been my views all along."

Judge Key was brief but emphatic in favor of a declaration such as I had indicated.

Gen Devens, was compelled to leave to attend a case in the Court of Claims but as he rose to go explicitly assented to the course I had suggested.

Gen Schurz warmly approved. He said "No European nation under similar circumstances would hesitate an instant to assert its rights in such a case, and to give decided expression of its purpose to maintain them.

So that practically the Cabinet is a unit on my side of the question.

12th February, 1880.—The [vicuna] robe given to Lucy by Mrs S. Newton Pettis of Meadville, [Pa.], is made from skins of the Guanaco a So[uth] Am[erican] animal of the Camel species—a wild variety of the Llama—three feet high and extremely swift.

17th February, 1880.—The President of the Panama RR gave me yesterday a very interesting account of the Isthmus, of his Railway, of Mr De Lesseps and his Surveys, and of the prospects of the enterprise. He thinks a canal can be built at tide level from Aspinwall [Colon] to Panama—that it will not pay as an investment but would be very useful to the U.S.

20th February, 1880.—The true policy of the United States as to ~~the~~ a canal across any part of the Isthmus is either a canal under American control, or no canal. We cannot allow the geographical relations of the ~~canal~~ N.A. continent to be essentially changed. ~~No~~ European ~~no~~ control of this thoroughfare between the different parts of the U.S. is wholly inadmissible.

Clark Centre [Center] says [Robert Bruce] Langdon of Minneapolis cast the Minnesota single vote for me on the final ballot.

The Isthmus canal would change essentially the geographical relations between the East and West Coast of N.A. and between N.A. and the rest of the world. This important change in the Geography of the Continent can not occur without gravely affecting the power, the prosperity, the means of defence, the peace and the safety of the U.S.

That canal must be controled by the U.S.

The U.S. can not consent that it shall be under European control.

Either an American canal ~~control~~ or no Canal must be our motto with respect to this subject.

4th March, 1880.—Three years of my term gone today. Only one year of it remains. The past has been on the whole more satisfactory, as I now look back, than I hoped it would be. For the future more care, more determined adherence to strict duty, and all will be well.

6th March 1880.—Monday last Lucy and Webb with Mr & Mrs [Jay O.] Moss of Sandusky left for Ohio. They will be absent another week. The two young children are with me, also Miss Lucy Cook & Miss Betty Ballinger of Texas. We are a nice party, but Lucy is greatly missed.

For two or three weeks I have had a dull pain extending through the body from the right breast to the right shoulder blade—occasionally there is pain in the right elbow. It seems to be rheumatism, and Dr [J. H.] Baxter is treating it as such. It interferes with sleep and comfort & grows no better. In other respects I was never in better health.

Sunday, 7th March, 1880.—Rainy & gloomy. About a month ago I missed the volume of my diaries which precedes this— beginning in May, I think, 1876 and ending about a year ago. It was a black flexibly bound volume not so thick as this and about the same shape and size in other respects. It contained what little I had to say during the Presidential canvass, and the first two years of my term of office. I fear if lost it will get into the newspapers. It contains few things that would be embarrassing in print, but undoubtedly has some. I do not recall more than two of this sort—and yet there must be much in it that I would prefer not to see in print.[5]

———

Mr Francis Brown Hayes of Boston is a collector of rare old books & is also a scientific Horticulturist. Alonzo Hayes Quint of New Bedford is a genealogist. John L. Hayes of Cambridge, brother of Francis, is a geologist &c &c &c.

———

Saturday, 13th *March,* 1880.—A wintry morning. Snow covers the ground and trees. Fanny and Scott ~~with their sled~~ are out, before breakfast, with their sled enjoying it. It snowed all day yesterday. For three days we have had winter weather. Lucy will probably leave Columbus today ~~for~~ to return here.

———

Fanny and Scott night before last appeared at a costume ball for children given by their dancing master. Fanny was beautiful as Martha Washington, and Scott as an orderly Sergeant of the 23d [Regiment, Ohio Volunteer Infantry]. Fanny copied the picture in the East room.

16th March, 1880.—Lucy and Webb returned Sunday morning. Mrs [Linus] Austin came with them. The weather in Ohio, during our March winter, has been very fine.

The home place they found looking its best. Now for tree planting.

White Birch—Maiden-hair—Weeping Willow—[incomplete list].

18th March, 1880.—Almost every one of the first sixteen days of March were dismal cold days. Yesterday and today, bright and bracing.

In the Fitz John Porter case the Debate in the Senate is virtually a rehearing of the case. The bill restores him to his regular army rank—that of Colonel—with pay from the date of his dismissal Jany 1863. He has been out of service during all of that period. The passage of the bill is therefore a reversal of the judgment against him and something more. It is a declaration that he did his full duty in those last days of August 1862 and is therefore entitled to be signally honored and rewarded for his conspicuous merit and services as a Corps Commander in the battles referred to. This is the recommendation of the Board of Officers whose respect and findings were sent to Congress by me. The question I am now to consider is whether such merit was exhibited and such services rendered by Fitz J. Porter.

On receiving [and] reading the report of the Board this was the conclusion which I felt myself compelled (inclined) to adopt.[6]

20th March, 1880.—There is a strong disposition in the House to renew the contest of last spring over the election laws. They have attached as a Ryder [rider] to an important appropriation bill a proviso that will prevent the appointment of more than two or three deputy Marshalls in any one election District.No formidable riot or mob can be prevented or suppressed or held in check by such a force. If this is passed I must veto it. I will set out the law as it is—the change made by the bill—the opinion of the Supreme Court, and the duty to sustain it.

Let me examine [Alexander H.] Stephens['] and [Emory] Speer[']s speeches.

24th March, 1880.—The extreme Eastern part of the United States in Maine is *about* 69° [67°] west of Greenwich & the Extreme Western part, one of the Aleutian Islands is about 189° west of Gr'wich or in other [words] the U.S. extends from W[est] to E[ast] about 120°. The central point is in the Pacific Ocean about 90 miles west of the coast of Washington T[erritory]!

1st April, 1880.—We returned from N[ew] Y[ork] yesterday afternoon in the Limited Express, reaching here on time —4 P.M., after a pleasant ride of six hours, and a notably happy visit of in the great city. We took lunch with Mr John Taylor Johnston Prest of the Metropolitan Museum of Art at 1 P.M. Tuesday—attended the opening exercises of the Museum at the Central Park at 3½ to 5½ P.M., dined at Mr John Jacob Astor's at 7 P.M. and a reception at the same place until 11½ P.M. In the A.M. I had photographs taken by Frederick [Charles D. Fredericks]. (Party: Lucy, Mr   Andrews, Gov & Mrs   Andrews, Mrs [Linus] Austin and Gen [Albert J.] Myer.)

Monday evening, at a quiet & beautiful party at Mrs [Edward] Parsons.

8th April, 1880.—After walking before breakfast, pockets emptied, in winter clothing, light boots[:] Weight, 195½ lbs.

A cold snap but I hope no severe frost.

10*th April*, 1880.—This morning at 8½ A.M. I planted two American Elms perhaps six feet North of the drive way in front of the North front of the White House. One is due north from the North East Corner of the House and the other is due North of the N.W. corner. I was assisted by [Henry] Pfeister and two laborers and by Scott. Scott also planted an elm a little N.W. of my N.W. Elm.

11*th April*, 1880.—In the Phila. Times of March 29, an article was published entitled "White House Gallery"—"Rutherford Birchard Hayes of Ohio" "a pen picture" &c, by Gen H. V. Boynton. It seems to be by a friendly hand and contains many things a friend might have written. But in truth Gen B[oynton] who has been, and I hope, will be again, sincerely friendly, was at the time deeply offended with me. His nature makes it impossible for him to see fairly the character and merits of those he dislikes. The great defects of the sketch, as I see it, are due to the unfortunate quarrell between Gen Boynton and Gen Sherman. I had no connection with the controversy except to refuse a Court Martial to decide the merits of the affair between the Correspondent and the Commander of the Army. I did this without any thought that my judgment, clearly right, would alienate Gen Boynton. I regret that it has had that effect.[7]

His leanings ~~first~~ appear ~~the part~~ in many parts of the Pen Picture.

1. The Southern policy is represented as very different in practice ~~and~~ from what "its friends" understood it would be when they supported it.

I know, of course, very little of what was expected. The truth is I had no confidants in regard to it. My judgment was that the time had come to put an end to bayonet rule. I saw things done in the South which could only be accounted for on the theory that the War was not yet ended. Many Southern people evidently felt that they were justified in acts which could only be justified ~~ago~~ in time of war towards the common enemy. The Republicans, the North, the colored people if active in politics, were regarded and treated as the public enemy. My task was to wipe out the color line, to abolish sectionalism, to end the war and bring peace. To do this I was ready to resort to unusual measures, and to risk my own standing and reputation with my party and the country. For the first time in our history a gentleman who had opposed ~~my~~ the election of the President was by that President invited into his cabinet. Judge Key a confederate soldier and a Democrat who had ~~of~~ supported Mr Tilden against me was made Post Master General and one of my Constitutional advisers. A number of other appointments were made of Southern Democrats. My object was to end the War—to restore confidence in the South in the justice and good will of a Republican Administration. The army was withdrawn because I believed it a constitutional duty and a wise thing to do. I know of no friend, unless it is Gen Boynton, who supported the policy when it was inaugurated who does not sustain it now. On the other hand I meet constantly men who now applaud it, who were at the beginning of it, strongly opposed to it. It is not true that ~~that~~ tried Republicans at the South were totally abandoned. The possible support which could lawfully be extended to them was their appointment to office. Altogether the loudest complaints I have heard is that so many of "the tried Republicans" referred to have been appointed to office. I am not aware of a single instance in which a conspicuous Republican of the South can be said to have been abandoned. Gov Chamberlain alone has not received office, and he placed himself in an attitude of antagonism which precluded it. The practical destruction of the Republican organization in the South was accomplished before my Southern Policy was announced and before Order No. 1 was heard of. I repeat no man who favored the policy, except NOW Gen B is now dissatisfied with the Administration on account of it. I am confident that Gen B. never expressed discontent with it, or with Order No 1 until after the refusal of a Court Martial on his charges against Gen Sherman. If he did it never reached me. And certainly for the six months next before the Sherman affair Gen B. constantly expressed the warmest admiration of the ~~whole~~ conduct of the Administration, and his ardent desire that I should consent to be a candidate, or at any rate to accept a nomination a second time. I always replied to him in substance that if the nomination, and the election, and the commission ~~could be~~ were offered to me I would refuse under all circumstances to depart from my avowed purpose not to be my own successor. In no way could I do the country so great a service as by setting a precedent against a second ~~successive~~ term. Several presidents have declared themselves when candidates, or when elected, opposed to a second term. I shall be the first who has adhered to the rule when the question arose at the end of a first term.

If I were to here enumerate the points in which the Administration has been successful in a marked degree I would name

1. Judicial Appointments
   Mr Justice [John M.] Harlan ~~of~~ Supreme Court
   [John] Baxter Cir[cuit] C[our]t, Tenn.
   [Samuel Blatchford], Circuit Court, Mass.
   /   /, Dist[rict] C[our]t, Penn'a.
   /   /, District Court, Penn'a.
   /   /, District Court, Md.
   [John W. Barr], District Court, Ky
   /   /, District Court, /   /
   /   / Haguer, Dist[rict] of Col[umbia].
   /   / Cox, District of Columbia
   /   / James, District of Columbia

2. Foreign Missions
   England–[John] Welch & [James Russell] Lowell
   France–[Edward F.] Noyes
   Germany–Bayard Taylor & [Andrew D.] White

Italy–[George Perkins] Marsh
Spain–[James Russell] Lowell & [Lucius] Fairchild
Russia–[Edwin Wallace] Stoughton & [John Watson]
  Foster
Austria–[John A.] Kasson

3. Cabinet–able gentlemen free from Scandals
4. No nepotism in the Presidents appts.
5. Good morals in the White House
6. Maintaining the authority of the President in appointments agst Congressional dictation, and especially agst Senatorial dictation.

7. Maintaining sound doctrine in Vetoes of of bills designed to coerce the Executive.

8. Veto of Chinese Bill
9. ditto of Silver bill
10. Firm adherence to resumption and successfully carrying it out.

11. The Mexican policy securing peace and safety on the Texas border

12. The true Doctrine asserted as to European Control of an Isthmus Canal.

13. An Indian policy [of] justice, & fidelity to engagements, and *placing the Indians on the footing* of citizens.

14. A constitutional just and liberal policy upon the Southern question.

15. Non partisan appointments in greater number than any president since Washington. Key in the Cabinet, a marshal for Georgia–a Judge for D.C.–a Commissioner of D.C.–members of Board of Health–of Miss[issippi] River Com[mission] –Visitors to W[est] P[oint] & Annapolis–Minister to Brazil –Post Masters, many–Census Supervisors–several hundred in all–.

16. The prompt and firm suppression of the great riots of 1877.

17. Raids into the Indian Territory prevented.

18. The true policy with respect to Mormonism and polygamy.

19. The administration has never had a newspaper organ in Washington or elsewhere. As Mr Evarts said "the administration has not been well edited." This is good as a joke, but with the newspapers so enterprising and able as they now are, *no organ* is wisdom. It gives all a fair chance, and gives the administration a fair chance with all.

20. In fine, I have not done as much to improve the System and methods of the Civil Service as I hoped and tried to do, but I have improved the Service in all of its branches until it is equal to any in the world—equal to that of any previous administration. ~~Compare~~ Look at its purity, efficiency, freedom from Scandals, ~~with~~ and decide as to its merits.

28th April, 1880.—Yesterday when we were sitting at lunch a dispatch was handed to Lucy which she seemed to divine contained bad news. She handed it across the table to me and I read

Minneapolis April 27, 1880

To Mrs R B Hayes
  Executive Mansion
    W[ashington]

Doctor [Joseph T. Webb] had an apoplectic stroke this morning. Unconscious—condition dangerous.

Annie M. Webb.

Soon after we received a dispatch that the Doctor died about noon.

Lucy immediately made preparations to start for Minneapolis. We sent dispatches to Birchard at Toledo and Webb at Fremont and received replies. Hearing that the Doctor's remains would be buried at Cincinnati, Lucy and Lucy Cook with our servant, Isaiah, about ten O'clock last night in ~~Pres~~

ident Mr [John] Garrett's pul private car left for Cincinnati. Our friend John W Herron sent word that he would meet Lucy at the Depot and take her to his home.[8]

Dr Joseph T. Webb has been out of health several years. He was Superintendent of Long View Asylum about 187[1]. The location was a bad one for being near the Canal. Chills and fever prevailed. Doctor Webb was never rid of chills and fever after he left Longview. In addition to this he had severe headaches. He was of a bilious temperament, and quite corpulent. His sudden death was therefore not a surprise to us.

As a young man he was very fine looking. He weighed over 200 before he was twenty years old, was about six feet tall, dark complexion fine large black eyes, or dark hazel, good regular features, black hair, and was a friendly, social man of popular ways. His fondness for sports was un a noticeable trait. He played ball, was an excellent fisherman and horseman. and He was a tender hearted and skilful physician. In the army he was an almost universal favorite. His laugh was contageous and full of happy humor. I often meet our old comrades who say "I would give anything to hear the Doctor's laugh.["] He occasionally had fits melancholy spells but until after the loss of his health they were of short con short continuance and not very frequent. Since After the failure of his health the morbid tendency of his nature became strong —almost predominant. I sometimes feared that he would become insane. There were occasional symptoms of it. He distrusted at times his nearest friends. Dr [Cornelius G.] Comegys, a friend and connection, feared that he might glide into insanity. Judge Matthews [his brother-in-law] felt the same apprehension. Some months ago he wrote of his general good health but spoke of severe shooting pains in his head. These no doubt were symptoms of the appolexy [apoplexy] which killed him. We will remember him as he was until after the war—an affectionate, warm hearted, honest and brave man, possessed of uncommon talents of observation, good judgment, and the faculty of making those around him happy to a degree rarely met with.

He died childless leaving his widow, Annie Matthews, his sister (my wife) and numerous friends to mourn his loss.

Age 53 last January. Buried in Spring Grove, Cinti.

NOTES

CHAPTER XII

[1] Despite the preference here expressed, Spiegel Grove became the permanent name of the home.

[2] Hayes means to elect a Republican Senator in place of Democratic Thurman.

[3] Cornell was elected governor, and the Republicans won four of the seven state offices.

[4] In 1870, a French company prepared to construct an isthmian canal across Panama. American resentment was instant and intense. Hayes shared this common reaction. His action at this time revealed the strength of his feelings. Shortly he would speak out specifically on the issue, sending on March 8 a special message to Congress stipulating that any canal connecting the oceans must be under American control.

[5] The volume was not lost. Probably Hayes had mislaid it.

[6] The bill referred to eventually passed the Senate but failed in the House.

[7] Boynton was the Washington correspondent of the Cincinnati *Gazette*. During the disputed election he had been one of Hayes's firmest supporters and shrewdest advisers. His greatest service had been in bringing together behind Hayes the Texas Pacific lobby and the Southern Democrats. Since then, however, he and Hayes had disagreed on matters of patronage and legislation. Boynton had made a violent attack on General Sherman's war memoirs when they appeared, going to the length of writing a book of refutation called *Sherman's Historical Raid*.

[8] Joseph Webb was Lucy's brother and had served as surgeon with Hayes during the Civil War. Garrett was head of the Baltimore and Ohio Railroad.

Chapter XIII

APRIL 29, 1880—AUG. 30, 1880

29th April, 1880.—Mrs Sarah Moody Kilbourn, of Delaware, O., my cousin, came to visit us after Lucy had started for Cincinnati. I am glad to have her here during Lucy's absence. I only regret that her mother, Aunt [Clarissa Hayes] Moody did not come with her. Although in her *ninetieth* year, and somewhat deaf from age, she is a most interesting woman. She not merely remembers well and relates in an interesting way the events of many years ago, but she also is well informed and has an accurate memory as to current affairs in the Country and abroad.

8th May, 1880.—I vetoed the Deficiency bill on account of the permanent legislation attached to it in regard to the election laws. It was a measure of coercion thinly disguised. Now I anticipate the passage by the Democrats of a bill to change the mode of appointing the Deputies of Elections, their number, &c &c. I can sign an *efficient* measure containing suitable provisions if its only object is to secure non partisan Deputies.[1]

11th May, 1880.—Walked with [William Dean] Howells to the new building for the Bureau of Engraving & Printing, to the new Museum building and thence home. Two miles or more between 6 & 7 A.M.—before breakfast.

The name of a very young writer ~~for~~ in the Atlantic [Monthly:] Belton O. Townsend, Society Hill, S.C.

17th May, 1880.—Mr & Mrs Howells left us Thursday evening—we had a delightful visit from them. Mrs Kilbourn left Tuesday.

We hear from Rutherford at Santa Fe. He will return to College this week.

Hon Thos A Osborn, Minister to Chili, sends me by his wife, a cane—the stick cut from near the mouth of the cave of Alexander Selkirk in the Island of Juan Fernandez.

26th May, 1880.—The Magnolia south of the White House had its first large white blossom this morning.

30th May, 1880. Yesterday I went in special car to Philadelphia to take part in a meeting of Geo G Mead[e] Post No. 1, G.A.R., at Academy of Music for the purpose of raising a fund for a Meade Memorial. Secy of War [Alexander] Ramsey, Gen Devens, Atty Genl, Gen   Bingham, Judge   Kelley, Judge   McCammon, and a Mr Russell constituted the party in the car. Gen D[evens] & I went to the house of Hon Ch Gibbons. A pleasant dinner party—a ride in the noble Park, and in the evening Gov [Joshua L.] Chamberlain made the regular address. Rather didactic in the main, but with ~~much~~ noble sentiments and much deep feeling in the closing paragraphs about the dead. I followed with a short talk on Mead—was exceedingly well received by the fine audience. Gov [Henry M.] Hoyt presided. Gen [W. T.] Sherman & Mr [Stewart L.] Woodford followed me.

Saturday, 5th June, 1880.—This is the fourth day of the Chicago Convention. It is probable that no nomination will be made today. The friends of Grant are apparently working for delay. It now seems impossible to nominate Grant. Blaine's chances are good. It may be Sherman or a fourth—either Edmunds or Windom.[2]

The defeat of Grant is due to the unpopularity of the managers of his canvass, and of their methods. The third term and the general lack of availability on account of his failure as President are also powerful elements in producing the result. The immediately valuable result is the condemnation of the machine as organized & managed by Conkling and [James Donald] Cameron. The latter is in all respects a failure as a politician. The final overthrow of the Unit rule is a solid achievement. I greatly regret that Grant—our first soldier and a man of many sterling qualities should be so humiliated and degraded as he has been by his unprincipled supporters.

Let me emphasize in my last message the idea that

The Constitution should be so amended as to lengthen the ~~Presidential~~ term of the President to six years, and so as to render him ineligible for a second term.

11th June, 1880.—Gen Garfield's nomination at Chicago was the best that was possible. It is altogether good. The Convention accomplished a great deal of good. The defeat of the unit rule was an important achievement. The defeat of the rule or ruin Senators, who usurped the power of the people. The defeat of a Third term ~~even for~~ agst so great a chieftan as Grant. There is much personal gratification in it. The defeat of those who have been bitter against me. The success of one who has uniformly been friendly. Ohio to the front also and again! The endorsement of me and my Administration. The endorsement of Civil Service reform. The sop thrown to Conkling in the nomination of Arthur, only serves to emphasis the completeness of his defeat. He was so crushed that it was from sheer sympathy that this bone was thrown to him.[3]

But now how to win. The contest will be close and fierce. We may be beaten. Oregon begins the campaign with a good first gun.

We must neglect no element of success. There is a great deal of strength in Garfield's life and struggles as a self made man. Let it be thoroughly presented. In facts & incidents, ~~in~~ in poetry and tales—in pictures—on banners, in representations, in processions, in watchwords and nicknames.

How from poverty and obscurity—by labor at all avocations he became a great scholar, a Statesman, a Major General, a Senator, a Presidential Candidate. Give the amplest details—a school teacher—a laborer on the canal—the name of his boat. The truth is no man ever started so low that accomplished so much in all our history. Not Franklin or Lincoln even.

Once in about twenty years a campaign on personal characteristics is in order. Gen Jackson in 1820–24—Gen Harrison in 1840—Lincoln in 1860—now Garfield in 1880. I know we cant repeat in details, but in substance we can. In this instance we stand on the rock of truth. Such struggles with adverse circumstances and such success! The boy on the tow path has become in truth the scholar and the gentleman by his own unaided work. He is the ideal candidate because he is the ideal self made man.

If he were not in public life he would be equally eminent as a Professor in a College, as a lecturer, as an author, ~~and~~ an essayist or a Metaphysician.

Quote in talking of him Buells article in the Capital of the 13*th* of June.

15*th June* 1880.—Gen Garfield returned from Ohio this morning & spent several hours with me & took dinner with us. He is a little hoarse from much talking but is natural and sensible. I told him I thought the nomination would be ratified at the election with enthusiasm.—that his personal history as an ideal self made man would be a most popular feature of the canvass. He was anxious to know the feelings of Sherman as to his (G's) loyalty to him. I assured him on this point that it was as he would wish it to be.

He told two omens. As he entered the Convention the day of his nomination a man distributing leaves of the New testament handed him a leaf which he (G) put in his pocket. Long after the nomination, emptying his pockets the leaf was found. The verse that was uppermost as it was folded read

"~~This is~~ The Stone which the builders rejected &c &c

At one O'clock P.M., the hour of the nomination, an Eagle lit on Garfield's house in Washington and sat there several minutes and was seen by many persons.

John Hoar and Abram Garfield "embattled farmers" of Massachusets sent their affidavits to the Continental Congress as to the fact that the British began hostilities on that famous 19th Apr. '75.

Webster will resign as Register of Wills. Let Theo[philus] Gaines have his place.

26th June, 1880.—Returned yesterday from Ohio. Lucy and Fanny spent the time with Laura at Columbus. I went to the Commencement of Kenyon College. A most enjoyable time. Bishop [Gregory Thurston] Bedell and his hospitable home contributed largely to the happiness of the time. Mrs B[edell] sick and absent, and greatly missed. Received warmly by all on Commencement day. Spoke easily and apparently acceptably for ten minutes.

I go today to Yale College Commencement and to visit my kinfolks, the Trowbridges.

9:30 A.M. on limited Express with Ruth'ford, Lucy and Isaiah to New York.

3:30 P.M. met by Gen [Thomas L.] James, and two gentlemen of Railway mail service at Jersey City. Carriages to New Haven Depot [in Jersey City]. Met Wm Rutherford & Ruth'fd Hayes Trowbridge at Depot—sons of my Kinsman at N[ew] H[aven]—also Mr   Watrous, Prest of the R.R.

En route near N[ew] H[aven], met Mr   Cook & Mr
Kimball.

Met at Depot by Mayor [Hobart Baldwin] Bigelow, Prest [Noah] Porter, Proff. [Charles Henry] Northrup & Mr & Mrs T[homas] R. T[rowbridge], a band & vast crowds.

Escort of Grand Army.

Sunday at Centre Church—Dr [Leonard] Bacon made handsome mention of me [in his address]. Visited the Crypt where seven of my ancestors repose. It is under the Church and is interesting. [In the] P.M. rode out Hillhouse Av. and saw East & West Rocks and ["Edgewood"] Ik Marvell's place.

Monday, 5th July, 1880.—The 4th celebrated today. The day opened with the firing of one hundred guns south of the Treasury. It is cool with a strong N.E. wind.

We returned from a delightful trip to New Haven at 10½ P.M. Saturday. We were received warmly. With Thomas R. Trowbridge's family Saturday night, Sunday, Monday and until Tuesday afternoon. A rare family we found our Kinsfolk the T[rowbridge]s. Several families—all in business together —the business dating back about 240 years, and the present firm and form of it about 80 years. The older brothers, Thos, Henry, & Ezekiel all men of character, and their sons apparently worthy of them, with ladies and grandchildren all that could be desired. Sunday attended church at the Centre Congragational. Mr [Edward G. Seldon] preached a *trial* sermon. Dr Bacon after the regular sermon called attention tastefully to my presence. After service visited the Crypt where are, I believe, ~~are~~ seven of my ancestors, viz four named Trowbridge—husbands & wives—one Ezekiel Hayes & two (probably) Russells and (perhaps) Whitings. This is well kept immediately under the church.   Monday we visited Branford, a fine farming town. We were received in the large brick house built by my Gr Grandfather Ezekiel Hayes, and saw the graveyard where are buried Rev Saml Russell and other ancestors. A pleasant welcome by a large number of people at Mr [E. F.] Jones, Landlord of the [Totokett House], the old [Ezekiel] Hayes mansion. Eve[ning], a Recep[tion] at T[rowbridge's].

Tuesday P.M. we went to the quiet and admirable home and family of Prest [Noah] Porter. Attended Law School and Scientific School commencements—College ditto and Alumni meeting. Received the Degree of L.L.D. I made a successful little speech which was well applauded at the Alumni meeting. It was badly reported.

July 2, dined on the Moselle, ocean steamer of the Lloyd [North] German line at Hoboken. Capt   and Mr [Gustav] Schwab were specially interesting. It was all managed by Gen [Thomas L.] James, the P[ost]M[aster] of New York.

3d breakfasted at Manhattan Beach with Gen S[tewart] L. Woodford. The most useful, enjoyable and attractive watering place I ever heard of.

Thursday, 8th July, 1880.—Sol[dier]'s Home Yesterday we came out to the Home bag & baggage. Weather fine. This morning have risen before 6 A.M. and will begin my morning walks. I weighed yesterday 190 lbs. Warm morning walks will take off during this month at least five or eight pounds.

I walked this morning over to the National Cemetery, and eastwardly, until the clock struck 7 A.M., when I returned by the Presidents Gate—the gate kept by Gen [Winfield] Scott's orderly Serg[ean]t.

Friday, 9th July, 1880.—Last evening we sailed in a steam Yacht down the Potomac from *7th* St wharf almost to Ft Washington and reached home about half after nine. The party consisted of Gen & Mrs [Albert J.] Myer & a young dau[ghter] of nine, Mr [William King] Rogers, Phebe & Andrews, and Lucy, Ruther'fd & myself. We were guests of Gen Myer. The weather was favorable. Rain threatened but none fell until during the night after our return.

In my last message why not show that the Civil Service

cannot be what it should be without legislation in aid of the reform. There should be a Board, or Commission, to make rules and to investigate fitness of candidates, charges agst incumbents and the like, with power to make the investigations thorough. There should be legislation as to the interference of Members of Congress with appointments.

Sunday, 11th July, 1880.—In the Nation of the 8*th* are criticisms of my course on the Reform of the Civil Service. Agreeing generally with the Nation on this subject, I would like to make it clear to all such friends of the Reform, that public opinion and Congress must be right on the question before we can have a thorough and complete Reform. The President has neither time, nor authority, neither means nor men, to gather the information required to make appointments and removals.

In my last message I may frankly admit my own shortcomings (albeit they are not what the *Nation* supposes) enlarge on the importance of the reform, and urge that my successors shall have what I have not had a Board of well paid, able men, to supply the information required to ascertain qualifications of applicants for office, and to furnish ways to examine as to the conduct & qualifications of the incumbents.

Monday, 12th July, 1880.—Yesterday Gen [Thomas L.] Casey & Mrs. Casey dined with us. After dinner a long talk with the General on the Washington Monument, which he has charge of. The condition and want of West Point, the retirement of old officers and other army matters.

The Chaplain at W[est] P[oint] should be retired and a young and vigorous preacher of real character should take his place. A larger attention should be given to General literature. Our officers should have higher resources for happiness than are now resorted to in the Western Posts.

Let me try in my annual Message to give a fair picture of the present condition of the Civil Service. The party now in power has had the offices of the Gov't longer than any party since the introduction of the spoils doctrine into our system of

Administering the Gov't—since 1829. The party of Jackson and Van Buren after their Presidential terms—12 years were succeeded by the party of Harrison and Tyler upon whose inauguration a general sweep out of offices began. They in turn were Superseded by Polk in 1845 after only four years of power, and a new set of officers were brought in. After four years they in turn were changed and the appointees of Taylor and Fillmore took the offices in 1849 and held them ~~pub~~ until displaced by Pierce. For eight years no general removal took place. In 1861 the appointments of Republicans in the place of the officers of Pierce and Buchanan was begun by Prest Lincoln. Many changes were made in 1866 and 1877 but no general sweep out has occurred for twenty years.

Let me ascertain the number of office holders in each Department of the Gov't—the length of time they have been in the public service, and the general condition of the Service as to efficiency illustrated by special facts, such as the amount of money collected and disbursed, the amount lost ~~by in~~ &c &c &c.

The points to be considered are

1. Appointments—on what showing, or examination to be made

2. Removals—for what causes & how the facts are to be shown, or ascertained

3. Political action (conduct) of officials

4. Assessments &c &c

5. Congressional patronage. What it means. Its practical working.

The President has the authority to do a great deal in promoting a reform of the Civil Service. But the great mass of evils to be dealt with require means, time, agents, the work of intelligent & able officers, none of which the President has unless they are furnished by Congress.

As at present situated the great evil is Congressional patronage. This I have resisted as a usurpation of Executive prerogatives, until now few Congressmen assert openly their claim to it. But they withold from the Executive the means to get information from other sources, than through Congressmen.

My action has been mainly directed to these points:

1. To restore to the Executive department the appointments and removals, and to take it from Senators and Representatives

2. To take the office holders out of Political work.

3. To give to men in office security in their *tenure* as long as their official and personal conduct are good.

4. The ~~unsparing~~ thorough investigation of abuses and the dismissal & punishment of unworthy officers, without regard to political influences.

5. ~~Carefully~~ Judicious appointments without regard to "influences."

6. To abolish the practice of making assessments upon public ~~purpose~~ officers for political or other purposes

13th July, 1880.—This is the anniversary of the adoption of the Ordinance of "[17]87" by the Congress of the old Confederation. In the early days of the Republican Party this day was always remembered. Twenty five years ago—in 1855, "the Anti-Nebraska Convention," the Republican Convention many called it—the Fusion Convention as it was of anti-slavery men, Know Knothings, &c &c was held at Columbus, Ohio, and Salmon P Chase was nominated for Governor.

I have been asked for my crest. In honor of my ancestors according to the Hayes traditions—and especially in honor of my grandfather, a Blacksmith, and my Gr Grandfather, a scythe maker—why not say?

Crest.—A Falcon displayed sitting on an anvil—the right side of the anvil supported by a Scythe and the left side by an ox yoke.

Motto—(under the anvil), *Recte.*

Nothing is more certain than this. The principles of Mr [Thomas A.] Jenckes, and Mr [Dorman B.]Eaton—in short the principles of a true Civil Service reform can not be carried out if both Houses of Congress are hostile ~~to the Reform~~ to those principles.

If a decided majority in each house is opposed to the Reform it cannnot be established. It can only be made radical, thorough, and complete by the support of a majority ~~of~~ in both the House and Senate.

The first great step in the reform is to abolish Congressional patronage—to restore to the Executive the appointing power which has been usurped by Congress, and especially by the Senate.

"Experience has proved, says Gen Garfield, that with our frequent changes of Administration no system of reform can be made effective and permanent without the aid of legislation. Appointments to the military and naval service are so regulated by law and custom as to leave but little ground for complaint. It may not be wise to make similar regulations by law for the Civil Service." Undoubtedly Gen G is right in the first part of his statement. Experience has shown the necessity of legislation by Congress to establish ~~an es~~ an effective and permanent reform of the Civil Service. And nothing is plainer than that Congress will ~~do~~ enact no ~~such thing~~ useful legislation on the subject unless actually driven to it by the force of public opinion, as long as what is called the offices of the Government are mainly under the Control of Members of Congress. The offices are regarded as part of their perquisites—by far the most important part, in the case of Senators, of the emoluments of their offices. They will not voluntarily give up that part of the compensation of their offices which they most highly prize.

14th July, 1880.—The end I have chiefly aimed at, has been to break down Congressional patronage—and especially Senatorial patronage. The contest has been a bitter one. It has exposed me to attack, opposition, misconstruction, and the actual hatred of powerful men. But I have had great success. No

286

member of either House now attempts even to dictate appointments. My sole right to make appointments is tacitly conceded. It has seemed to me that as Executive I could advance the Reform of the ~~way~~ Civil Service in no way so effectively, as by rescuing the power of appointing to office from the Congressional leaders. I began with selecting a Cabinet in opposition to their wishes, and I have gone on in that path steadily —until now I am ~~appointing~~ filling the important places of Collector of the Ports, and Post Master at Philadelphia almost without a suggestion even from Senators or Representatives! Is not this a good measure of success for the Executive to accomplish almost absolutely unaided in Congress. Mr Edmunds, *conspicuously* Messrs Hoar, [Ambrose E.] Burnside, [Henry L.] Dawes, [Justin S.] Morrill, [Nathaniel P.] Hill, of Colorado, ~~also~~ have aided in the work, and many other Senators have in the outcome cheerfully acquiesced in my course. Among them are [Samuel J.] Kirkwood, & ~~Allis~~ [Preston B.] Plumb, [Henry P.] Baldwin, [Thomas W.] Ferry, [Samuel J. R.] McMillan, [William] Windom, [Alvin] Saunders, [Henry W.] Blair, [Angus] Cameron of Wisc., [incomplete list].

The greatest heat of this summer in Washington was on the 13*th* of July. About 2 P.M. the thermometer at the front window near the entrance to the East Room was at 98° in the shade. In the hall, the thermometer at the entrance to the Blue Room was 88° +.

19*th July*, 1880.—[W. K.] Rogers returned from Atlantic City yesterday. He left his family there. He says that in an interview Gov [Marshall] Jewell is reported to have said that the President is not so decided in his Civil Service reform views as he was, and that he, Jewell, hoped for greater activity on the part of office holders.

I do not believe Gov Jewell said this. Certainly it is without foundation. I am not in the habit of talking otherwise than squarely and with distinctness, if I speak at all on any public question. The politicians are often anxious to be politic—to trim—to talk so equivocally as to have the benefit of opposing no body. This is of course contemptible, and does not usually avail. The man of policy is pretty sure to be found out. The true course is respectful, but explict statements of opinion. I think that Gen Garfield has made a mistake in not speaking more explicitly on the Civil Service. I do not doubt the soundness of his real opinions on the subject, but his letter [of acceptance] does furnish some ground for doubt on that subject.

20th July, 1880.—Last night we had the first copious shower that has fallen since we came out to the Home about two weeks ago. Soaking rains are much needed.

The practical success of this administration in giving the Country as good a Civil Service, for the time being, as that possessed by any Country—as that of any previous administration is due mainly

1. To the character of the Cabinet—all ~~personally~~ men of the strictest integrity, and only one of them with political ambition.

2. To the fact that all officeholders soon were made to know that efficiency and honesty were their best titles to security in their positions, and that if inefficient or dishonest their lack of fidelity would be promptly and thoroughly investigated, and unsparingly exposed and punished. No amount of influence, or political power ever saved the unfaithful.

21st July, 1880.—Showers yesterday—not copious here, cool weather.

I think an effective speech could be made for Garfield by showing by facts and figures how the Democratic party sanctions in both Houses of Congress the practical nullification of the 15*th* amendment. Let it be calmly done. Quote the resolutions of the Democratic National Conventions on the subject —the 5*th* plank of their last platform, and then show in detail what is done in South Carolina, Mississippi, Louisiana and other States. It could be clearly proved that by a practical nullification of the 15th amendment the Republicans have for several years been deprived of a majority in both the House and Senate. The failure of the South to faithfully observe the 15th amendment is the cause of the failure of all efforts towards complete pacification. It is on this hook that the bloody shirt now hangs. This causes the immigrant to avoid the South. Only one city out of the *twenty* which now have a population exceeding one hundred thousand is a Southern City. For all this the Democratic party of the North is responsible. If they would refuse to seat Southern Representatives and Senators whose seats had been obtained by a violation of the Constitution, the question would be rightly settled.

22d July, 1880.—Copious rains today.

25th July, 1880.—Webb came this morning. The addition to the House at Fremont goes on well. Two things

1. Double windows in our sleeping room—also—the new part of the House—Library & Drawing room.

2. Floors in first story to be fireproof—brick & mortar below the boards of the floor.

If I talk to the soldiers ~~of the~~ why not speak of the fruits of their services on the right side of the good cause. It is now true that this is God's Country, if equal rights—a fair start and an equal chance in the race of life are every where secured to all. If clouds cast their shadows on our path, we are cheered also by the sunlight of prosperity. What is our condition now. The debt, failures, incomes employment for skilled & common labor, at fair prices—a fair days wage for a fair days work. What we fought for was to make us one people —a free people with an equal start and a fair chance in the race.

Just in proportion as the results and true principles of that combat have been fully and cheerfully accepted, just in that proportion is our Country in its several parts properous and happy.

29th July, 1880.—Proff. [John Ferguson] Weir of Yale

College suggests to paint a portrait of Lucy, Benjamin C Porter, Studio building, Boston.

Webb came 25*th* July and left Wed 28*th*. He seems to be getting along with the building [in Spiegel Grove] satisfactorily.

Rutherford went to Ithaca to gather up his traps, &c &c &c. Will return the 31*st* July.

30th July, 1880.—Weather very cool for several days.

2d August, 1880.—R. E. Trow[bridge at] 26 B, N. E.

3d August, 1880.—The sentence in my inaugural message which has been often quoted viz "He serves his ~~country~~ party best who serves his Country best," occurred to me as I was walking east on the North side of Broad Street in Columbus with a small party of friends in February 1877. I was pondering the inaugural address, and talking of it ~~to~~ with, I think, [W. K.] Rogers, Dick Anderson, Denny Rogers, and perhaps [Gen. John G.] Mitchell—perhaps also Gen [John] Beatty. We were going from my residence to Gen Mitchell's. "Serve your party by serving your Country." "You will ~~best~~ serve your ~~Country~~ party if you Serve your Country.["] ["]To Serve one's Country is the best way to serve one's party,["] are among the forms of statement that occurred to me. The best service of ~~your~~ party is service to the Country.

Thursday, 5th August, 1880.—Heavy rains which were much needed for two days—very cool this morning.

Lucy and Rutherford went on limited express [train] last night to New York to prepare for our Pacific Coast trip in September. Fanny will go with Augustus D Shepard this morning to his home at Plainfield (P.O.Fanwood) in New Jersey. I will get ready for the Soldiers Reunions at Columbus and Canton in Ohio.

P.M., *5th*. About 7 P.M. a cool wind from the West cleared up the sky. There never was a finer sunset. The sky and clouds were brilliant and beautiful. Near the western horizon the sky was green, higher up silver, gold, blue and crimson. The freshened grass and foliage added to the scene. [W. K.] Rogers dined with me. We visited [Rowland E.] Trowbridge on B. Street N.E. near the Capitol. Some day there will be fine houses around the Capitol East and N.E. and N.W. and they will be the favorite sites.

I printed today my fifteen minute speech for the Ohio Soldiers reunion at Columbus on the 11th. Rogers who thinks well of almost anything I do says "it is so good" and repeated it, "and with emphasis."

My hobby more and more is likely to be Common School Education, or universal education.

A tract of Gen [John] Eaton, 1872 "The relation of Education to labor" shows that a common school education adds 25 per cent to the value of labor.

Carlisle [Thomas Carlyle] says "I warmly second that wise advice of the wisest of men 'seekest thou great things, seek them not.' 'Dont be ambitious, dont too much need success.' "

8th August, 1880.—Lucy & Rutherford, returned this morning from their New York trip. They spent one night at Plainfield with our kinsfolk the Shepards, and one night at Tarrytown with [Russell] Hastings—both delightful.

Yesterday the first stone was laid in continuance of the Washington Monument—a corner stone on the N.E. corner. Present, Col [Thomas L.] Casey, Capt [George W.] Davis, the workmen, Admiral [Daniel] Ammen, and myself. I placed under [the stone] a half dollar marked on one side R.B.H. and on the other 1880. The marking was done on the top of the Monument, and a similarly marked piece I keep as a token.

————

[Thomas] Jefferson to Yancey VI, 6 Jany 1816 "If a nation expects to be ignorant & free, in a state of civilization, it expects what *never was and* never will be."

[James Monroe] To W[illiam] T. Barry 4 Aug. 1822 "A popular government without popular information, or the means of acquiring it, is but a prologue to a farce or *a* tragedy, or perhaps to both."

"Knowledge will always [forever] govern ignorance." *Ib*[*id*].

> —[Quoted from "Education for the Colored Population of the United States," in *Proceedings of the Trustees of the Peabody Education Fund, 1874–1881*, Volume II, pp. 274–275.]

"Common schools fostered and protected."

> Last clause 3*d* Section, Cin[cinnati] Dem[ocratic Party] Platform

"Wherever a citizen is born some chance should be offered him of becoming a man."

> Carlyle

"The want of public schools in any quarter of the Union is an injury to the whole Union, as the success of republican institutions rests upon the intelligence & capacity for self government of the whole people & of all the States."

> —Dr [Barnas] Sears' Report to the Peabody [Education Fund Trustees] &c '79

———

14*th August*, 1880.—I returned last night from Columbus. The Soldiers' Reunion was very successful. The reporters speak of fifteen thousand veterans in line and seventy five thousand spectators. Certainly no such numbers have assembled before since the war on such an occasion. Each Regt in the great procession marched under its own old tattered banners—a very affecting sight—great joy and great enthusiasm. I took on as my guests in my car Gens Sherman, [Emory] Upton, [William Babcock] Hazen, [Charles Henry] Crane (Asst. Surg[eon] Genl), [Robert] MacFeeley,

Col[Almon Ferdinand] Rockwell, Maj [Azor Howitt] Nickerson, Lt [John Lincoln] Clem. Col [Henry C.] Corbin was in charge of the Party. All went of[f] well with us and gloriously with the grand reunion.

I had a most enjoyable visit with my hosts, our nephew & niece Dr & Mrs [Erskine B.] Fullerton. The two children, old enough to climb on my knee are very fine little folks. The baby boy Rutherford is a handsome babe of six weeks. Laura and her family came down from Gambier. The General and Mr [William A.] Platt were also often there, thus making the family party complete, and the family happiness complete.

Laura will go with us on our trip to the Pacific Coast. Altogether, I find myself very well satisfied with my Journey. Our route was via Harrisburg & Pittsburgh. The great Penn'a R.R. is in excellent condition. Time to Columbus from 11 A.M. Tuesday to & A.M. [?] Wednesday. Returning 12 midnight Thursday night to 9 P.M. Friday.

Suspicions are expressed as to the fidelity of the Census enumerators in Southern States, especially in South Carolina. It must be thoroughly examined. Doubtless the natural increase in the South is large. When the modes of living are inexpensive, land plenty & cheap, & population sparse the natural increase is always large.

Sunday, 15th August, 1880.—Sol[dier]s Home near Washington We had a beautiful shower last night—and it rained several hours during the night. This morning it is cool, bright, and bracing. We start for Ohio in less than two weeks, and for the Pacific Coast the 2d of September, or rather the evening of the first from Canton. The preparations for so long a journey and absence from the Capital will keep me very busy the rest of the Summer.

19th August, 1880.—One week from today, Thursday, we expect to start for Ohio and thence on our tour to the Pacific Coast. When I meet assemblages of citizens, of necessity, I must talk to them. Brief as these conversations must be I ought to be in some measure prepared for them. As I now see it congratulations on the condition and prospects of our Country will almost always be appropriate. In order to make them of some interest let me gather facts as to restored Union, sound financial condition, ~~and the like~~ increase of exports of Agricultural & Manufacturing products—balance of trade and the like. In order to make the talks practically useful, not merely vain boasting, let me trace the favorable conditions to the adoption of sound principles, and warn the people of some of the evils existing which threaten our future, such as clipped silver dollars—unredeemed government paper—a redundant currency, popular illiteracy, Sectional and race predjudices &c &c.

24th September [August], 1880.—We are preparing for our long absence. We go Thursday 26*th* to Fremont; remain there until Tuesday p.m.; thence to Cleveland staying with our Kinsfolk, the Austins that evening; and on Wednesday to the 23*d* [Regiment, Ohio Volunteer Infantry] Reunion at Canton on the 1*st* September. That night after the reception we go ~~to~~ on to our cars and start on the tour to the Pacific Coast.
I prepare one speech on National aid to Education to the education of the colored and other illiterates at the South—

When strangers meet in Mixed assemblages their talk is about the weather, their health, the Crops, the condition and prospects of business and the current news foreign and domestic. It is only after they are more intimately acquainted that in mixed companies they talk of religion and politics. For my general talks on miscellaneous occasions this usage must govern. All of my audiences must of necessity contain men of different creeds and parties.

Fremont, 28th August, 1880.—We reached here last night at 8 P.M., 22½ hours from Washington in the new car of Mr [Charles Edmund] Pugh Superintendent of Inspection of Penn'a R.R. We brought my old friend [Rowland E.]

Trowbridge sick (sciatica or Brights disease), Comm[issioner] of Indian Affairs, and Mr [John] Jameson of Railway Mail Service with Fan, Scott, and the colored servants, Winnie [Monroe] & Scott. At several points in Ohio, although all my movements were kept private, we were met by good crowds who cheered us heartily. I was pleased when cheers were heartily given on a call of "Three cheers for the model President." We got home after dark. Rud had the house in as good case as could be in view of the improvements. They strike us both well—particularly the external appearance, the porch and the rooms in the bay window addition on the South side.
Lucy is forty nine today. I never loved her so much as now.

Fremont, 30th August, 1880.—A heavy rain yesterday, last night and this morning. We attended ~~church at~~ the M E Church. Mr [Thomas H.] Wilson in tender sweet tones and words portrayed the consolations of the Christian in time of affliction. Text was a comparison of the Christian to the Palm tree and the Cedar of Lebanon.—My old friend Wm Henry Smith came from Chicago & spent several hours with me returning last night. He gave me the inside history of the Chicago Convention.—and of many other political movements. On the whole nothing unpleasant for me to hear.

———

The course of the drive to the [Spiegel Grove] house is one of the questions here. Now it is in front of the long porch, and all strangers whose curiosity leads them here will drive near the principal sitting place of the house. Cant I abolish this, and arrange a porte coche at the North end of the porch, and a drive past the North end of the House, and so around the garden? Abolish the drives South of the house, and with steps and a walk make a route for foot passengers to the Southwest Corner of the grove. Renew the evergreen trees in the N.W. angle between new & old house.

Trim off the lower branches of many trees near the house,

295

so as to open a view under the trees and let in the air freely. For the benefit of those who visit the place, cant I make an earth drive near the front fence, in front of the house to the edge of the ravine as ~~you~~ it runs South westerly parallel to Buckland Avenue, and at the ravine turn to the West towards the South East corner of the garden, and so around by the Stable & return on the main stone drive.

NOTES

CHAPTER XIII

1 The deficiency referred to was the failure of Congress in the special session of 1879 to provide money for the fees of federal marshals. A bill to supply the money contained a rider concerning the employment of the officers, and Hayes felt constrained to veto it. Later Congress voted the appropriation with no restrictions.

2 Hayes followed with interest the proceedings of the Republican convention. Two of the candidates, Sherman and Garfield, were his close friends.

3 Arthur was nominated as the vice presidential candidate to conciliate the Conkling faction.

Chapter XIV

NOV. 7, 1880—MARCH 10, 1881

White House, Sunday, 7th November, 1880.—We left W[ashington] on our Pacific tour Thursday evening *26th* August and returned Saturday morning 6 November after an absence of Seventy one days. Our trip was most fortunate in all of its circumstances. Superb weather, good health and no accidents. A most gratifying reception greeted us everywhere from the people and from noted and interesting individuals.[1] I must not forget to make acknowledgments, as follows

San Francisco

Gov Leland Stanford
Senator Wm Sharon
Gov A. A. Lowe [Low]
James B. Stetson
Mrs Sam'l Q. Hunt (at Oakland)
Gen & Mrs Irving McDowell
Rev Dr M. C. Briggs

Portland, Oregon

Mayor [D. P.] Thompson
Henry Failing
     Hill, artist
Capt [George J.] Ainsworth
T. F. Oakes

his father John Quincy Adams habitually spoke of his Presidential term as the unhappiest four years of his life.

Theodore R Noyes, son of [Hayes' first cousin] John H[umphrey] Noyes is here with his wife. They appear to be nice people.

1st December, 1880.—I have just reached home (7.30 A.M.) after a short trip to Easton to attend the reopening of Pardee Hall of Lafayette College. On the urgent invitation of the President, Mr [William C.] Cattell, I left Washington at 10 P.M. Monday night—reached Easton at 10½ A.M. *30th*—remained until 7 P.M. dined with the St Andrews Society in Philadelphia from 9½ P.M. until 12 M. and thence home again. A busy but delightful tour.

Gen Sherman, Gov [Alexander] Ramsey, Mr [Horace] Maynard, Mr [John] Jameson, Mr [A. D.] Hazen and Rutherford [Hayes] were ~~with me~~ of the party. Mr [Ario] Pardee some years ago for college uses built Pardee hall. It was completed at an expense to him of $300,000. It was burned five years ago. Now out of the insurance money it is rebuilt. An excellent address was delivered by Prof [Francis A. March]. Several—many addresses were made—for the most part they were very good. Gen [Robert] Patterson, [President of the Board of Trustees] was bright and vigorous—intellectually as ever. He spoke at the College banquet, and at the Scotch dinner. A man of 87!!

4th December, 1880.—Dined last evening at Mr Evarts with the members of the Cabinet. Mr Maynard, the P.M. Genl was absent. Mr [John] Hay, Asst. Secy of State, was also present. Mr Hay tells anecdotes capitally. He is timely and apt in using them and his fund is prodigious. Col Thompson said a Baptist Minister at the head of a Bureau allowed the first extra compensation for carrying the mail to Hon Wm Smith of Va. who was after that known as "Extra Billy Smith." The same Brown, (Baptist preacher) wrote Col R. M. Johnson's famous Report ~~age~~ on Sunday Mails.

I am to go to the New England dinner in Brooklyn 21st December. Why not say that the best New England idea in the present condition of suffrage and citizenship is that which requires Government to furnish all of the young sufficient instruction to enable them to be good citizens? The school schoolmaster is as essential ~~to good government~~ in a Republic to its safety and good Govt as a legislator, or judge, a soldier, or a Sheriff.

8th December, 1880.—A great and grevious wrong has been done to the Poncas [Indians]. Mr [Henry L.] Dawes thinks that Mr Schurz ~~and the In~~ is chiefly to blame for the wrong, and for the fact that no decisive steps have been taken for its redress. Mr. Schurz thinks that Congress is chiefly to blame in the premises and in particular that Mr Dawes is himself more in fault than the Indian Department.[3]

Let me look into this. Certainly if Mr Dawes thought Mr Schurz was so greatly to blame he should have called the attention of the President to the neglect or ~~crime~~ offense of the Interior Department. He was friendly to the Administration. He often brought matters of smaller importance to the President's attention but this affair he never mentioned to President Hayes, until in December, 1880 after the Worcester meeting.

Get all the [Congressional] Globes—the [Congressional] Records since Dec 1, 1876.—Also the Reports of the Comm[issione]r of Indian Affairs for the last four years.

The New England idea is universal education. Let it not be confined to any one State or Section. Let it be the National idea and be embodied in the legislation and institutions of the whole Union.

Liberal education will follow free school education as surely as the light of day comes with the sun.

When it was announced that an unknown and common place person had been appointed to an important office,

Tallyrand said "To have done and to have said nothing is I know a tremendous power but it ought not to be abused." This is a favorite anecdote of Mr Evarts'.

14th December, 1880.—The VP says if Garfield fails to appoint Sherman to the Treasury it will be regarded as a weak yielding to Conkling, as ungenerous to Sherman, and as a disregard of the wishes and interests of the Country. "This is the opinion of every man I have talked with.※※※※If he will be President all will be well, but if he merely does what Conkling wants he will be a failure. ※※※I have said forty times, if he had ~~your~~ one tenth of your amiable obstinacy and independence he would be a great success. All he needs to do is to be firm in the right and he will have the whole people at his back."

The Senate yesterday passed a bill in relation to Fitz John Porter. It is far less objectionable than any bill heretofore offered. Mr Dawes Rep offered the amendment, which was accepted by Gov [Theodore Fitz] Randolph. But on the final vote Judge [David] Davis and all Reps voted no. It probably presents again the old questions, 1. The power of Congress to set aside or disregard a Court Martial. 2. The merits of the case. The former bill was Extraordinary. It was a ~~veto~~ bill to *honor* Porter. This is not that. Is it simply to do him justice, or is it clemency? I am not averse to clemency. But on the merits, as I now see the case, Porter has no claims.

15th December, 1880.—With Gen [George] Crook walked to the top of the Washington Monument.

We dine Gen and Mrs Grant and thirty four others—mostly noted people, tonight. Lucy is well enough in all respects in the duties of a State dinner, but she feels unequal to them, and therefore *hates* State dinners.

16th December, 1880.—The dinner passed off in good style. The floral decorations of the table were very fine.

17th December, 1880.—Dined last evening with Gen Grant, and others, at Mr. John B Alleys. Gen Grant was interesting and talkative. Senator Edmunds tells good anecdotes, and is *both* witty and humorous—a rare combination. The stories which made most fun were Judge Williams to Senator Nye, "*I am losing flesh!*"; "He found a dam by a mill site, but no mill by a dam sight!"

Xmas, 1880.—As usual the gifts were collected in one room (in this case the red chamber) and the children servants and friends in another (the Library) and on the ringing of a bell at the door, ~~the~~ Scott & Fan ran and brought a single article well concealed by wrappings to me. After some delays and guesses, it is found ~~that the gift~~ whose gift it is. ~~for~~ All got some thing. Scott & Fanny, many things. All at least a $5.*oo* gold piece.

My visit to Brooklyn on the occasion of the N[ew] E[ngland] dinner at Mr A. A. Low's was a most happy one. I got off a satisfactory short speech, that was well received on "New England ideas."

26th December, 1880.—If I speak on leaving here to friends I may perhaps at Columbus enumerate the things done or acted upon during my term—not to discuss, or boast of them but merely to name them. I may speak of returning to Private life as Washington, Adams & Jefferson did—not to shirk the duties of a citizen, but not expecting or seeking again to fill con-spicuous offices—offices provoking competitions, but ready to do what I may in private life, or in humble stations, or if generally called to higher duties.

How will you pass time? Or that other unwarrantable phrase how will you kill time? A man with proper notions and training with books, and grounds and neighbors—and with the interests that are crowding around all who have a sense of duty to their fellow men, will have more trouble to find time for his work, then to find work ~~for~~ to occupy all the time at his command.

Sunday, 2d January, 1881.—Our New Years ceremonies passed off well—the papers say with "unwonted brilliancy." Lucy had gathered a fine bevy of young ladies as our guests for a fortnight or so. Three young girls still in school, viz Maria C Herron of Cinti, Aggie Devens of Cambridge, and perhaps our cousin Dora Scott of New Orleans—probably she is not to be called "a nestling," but a young lady "out," and three of the nicest young ladies in the world. Kate Morgan, dau[ghter] of Rev. Dr.   Morgan, of N.Y., & a cousin via the Trowbridge family. Lizzie Mills, dau[ghter of] D. O. Mills of Calif. now living in N.Y. City. Carrie Russell of Newport, R.I., and Lucy Cook of Chil[licothe], O. Seven fine young people. Our two lads, Webb & Rud with Fan and Scott make up the Household. A very fair promise of enjoyment for the next few weeks. We begin to long for home and freedom, more and more as the time draws nearer.

Very cold weather for two weeks—lately the coldest known in Washington in many years. 30*th* Dec., 10½ below zero; 31*st* d[itt]o & Jany 1, 13½. Snow a foot deep and good sleighing. Twice riding with   Hawkins, once with Mrs Senator [N. P.] Hill, and today with Sherman.

About the middle of October last, one fine morning as we were passing on the noble steamer Columbia out of the Columbia River into the Pacific Ocean we passed a beautiful Ship, the Valiant from Boston, Capt.   . Her flags were all up in honor of the President, and when we were nearest to her she gave us three rousing cheers. She turned northward towards Puget Sound, and we headed Southward for the golden gate! It impressed me deeply.

I am soon to become a private citizen—to be entitled to the privileges and immunities of that honorable and enviable position. To have a right to manage my own private affairs without intrusion. If not one of the wealthy citizens of our State, I trust I shall always be ready to offer to friends that best part of hospitality a hearty welcome to my home, and to those who need it that part of charity ~~a cheerful~~ aid cheerfully given according to my means.

9th January, 1881.—Lucy had her first reception yesterday afternoon between 3 & 5 P.M. This is an affair which if merely formal and stiff is stupid enough. But Lucy by ornamenting the rooms with flags and flowers, and by gathering a number of her most entertaining friends, ~~and~~ young and old, to assist her has succeeded in making it an enjoyable social reunion.

Sunday, 16*th January*, 1881.—The [New York Daily] Graphic said a few days ago

"Take him for all in all Hayes will step out of office on the 4*th* of March next with more peace and blessing than any President in fifty six years. Who since Monroe has gone out both *willingly* and regretted?"

That the White House will be left *"willingly"* by both Mrs Hayes and myself is perfectly true. Indeed "gladly" might truthfully be substituted for "willingly." We have upon the whole enjoyed our four years here. ~~upon the whole.~~ But the responsibility, the embarrassments, the heart breaking sufferings which we cant relieve, the ever present danger of scandals and crimes among those we are compelled to trust, and a thousand other draw backs to our satisfaction and enjoyment by which we are constantly surrounded leave us no place for regret upon ~~leaving~~ retiring from this conspicuous scene ~~for~~ to the freedom independence and safety of our obscure and happy home in the pleasant grove at Fremont.

It is said Gen Garfield will restore wine and liquor to the White House. I hope this is a mistake. I am no fanatic on this subject. I do not sympathise with the methods of the ultra temperance people. I believe that the cause of temperance will be most surely promoted by moral, religious, and educational influences and by the influence of example. I would not use the force of law as an agency for temperance reform. If laws on the subject are ~~for~~ enacted let them be for the security of the community—to protect the public from nuisances and crime. Let the temperance reformer keep to the text influence, argument, persuasion, example.

When we came here we banished liquors from the house

1. Because it was right wise and necessary
2. Because it was due to the large support given me by the sincere friends of the Temperance reform
3. Because I believed that it would strengthen the Republican party by detaching from the Political temperance party many good people who would join the Republican party, and would save to the Republican party many who would otherwise leave it to join the Temperance party.

If Gen Garfield rejects the practice I have inaugurated, he will offend thousands, and drive them into the hands of the Temperance demagogues. He will lose the confidence of thousands of good citizens and gain no strength in any quarter. His course will be taken as evidence that he lacks the grit to face fashionable ridicule. Nothing hurts a man more than a general belief that he lacks "the courage of his convictions."

If there are any two men in the Country whose opposition and hatred are a certificate of good character and sound Statesmanship they are Conkling and Butler. I enjoy the satisfaction of being fully endorsed by their hatred and opposition of both of these men.

Hon John D Defrees has been in public life more than forty years, and is full of information of the great men of the past in our politics. He was in the conference which formed Gen [Zachary] Taylor's cabinet in 1849. It was held at Gov [John J.] Crittenden's house in Frankfort, Ky. Gen T[aylor] was not well informed in the details of political life and relied very much on the information and advice of Mr Crittenden.

He tells this of Mr Lincoln. In 1849, Mr L. was very anxious to get the place of Comm[issione]r of the General Land Office. Mr Defrees came to Washington to get it for him. He would probably have been successful if he had reached W[ashington] a few days earlier. He found it already disposed of. Mr Lincoln was greatly disappointed. Success then would probably have lost him the Presidency—and immortal fame.

Sunday, 23d January, 1881.—Coming in, I was denounced as a fraud by all the extreme men of the opposing party and as an ingrate and a traitor by the same class of men in my own party. Going out, I have the good will, blessing and approval of the best people of all parties and sections. The thing that seems to me unaccountable is that with more than usual distrust of my own powers, I ~~always~~ had a strong and comforting faith that I should be able to organize and conduct an administration which would satisfy and win the Country. This faith never deserted me. I had it before either the election or the nomination. Doubtless it was founded on my experience. I have often said that I never fail to gain the confidence and friendship of those I wish to win if I have time and an opportunity to do so.

I have for the present lost the friendship of Gen Sherman. Several things have occurred to which this may be attributed. 1. I recommended the promotion of Gen Grant to a Captain Generalcy. 2. I retired certain officers, notably Gen [E. O. C.] Ord, against his advice and wish. 3. I promoted Gens [William B.] Hazen and [Nelson A.] Miles against his wish.

In all this there was no intention to slight Gen S. In fact during all the time I was most desirous to have his approval and friendship.

5th February, 1881.—A beautiful winter morning. Snow everywhere—good sleighing yet. Took a sleigh ride yesterday with Gov [Eli H.] Murray of Utah and Gen [E. A.] Merritt. The snow now on the ground fell, much of it, as early as Dec 2oth!

9th February, 1881.—Snow going of[f] rapidly. Garfield declared President without hitch or difficulty.

307

Lucy has got, we are told, an excellent portrait by [Daniel] Huntington. It is painted for the Temperance ladies. Miss ˹Frances E.] Willard Pres't of the Womens Temperance ˹nion of the U.S. called today with Mrs. [C. L.] Roach Miss W[illard] talked intelligently about the whole affair and in the best taste and disposition. I am glad to find she is so capable and discreet. We shall have no trouble with such a lady.

11th February, 1881.—We have dined out a number of times this winter. We thought we might depart from custom our last winter. Last night we dined with Mr Geo[rge] Bancroft the historian. The company at table was not large, but it was notable. Mr Bancroft lively, full of conversation and vigor at 82 or more, is noticeable always. He said "in 1821 I met Mrs Jerome Bonaparte neé Patterson, then a very beautiful and attractive woman in Rome." "[William Winston] Seaton told me a conversation he had with Calhoun." "Calhoun was a candidate for President when he was a comparatively young man. I, said Seaton, told him he was too young—that after his two terms he would still be young, and he would find it hard to be laid on the shelf so young. Calhoun replied 'I would go home and write my Memoirs.' " "So characteristic!" said Bancroft. He said when Clay was an old man and expecting soon to die he expressed a wish to be reconciled to Calhoun. A meeting at Clay's chamber was arranged. Clay met Calhoun with the friendliest courtesy. Calhoun was stiff—he couldn't say what ought to be said, or do what ought to be done— C[lay] was all the opposite.

After Mr Bancroft the other notable ~~guests~~ persons present were Mr & Mrs Evarts, Senator & Mrs Hoar, Sir Edw[ard] Thornton, Senator [William B.] Allison, Col [Jerome Napoleon] Bonaparte, the gr[and]son of Prince Jerome [Bonaparte], Mrs [Caroline Edgar] B[onaparte], the gr[and] dau[ghter] of Daniel Webster, Mrs Bancroft Davis, dau[ghter-in-law] of Senator ("honest John") Davis of Mass. and gr[and] dau[ghter] of Rufus King. Henry Adams, gr[and] son of John Quincy Adams & his wife, niece of Mr Hooper. Ex Secy of Navy [George M.] Robeson & wife, Mr Thayer of Worcester, Mass. & his wife, a Livingston. Mrs Hayes and myself. More "family" than we have met. Very agreeable and intelligent people.

Mrs Bonaparte said her Gr[and]father Daniel Webster the night before his great speech in the debate with Hayne went to bed at 8 P.M. and slept soundly four hours. He then rose and began his preparation [of] the great reply. The whole subject poured at once through his brain. Only one day for that speech! Mrs B[onaparte] said her grandmother on her deathbed at 95 or 96 said to Col Jerome [Bonaparte] "The end of royalty will soon come—there will be no more Kings or dynasties—the world is now to be Republican."

Mr [Henry] Adams said "Our system of Govt has failed utterly in many respects. The House is not what it was intended to be a deliberative body. The majority cant control its action. Nothing less than two thirds can control it. Our army is as it ought to be a mere police. It ought to be called a police. Our Navy is nothing. In all ages the difficulty has been how to decide who shall be ruler. It is the same here. No means has yet been discovered of doing it peacefully. We have not got it. Our reliance is on the people being so as to need no government. When that is the case we are safe."

13th February, 1881.—Visited Baltimore yesterday. Met at Depot by the Mayor [Ferdinand C.] Latrobe, Prest [Daniel C.] Gilman of the Johns Hopkins University, and Mr [William] Keyser of B & O [railroad]; drove to Prest Gilmans; the old home of Johns Hopkins. Visited with "friend" [Francis T.] King the hospital (J[ohns] H[opkins]), unfinished but with a commanding site and on a noble plan, the Peabody Library &c, and Lunched with Prest [D. C.] Gilman with perhaps thirty or forty of the best people. At my table

Judge   , Revedy Johnson, and   Hopkins, a nephew of [Johns Hopkins]. In the evening dined with the [Baltimore] Press Association. Prest [C. K.] Fox of [the] Associated Press [of Baltimore] in chair. Senator [Thomas F.] Bayard, Gov [William Thomas] Hamilton, and the mayor [Latrobe] near or opposite to me, with John L Thomas at my right. The P[ost]M[aster, E. B. Tyler] and Treasurer [Joshua Vansant] also. A liberal courteous company of over fifty at Eutaw House. Mr [J. W.] Simonton, Senator Bayard, Thomas, & [Major Innes] Randolph and Judge [Hugh L.] Bond & Rev Mr [Samuel K.] Cox made good speeches—Mine was well received, and with much enthusiasm viz three cheers as I closed. Altogether a happy occasion.

15th February, 1881.—I attended the Yale dinner at the Arlington last night. Among the guests were Prest [Noah] Porter, the C[hief] J[ustice, Morrison R. Waite], Mr Evarts, and a number of Senators and Rep[resentative]s with scientific men &c &c &c. The young men enlivened the occasion with college songs. Two of the good speeches were by the young men, Mr [Edward M.] Bentley and Mr [Henry Kellogg] Willard. I signed the Constitution and so became a member of the Washington Yale Association.

A word or two on the Temperance question.

When I became President I was fully convinced that, whatever might be true in Europe and of Europeans, in our climate, and with the excitable temperaments of the Americans, the habitual use of intoxicating drinks was not safe. I regarded the danger of the habit as especially great in public political and official life. It seemed to me that the example of excluding liquors at from the White House would be wise and useful and would be approved by good people generally. I knew it would be particularly gratifying to Mrs Hayes to have it done. We had never been in the habit of using liquors in our own house and we determined to continue our home custom in this respect in our official residence in Washington. Mrs Hayes has been from childhood a total abstainer. I was not a total abstainer, when I became President. But the discussions which arose over the change ~~which~~ at the ~~executive m~~ Presidents House soon satisfied me that in this matter if our example was to be useful there was no half way house for me. During the greater part of my term ~~certainly~~ and at least for the last three years I have been in practice and in theory a consistent total abstinence man, and I shall continue to be so. ~~through the remainder of my life.~~ All statements ~~such as those you refer to~~ inconsistent with the foregoing are without foundation.

25th February, 1881.—Our Diplomatic Reception last evening was very beautiful. It began promptly at 8 P.M. a large number of guests having arrived as early as 7½. The stream of hand shakers poured incessantly past us two hours. The entertainment in both dining rooms was unusually well done. We passed down to the East Room in the following order *1st* Mrs H[ayes] & myself, the Cabinet & families and our guests, then the members of the Diplomatic Corps, and finally the guests generally. There was very little crowding all the rooms of the House and the Conservatories being open, but the number was between two and three thousand. The members of the House for the most part were prevented from attending by a night session and deadlock over the apportionment bill. Towards the close of the affair several officers of the House entered to arrest members fifteen or so, of whom had come down to the Reception. Present[:] All of the Cabinet with many ladies. Judges Supreme Court[—]Ch[ief] J[ustice] Waite, [Samuel F.] Miller, [Stephen J.] Field, [John M.] Harlan, [William B.] Wood[s] [Joseph P.] Bradley, [Noah H.] Swayne, [William] Strong, Ex-[Justice].   Cox,   James,   Wiley, (District C[our]t). Senators [Senator-Elect Eugene] Hale, Me., [Henry W.] Blair, N.H.,

[George F.] Hoar & [Henry L.] Dawes, Mass., [Justin S.] Morrill, Vt., [Orville H.] Platt, Ct., the ladies of [George F.] Edmunds of Vt. who was sick, Miss Barnum of Ct., [Francis] Kernan of N Y., [Theodore F.] Randolph of N. J., [Thomas F.] Bayard of Del., [William A.] Wallace of Penna., [John W.] Johns[t]on of Va., [Zebulon B.] Vance & [Matt W. Ransom] of N C., [Joseph E.] Brown of Ga., [John T.] Morgan of Ala., [James E.] Bailey of Tenn., [Blanche K.] Bruce of Miss., [John S.] Williams of Ky., Mrs & Miss [George H.] Pendleton of O., [Benjamin] Harrison & [Joseph E.] McDonald of Ind., [Henry P.] Baldwin & [Thomas W.] Ferry of Mich. (Wisc[onsin's Matt H.] Carpenter[']s death yest[erday] prevented [Angus] Cameron['s attendance], [John A.] Logan, Ill., [Francis M.] Cocherill, Mo., [Henry G.] Davis, West Va., [Samuel J.] Kirkwood & [William B.] Allison, Iowa, [William] Windom & [Samuel J. R.] McMillan, Minn., [Henry M.] Teller & [N. P.] Hill, Colorado, [William] Sharon, Nevada, [John F.] Miller & [Newton] Booth, Calif., [Winkinson] Call, Fla., 1=32 & 2 new Senators.

———

Private

Washington, D. C.
17 Feby, 1881

My dear Mr. Welsh

I need not say that I am very grateful for the kindness of yourself and the citizens of Philadelphia in whose behalf you wrote to me a month ago. The invitation places me under great obligations. But after some consideration Mrs. Hayes and I are agreed in thinking that it is upon the whole best that we should return to Ohio immediately after the inauguration of Gen. Garfield. No terms can be too strong adequately to express my sense of the support I have received from men like yourself and those you represent in the difficult duties of the trust devolved upon me four years ago. Your approval of the

312

general course and purpose of the Administration will always be remembered among the most agreeable circumstances attending my official life.

With great respect, I am,

Sincerely,

R. B. Hayes

Hon. John Welsh

2d March, 1881.—My closing days are full of satisfaction. I have shaken hands with five hundred today. Many clergymen congratulate me. The burden of the talk on all sides is a clean, honest, independent and successful Administration. Mr [Alexander H.] Stephens of Georgia says he never saw an Administration go out so well spoken of. Senators, Representatives and Citizens say the same.

Capt Mc   gave me a cane with a cannon head from iron of [Admiral David Glasgow] Farragut's ship the Hartford and Rosewood shaft.

3d March, 1881.—A bright and beautiful morning. The Refunding bill reached me at 8 o'clock last evening with all of its objectionable features still in it. I shall veto it today. This will be my last important act. The signing of routine bills &c &c for a few hours more, and my official life closes.[4]

Never have I listened to as much commendation as I heard yesterday. Mrs Hayes seems to be a great and almost universal favorite. Would we were worthier. It is said by old public functionaries and by Citizens that no president and his wife and family ever left here so much and so generally regretted. Mr [Frank E.] Roff, Mr [Anthony Davis] Bullock & Mr [John W.] Herron, with Mrs. Garfield, the elder, & the sons of the General [Garfield] brought our list of guests at dinner last evening up to thirty (30)—a full house!

9th March, 1881.—Fremont Ohio We reached home last evening. The weather was bad—"nasty," as the Englishmen say, but the people turned out and gave us a hearty welcome to our home. Our trip from Washington, and our good bye in Washington had but one untoward event. The sad railroad accident near Severn by which two lives were lost, and two others are not yet out of danger. Our Engineer, *John M. Unglaub*, behaved in the most devoted and brave way. He staid by the engine, at his post, doing all he could to save us. Happily he will recover.

In consequence of the delay we dined the evening of the *5th*, Saturday, with our good friends at Mr Saml M. Shoemaker's. We then in a new car, a Pullman, went on till we reached Altoona, where we staid over Sunday. Monday we reached Cleveland, and staid with our kinsfolk, Mr & Mrs Linus Austin. We were called on by a good number (7) of the *23d* [Regiment, Ohio Volunteers], and by many of the best people. Gen [James] Barnett, Mr [John S.] Foote, [George H.] Ely, and many others.

At Clyde we were met by the Fremont Reception Committee just at dark Tuesday, *8th*, and found a large crowd with bands, torches and banners [awaiting us at Fremont]. We were heartily welcomed and taken home via Croghan Street, Main St, Birchard Av & Buckland Av., to Spiegel Grove, with a large throng of men, women, and children. I will put the names of the Committees with the programme in my Scrapbook of this date. Mr [Homer] Everett made a speech on my verandah to which I replied. After this Mrs Hayes and I shook hands with a large part of the meeting.

10th March, 1881.—Rose at sunrise. Yesterday and today the sun rose beautifully. Thermometer 30°. Walked rapidly around the North and West sides of the place, returned by the Harrison road, and stepped off the route of a new drive farther from the house than the present one, so as not to have people sitting on the Verandah disturbed by persons driving about the place. From the new route the house looks low—

rather "squatty." But this gives it an old fashioned look which is not undesirable.

Last evening we got forty-two letters. The most of them were congratulatory on the success of the Administration or upon our escape in the railroad accident near Baltimore. There were letters from Gen Sherman, Mr Schurz, our darling Fanny, John L Thomas, Mr [E. A.] Merritt, Col [Silas W.] Burt, Geo Wm Curtis [and others].

I suppose the list will soon fall off to reasonable proportions.

NOTES

CHAPTER XIV

1 Hayes was the first President to visit the Pacific coast. The journey was the longest one yet undertaken by a Chief Executive. Although it was an election year, Hayes avoided political themes in his addresses. Because of the extent of the tour there are no entries for the months of September and October.

2 The Crédit Mobilier was a company that did construction work for the Union Pacific Railroad. It was controlled by stockholders of the railroad who were using this device to milk extravagant costs from their own company. The chief promoter of the scheme, Oakes Ames, feared a possible investigation—the government had provided financial aid to the road—and decided to protect himself by distributing shares of stock in the Crédit Mobilier to key members of Congress. Nevertheless, the arrangement was exposed, and some high names were involved in the scandal. Garfield was named as one of those accepting the stock. He denied it, but the accusation clung to him.

3 Senator Dawes of Massachusetts was chairman of the Committee on Indian Affairs. The Ponca Indians had been moved from one reservation to another under conditions that caused them great suffering. Friends of the Indians in the East charged inefficiency and inhumanity, and hinted at fraud. Secretary Schurz replied that he had acted in response to a law of Congress, which he admitted was unjust to the Indians. Hayes finally appointed a commission which made redress to the Poncas.

4 Congress had passed a measure providing for the issuance of three and one half per cent bonds to refund the national debt. Hayes favored the purpose of the bill. But he was led to veto it by a section which he thought would harm the National Bank system by preventing the organization of additional banks.

EPILOGUE: THE RETURN TO SPIEGEL GROVE

At the end of his presidency Hayes returned to the estate at Fremont that he had inherited from his uncle Sardis Birchard. Spiegel Grove was a spacious and gracious house set in fifty acres of trees and lawns. Here he lived until his death on January 17, 1893. It was a comfortable and yet a curious life that he led in his retirement years. Assured of ample means through his family's and his own exertions, he could do pretty much as he wanted. He traveled widely. His greatest delight was to attend reunions of veteran societies of the Civil War. He was always a featured speaker at those affairs, and he invariably stressed one theme: The sacrifice, the devotion, the unselfishness that the soldiers had found among themselves during the war must somehow be maintained as a part of the national character during the peace. The war had given Hayes something that was precious to him —perhaps it was a realization that men were fundamentally good—and he was pathetically fearful of losing it. He liked to refer to the war as "the golden years," and it is probable that his military career was to him a more rewarding episode than the Presidency.

He served as an official of the Peabody Fund to further southern education and of the Slater Fund to encourage Negro education, and he continued his efforts for prison reform. But, and this is the curious phase of his life, he took no part in politics. He was not an elder statesman or a respected party voice. He sought no office and was offered none. No announced opinion of his could determine the fortunes of any candidate or decide the adoption of any principle in the party he had once headed. Nor did he seek to play the role of a dominating former chief. He was respected and admired, but in a real sense he dropped out of the political picture. There is no case quite like his in the whole record of American politics. Other previous Presidents have played their parts quite differently. Two have come back to win lesser offices, and others, while not seeking office, have insisted on giving their pronouncements, even if these have not always been heeded. But Hayes removed himself from the political scene, and he and the country were both content to have it that way. He was strictly a "one-shotter." Perhaps he knew this. He had been called to the Presidency for particular reasons. The politicians and the public, with that strange wisdom that sometimes marks Americans in their conduct of government, had sensed that he was the right man for a certain moment. He had done the job required of him, and then he stepped back to do other things that he liked better. It was fortunate for the nation, if not for his own fame, that it happened the way it did.

In a diary entry of December 29, 1881, Hayes looked back on his administration and tried to cast up its credits. His evaluation was naturally subjective and in part exaggerated. But in the round it was a fair judgment:

> What was the result of the Administration on the Country and on the Party which elected it. The Administration found the Country divided and distracted and every interest depressed. It left it united, harmonious and prosperous. The Administration came in with the Republican Party discordant, disheartened and weak. When the Administration closed its Party was united, strong, confident and victorious.
>
> At its beginning the South was solid and the North divided.

318

At its close the North was united and solid and the South was divided. At the beginning both houses of Congress had been lost. When it closed both Houses were regained. I can say with truth "I left this great Country prosperous and happy, and the party of my choice strong victorious and united. In serving the Country I served the Party."

INDEX

322

325

Nickerson, A. H., 293
Nixon, W. P., 221
Noyes, E. F., 45, 63, 79, 127, 142
Noyes, H. S., 151, 157
Noyes, Theodore R., 300

Obscenity in mails, 183-84, 188, 233, 237-38
Offices, policy on, and people appointed to, 85-86, 94, 97, 98, 99, 106, 112, 120, 126, 127, 134-45, 138, 140-41, 151, 158-59, 160, 271-72, 283-84
O'Neill, Charles, 124
Ord, E. O. C., 87, 307
Oregon, 55-56, 76
Osborn, Thomas A., 277

Packard, S. B., 55, 83, 84
Packer, Asa, 149
Pardons, Hayes's policy on, 18-19, 240
Paroll, J. B., 6
Parton, James, 241
Peabody Education Fund, 97, 162, 163, 292, 317
Pendleton, A. R., 166
Perry, Aaron F., 55-56
Pettis, S. N., 259
Phelps, W. W., 255
Pierrepont, Edwards, 36
Platt, Emily, 47, 52, 55, 56, 84, 92, 96, 108, 109, 128, 136, 145, 146, 147
Platt, Rutherford H., 47, 52, 56, 65, 92, 111
Platt, Thomas C., 59
Platt, William, 12, 45, 52, 56, 292
Plumb, Preston B., 287
Poindexter, James, 74
Pope, John, 88
Porter, Albert G., 127, 129
Porter, Fitz John, 216, 267, 302
Porter, Noah, 281-82, 310
Potter, Clarkson N., 141
Potter, Joseph H., 238

Potts, B. F., 91
Prescott, Benjamin F., 127
President, powers and functions of the, 85, 103, 122, 129, 193, 201, 206, 208, 283, 286
Presidential portraits, 260
Preston, Thomas L., 96
Pugh, Charles E., 294
Pugh, John M., 16

Quinby, G. A., 169

Rainey, Joseph H., 147, 164
Ramsey, Alexander, 235, 264, 277, 300
Randall, E. O., 24
Randall, Samuel, 193
Randolph, Theodore F., 98, 302
Ray, John, 55
Rayner, Kenneth, 84
Read, John M., 127
Redfield, Benjamin B., 40
Refunding Bill, 313
Religion: in campaign of 1875, 4-6; in election of 1876, 41
Republican Party, 7-8, 50, 58-59, 100, 114, 126, 250
Reynolds, Robert M., 127
Rice, Alexander H., 69
Roach, John, 132, 136
Robbins, William M., 143
Roberts, W. H., 52
Robeson, George M., 309
Robinson, Lucius, 152, 252-53
Rockwell, Almon F., 293
Rogers, Denny, 55, 290
Rogers, William K., 29, 37, 47, 81, 108, 113, 159, 165, 216, 282, 290, 291, 299
Roosevelt, Theodore, 87

St. John, John P., 246
Sargent, Aaron A., 86, 136-37
Saunders, Alvin, 287
Saylor, Milton, 97

327